# The Iroquois

# The Peoples of America

*General Editors*
**Alan Kolata and Dean Snow**

This series is about the native peoples and civilizations of the Americas, from their origins in ancient times to the present day. Drawing on archaeological, historical, and anthropological evidence, each volume presents a fresh and absorbing account of a group's culture, society, and history.

Accessible and scholarly, and well illustrated with maps and photographs, the volumes of *The Peoples of America* will together provide a comprehensive and vivid picture of the character and variety of the societies of the American past.

## Already published

*The Tiwanaku: A Portrait of an Andean Civilization*
Alan Kolata

*The Timucua*
Jerald T. Milanich

*The Aztecs*
*Second Edition*
Michael E. Smith

*The Cheyenne*
John Moore

*The Iroquois*
Dean Snow

*The Moche*
Garth Bowden

*The Nasca*
Helaine Silverman and Donald A. Proulx

*The Incas*
Terence N. D'Altroy

*The Sioux*
Guy Gibbon

# The Iroquois

Dean R. Snow

Blackwell
Publishing

350 Main Street, Malden, MA 02148-5018, USA
108 Cowley Road, Oxford OX4 1JF, UK
550 Swanston Street, Carlton South, Melbourne, Victoria 3053, Australia
Kurfürstendamm 57, 10707 Berlin, Germany

First published 1994 by Blackwell Publishers Ltd, a Blackwell Publishing company
First published in USA 1994
Reprinted 1995
Reprinted and first published in paperback 1996
Reprinted 1996, 1998 (twice), 2000, 2001, 2002

*Library of Congress Cataloging-in-Publication Data*

Snow, Dean R., 1940–
    Iroquois / Dean R. Snow.
    p.   cm. — (The peoples of America)
    Includes bibliographical references and index.
    ISBN 1–55786–225–7 (hbk: acid-free paper)—ISBN 1–55786–938–3 (pbk.)
    1. Iroquois Indians—History. 2. Iroquois Indians—Antiquities.
3. East (U.S.)—History. 4. Canada, Eastern—History. I. Title. II. Series.
    E99.17S63   1994                                    94–27890
    973'.04975—dc20                                     CIP

A catalogue record for this title is available from the British Library.

Set in 10 on 12pt Sabon
by Graphicraft Typesetters Limited, Hong Kong
Printed and bound in the United Kingdom
by MPG Books Ltd, Bodmin, Cornwall

For further information on
Blackwell Publishing, visit our website:
http://www.blackwellpublishing.com

# Contents

# List of Tables

# List of Figures

# Preface

This book is about the Iroquois, not about the non-Iroquois who interacted with them and who largely wrote their history as we now know it. However much we may know about figures such as Isaac Jogues and William Johnson, they are treated here as supporting cast, not main characters. In some sense this book is also my gift to the Iroquois. My training and experience have equipped me to provide evidence and insights that are not available from others, whether they be scientists or the Iroquois themselves. I know these people well as a people, and I know some of them well as individuals, but in some things I can never know them as they know themselves. In these things I will always defer to them, for it is one of their gifts that these master orators have always spoken eloquently for themselves. But in other things I have the useful objectivity of an outsider.

When dealing with ceremonies and other sensitive issues I have been careful to use only information that has already been published. I have used some information given to me directly by my Iroquois friends, but I have made every effort to avoid betraying confidence, or revealing those things that the Iroquois generally wish to keep private. As the Mohawks would say, they are *onkwehonwe*, "real people," and they deserve the courtesy one accords real people.

There are many ways to organize a subject as complex as this one, many paths that a narrative might follow. I have chosen to follow a time line, for that way I can discuss both large and small changes over time. This is what one should expect from an archaeologist/ ethnohistorian; it also seems to me to be the most interesting perspective, given the great depth and detail of historical information we have on the Iroquois and the magnitude of the change they have both initiated and endured. This approach has meant that I have had to break up some topics that might have otherwise been dealt with in sections of their own. For example, medicine masks ("false faces") and the League of the Iroquois appear in many places rather than having chapters devoted to them. However, I have tried to focus discussion of these and other topics in chapters where they are particularly relevant. No matter how I might have chosen to organize the book, some important subjects would inevitably be fragmented. I trust that readers will be able to use the index and boxed features to pull together scattered topics that might be of special interest to them.

I have also tried to structure the book in a way that is consistent with traditional Iroquois culture itself. The essential features of Iroquois ethos reflect duality, ecology, cyclicality, and equilibrium. I have structured the presentation as a cycle of thirteen chapters, and in such a way as to preserve throughout the sense of balance and adaptation over time that so permeates traditional Iroquois culture. The conflict of good and evil, and the inability of mortals to be sure which is which, finds its expression in endless factionalism. It is embedded in the mythological origins of the Iroquois, and it is embedded in the current conflicts over issues such as land claims and gambling.

I have given disproportionate space to certain subjects that I have judged will be of special interest to many readers. Morgan and the Iroquois made each other famous in the nineteenth century, and that relationship has been given special attention. Similarly, many readers are especially interested in the most recent history of the Iroquois, which continues to unfold in our daily newspapers. I have accordingly allowed space for more detailed coverage of these events than is the case for similar events in earlier centuries.

When archaeology came to America it left behind the Mediterranean world's emphasis on the elite, the great artists, and the great political leaders. American archaeology necessarily grew as a populist enterprise, for its subjects were largely anonymous peoples. This is an approach that fits well with Iroquois culture. Like my own ancestors (none of them elites), the Iroquois before the seventeenth century were people without history apart from oral tradition. Archaeology is rectifying that; it is finding history for peoples of the past who would otherwise not have it.

But even populist archaeology can be used for unpleasant ends. It has sometimes been used for the dubious purposes of nationalism and ethnic chauvinism. In the service of these ends some archaeologists have been lured into exaggeration, distortion, and even fraud. I have done my best to avoid these traps, even when it has meant that the Iroquois might read something they would rather not know about their ancestors. It is a difficult task, especially in an era when some authors have decided that there is no objective reality, only alternative visions and alternative voices. In contrast to this self-defeating fad, I maintain that there is an objective reality, even though I might perpetually misperceive it. Different versions of the past result from imperfect perceptions, imperfect uses of the evidence, and variable emphasis. I might choose to ignore an area that someone else thinks is important. However, if anyone disagrees with the factual content of what follows, one (or both) of us must be wrong. Time will probably prove me to be wrong on some points, but that is a small price for any particular scientist to pay in the common effort to expand knowledge. While I will not pretend to have a monopoly on the truth, neither will I repeat unsupportable views merely because they are earnestly held by honest people. Readers wishing to explore the implications of this position will find some leads in the endnotes.

As an anthropologist I can speak on two distinct themes. For a variety of reasons, the Iroquois contribute more to both themes than do many other societies. First, there are the generalizations about the specifics of past societies that we are able to make on the basis of what we know from archaeology combined with what we know about societies in general. The study of the cultural processes in extinct societies through archaeology is done anonymously, in the sense that we seek valid generalizations about societies of certain types or in certain circumstances, regardless of the specific meanings artifact types, settlement patterns, and so on, might have had for them individually. Thus the archaeologist might deduce from settlement patterns and patterns of ceramic decoration that people lived in multifamily residences that were organized along female lines. This is more than we would otherwise know, but it stops short of saying anything about the specific meanings that the ceramic decorations had to the people who made and used them. This situation has prompted some archaeologists to claim that "some general propositions . . . are, by their very general nature, trivial – hardly the focus for scientific enquiry" (Hodder 1986: 6). But such pessimism misses some very important general inferences about the nature of human cultural evolution. The comparative archaeological study of the Iroquois and similar societies provides many generalizations about things such as the development of farming, the origins of internecine warfare, and the evolution of social organization. That they are generalizations that do not speak to the rich specific histories of any one of the societies in the sample does not reduce them to trivialities. What is simple is not necessarily simplistic, as all real scientists can appreciate. They are, in fact, the fundamentals of anthropological science, and fundamental principles are at once simple and profound.

Some modern Iroquois grumble at the use of Iroquois archaeology for the development and testing of general propositions. They would rather that archaeological attention were focused on the elucidation of specific and meaningful generalizations about Iroquois culture. This is the second distinct theme of enquiry in Iroquois archaeology, and the one that archaeologists who quest for meaning prefer over the anonymity of scientific generalization. Because of the richness of documentary sources relating to the Iroquois, this direct historic approach is also possible in this volume. Yet its use must be carefully limited. Meaning changes over time, and we must be cautious lest we go too far back in time when trying to understand something like the medicine masks of three centuries ago in terms of their uses in the well-understood contexts of the nineteenth century. There is a limit to how far the archaeological fisherman can wade upstream against the flow of time without misrepresenting the past. Nonetheless, when used carefully, clues from documentary sources and living oral tradition can be used to illuminate the meaning of Iroquois archaeology, providing insights that would be unavailable to us if the Iroquois had been silenced by extinction in AD 1600.

Constraints on length have kept me from providing more than just a brief introduction to the vast literature on the Iroquois. I am unable even to provide a comprehensive list of references, for such a list would consume most of the volume. The sources I have cited will often lead serious readers to other more specialized sources. In addition, I recommend volume 15, *Northeast*, of the Smithsonian Institution series known as the *Handbook of North American Indians* (Trigger 1978). Key chapters in that volume are listed individually in the bibliography. I also recommend the three-volume *Iroquois Source Book* edited by Tooker (1985a, b, 1986) and published by Garland. The handbook volume provides summaries that were up to date as of the mid-1970s and the Garland series reproduces classic articles that are now difficult to find. Readers will also find that older bulletins in the New York State Museum series have been reprinted by various publishers and are now widely available for sale in museum shops as well as in libraries. Finally, readers should also refer to the general works of historians like Jennings and Richter as well as those of archaeologists like Ritchie and myself, whose works I have listed in the bibliography.

I have provided terms in various Iroquois languages throughout the book, but readers are cautioned that they are not linguistically consistent. For example, the Iroquoian *th* is never pronounced like either of its pronunciations in English, but neither have scholars been consistent in using it in Iroquoian languages. Orthographies have varied by language and over time, even when provided by the same authority. It seemed wiser to me to remain true to my sources rather than to try to impose a false consistency on them. Consult the sources cited to be sure of precise pronunciations.

I must thank, first of all, the Iroquois, who by being real people have made themselves worthy of all that has been written about them. I should also like to express special thanks to Ronald La France, William Starna, and Janet Snow, all of whom read this book in earlier manuscript form and provided me with many valuable suggestions for its improvement. Many of its better features can be attributed to them, but they remain blameless for any persisting errors.

I am also especially grateful for the advice and support of William Fenton, who was my mentor after I came to Albany as an assistant professor, and who remains so today. His tactful criticism has done much to improve my scholarship, my writing, and my fly casting.

Many others deserve acknowledgment for their help and constructive criticism over the years. They are all friends, mostly scholars, and in some cases they are lucky enough to be Iroquois as well. They include Thomas Abler, George Abrams, Kathleen Allen, James Axtell, Susan Bamann, Susan Bender, James Bradley, Jack Campisi, Wallace Chafe, Claude Chapdelaine, Norman Clermont, Patrick J. Crowe, Mary Druke Becker, Arthur Einhorn, William Engelbrecht, William Finlayson, William Fitzgerald, Raymond Fogelson, Michael Foster, Robert Funk, Charles Gehring, Douglas George, Raymond Gonyea, Barbara Graymont, James B. Griffin, George Hamell, Robert Hasenstab, Larry Hauptman, Charles Hayes, Reginald Henry, Francis Jennings, William Johnson, Dean Knight, Robert Kuhn, Gail Landsman, Floyd Lounsbury, Rob MacDonald, Marianne Mithun, James Pendergast, Tom Porter, Peter Pratt, Betty Prisch, Peter Ramsden, Daniel Richter, Donald Rumrill, Neal Salisbury, Lorraine Saunders, Martha Sempowski, Annemarie Shimony, Michael Stewart, William Sturtevant, Jake Swamp, Jacob Thomas, Elisabeth Tooker, Bruce Trigger, Laurier Turgeon, Robert Venables, Alexander von Gernet, Gary Warrick, Hanni Woodbury, James Wright, and William Wykoff. I hesitate to compile such a list, for I must inadvertently but inevitably leave out someone whose friendship I value, but there it is.

Finally, I thank my wife Janet and my children, Katherine, Barbara, and Joshua, for their love, support, and patience through the countless days and nights that I have deserted them to spend time in the field or in my study.

D.R.S

# 1

## Origins, AD 900–1150: The Midwinter Moon

The modern Iroquois are more than a nation. Historically they have been first five, later six, nations, and often referred to collectively as the Five Nations. In the seventeenth century they were a confederacy of the Mohawks, Oneidas, Onondagas, Cayugas, and Senecas that stretched from east to west across upstate New York. Later they took in the Tuscarora as a sixth member of the League of the Iroquois. Along the way they absorbed hundreds, probably thousands, of refugees and captives from other Indian nations of northeastern North America.

Linguists have used their name to identify a whole set of related languages, the Northern Iroquoians. Before the convulsions of the seventeenth century, Iroquoian languages were spoken not just by the Iroquois nations proper, but also by the five nations of the Huron confederacy, the five nations of the Neutral confederacy, perhaps three nations of Erie, and at least three independent nations, the Petun, Wenro, and Susquehannock. Together they numbered over 90,000 people spread across what is now New York, southern Ontario, and adjacent portions of Pennsylvania, Ohio, and Quebec.

The Iroquois come from ancient stock, but we would never have known them by that name were it not for the equally ancient Basques. Normans and Basques were among the now mostly anonymous fishermen who found and harvested the riches of the Grand Banks in the sixteenth century. This was a twilight century in the history of European exploration of North America, for few documents give us more than subtle hints about these early journeys. Archaeological evidence is just as scanty: a few European artifacts in an Indian site here, the remains of a tiny Basque fishing station there.

Basque fishermen came to know the Algonquian-speaking peoples that lived along the northeast coast from southern Labrador to New England, including the shores of the Gulf of St Lawrence. A simple trading jargon that was a mixture of Basque and Algonquian grew up between these transatlantic trading partners, a pidgin language that was recorded in fragmentary form by later travelers and missionaries. Among the words that survived from this simple vocabulary was one that referred to a feared nation of Indians that lived far to the interior. These warriors sometimes came down the St Lawrence to trade, and their dreaded visits increased when they discovered that European traders were likely to stop by during the warm months. The local Algonquians and Basques called them by the pidgin Basque name *Hilokoa,* "the killer people." Thus, like several other American Indian societies, the Iroquois became known first to Europeans through unflattering second-hand descriptions provided by rivals. That such descriptive aliases may not be complimentary seems rarely to have impeded their general acceptance.[1]

The Algonquian languages of the Gulf region lack the /l/ sound found in Basque and other European languages, so the name became *Hirokoa* to their ears. By the time the French followed Cartier's earlier route into the St Lawrence in the late sixteenth century, parties of Hirokoa men who were traders or raiders as circumstances dictated were even more frequent along the estuary. The French picked up the name for these formidable warriors from the local Algonquians, revised the spelling to fit their own language, and with that "Iroquois" entered the shared vocabulary of the region. Canadians still pronounce it thus, but speakers of New York English have long since changed it, as they have other French words, so that it now rhymes with "Illinois."

### Mythological Origins

*In the distant past, all the earth was covered by deep water, and the only living things there were water animals. There was no sun, moon, or stars, and the watery earth was in darkness. People lived above the great sky dome. A great ever-blossoming tree grew there in the cloud world, where it shaded the councils of the supernaturals. One day the Great Chief became ill, and he dreamed that if the tree were uprooted he would be cured. He further commanded that his pregnant daughter, Sky Woman, look down at the watery darkness. He told her to follow the roots of the tree, and to bring light and land to the world below. The fire dragon that floated in the hole gave her maize, a mortar, a pot, and firebrands for cooking. Then the Great Ruler wrapped her in the light of the fire dragon and dropped Sky Woman through the hole.*

*The animals of the cloud sea were stirred into action by the descending light. Waterfowl rose to cushion Sky Woman's descent with their*

*Figure 1.1    Sky Woman, by Ernest Smith*
*Source: photograph courtesy of the Rochester Museum and*
*Science Center, Rochester, New York.*

*wings. Beaver dove to find earth to make dry land for Sky Woman.*
*But Beaver drowned and floated lifelessly to the surface. Loon, Duck,*
*and others all tried and failed as well. Finally Muskrat tried, and came*
*back with a paw-full of earth that would spread and grow. "Who will*
*bear it?" he asked. Turtle rose to bear the growing earth, and the*
*waterfowl gently guided the falling Sky Woman to the new land.*
*Turtle, the Earth Bearer, is still restless from time to time, and when*
*he stirs there are earthquakes and high seas.*

*Time passed and Sky Woman gave birth to a daughter. The daugh-*
*ter grew rapidly, and when she reached maturity she was visited by a*
*man. He placed two arrows within her, one tipped with chert and the*
*other not. The daughter in turn bore twins. The handsome good twin*
*was born first the usual way, and he was called "Sapling" [maple*
*sprout]. The ugly evil twin forced himself out through his mother's*

*armpit, killing her in the process. He was called "Flint." In grief, Sapling created the sun from his mother's face. The Evil Twin made darkness to drive the sun west. Sapling drew the moon and the stars from his mother's breast, and created great mountains and straight rivers to grace the land. Flint jumbled the mountains and made the rivers crooked. Sapling set forests on the hills and fruit trees in the valleys, but Flint gnarled the forests and hurled storms against the land. Sapling created human beings, and planted maize, tobacco, and other useful plants. Flint created monsters, and made weeds and vermin to attack the plants made by Sapling. Sapling built a fire, which made Flint's legs flake. Sapling threw more wood on the fire and soon Flint's entire body began to flake, and he ran away. Eventually Sapling defeated his brother, striking him with deer antlers, and banished him to an underground cave. Yet Flint can still send out wicked spirits, and their persistence ensures that there is both good and bad in all things.*[2]

There are over 40 recorded versions of the Iroquois origin myth, beginning with one reported in 1632. As in any oral tradition, the essential themes remain but are subject to variation and elaboration. In an Onondaga version Otter is substituted for Beaver. In some versions Sky Woman gives birth to the twins herself and there is no daughter. In a Seneca version the earth comes not from Muskrat, but from the hands of Sky Woman herself, who grabbed it as she fell through the hole in the sky. Sapling can be called the "Older Brother," "the Good Twin," the "Good-Minded One," "Sky Grasper," and so on. Flint can be called "Ice," "Crystal," "Younger Brother," or "the Evil Twin." Various animals and supernaturals can be recast in key roles.

Although today many people vainly seek literal history in myth, origin myths tell us mainly about morality. Thus the genesis that this Iroquois myth tells us most about comprises the fundamental principles that underlie traditional Iroquois thought as it was recorded in the late nineteenth and early twentieth centuries. The coexistence of good and evil pervades the Iroquois cosmos, and the notion curiously fits the modern world better than modern mainstream American notions of evil. Many Euro-Americans still struggle with the paradox of belief in an all-powerful god and daily evidence for the existence of evil. Western philosophers have named the contradiction "theodicy," but giving paradox a name merely masks it. The irony remains that Euro-Americans cannot accommodate a clear definition of evil even if they give up belief in an all-powerful god; it remains relative, a thing for winners to attribute to losers and a thing to ascribe permanently to characters like Hitler and the wolf of traditional European folklore. The Iroquois waste little time grappling with this problem, for their traditional beliefs do not lead them to the paradox. Instead, the Iroquois cosmos is composed of good things, everywhere tainted by evil. The proportions can change; good men can become evil as the balance tips, and evil men can be made good by right-minded neighbors. The wolf is not pervasively evil, though he may appear to be to the rabbit; and the rabbit is not all good, for he destroys the young shoots of Iroquois crops.[3]

The origin myth also reveals other essential characteristics of ancient Iroquois society. The central character is a woman, who like later Iroquois women was the source of life and sustenance, and mother to the men who shaped the physical world. Sky Woman or her daughter gave birth to the men who would create most of the plants, animals, and inanimate things that, for better or for worse, constitute the world. From her body came some of the most important of these. Others, like the beaver and the goose, were already here.[4]

Although the number three occasionally turns up as well, the duality of the twins reflects a pervasive duality in Iroquois society. The twins dwelt together in the same lodge for a time, facing each other across the fire in a way that reflected family living arrangements, village moiety division, and even the structure of the League of the Iroquois.[5]

But Iroquois origins conceived as first principles tell us nothing about their physical origins in ancient North America. The nonliterate societies of the eastern woodlands prior to the sixteenth century have left us with no written records and with oral traditions that evolved to serve purposes other than the recording of factual history. To recover the ancient history of the Iroquois, we must reconstruct it from surviving vestiges, whether they be elements of living languages, documented behavior, or physical evidence recovered from repositories or archaeological sites.

## The Origin of Ritual

The earth of Iroquois cosmology lies on the back of a great turtle, and the turtle itself holds the secret to the annual passage of the new moons. Turtle's carapace is comprised of a mosaic of thirteen large plates, surrounded by a border of smaller ones. One counts the new moons of the year by starting above Turtle's left front leg and counting the large plates counterclockwise. The tenth new moon falls on the plate above his neck, and the next three follow down the middle of his back. In another part of the world, people divided time into quarter-moon weeks of seven days, but this division of the cycle did not interest the Iroquois. It is said that the border of small plates allows one to count off the 28 days of the lunar month. Turtle actually has only 25 small plates on the fringe of his carapace, but his imprecision is almost balanced by that of the moon itself. The lunar month is actually 29.5306 days long.[6]

A period of twelve lunar months falls about ten days short of marking off a complete year. So in addition to twelve named moons, the Iroquois inserted a "lost moon" every three years or so. The Iroquois did not use the moons as a precise calendar, for environmental cues were much better signals for changes in daily routine during all but the coldest months. The names of the moons were not so much names as brief descriptions of the kinds of activities that went on during each of them.

The year began with the midwinter new moon, which grew to fullness and then shrank once again to mark the first lunar cycle of the year. Men were usually out for the early winter hunt when midwinter approached, and they needed a signal to know when to come home for the year's most important ceremony. The signal came from the Pleiades, the winter constellation of seven stars that was never in the heavens while the crops were growing. The stars of the Pleiades still rise in the east just before dawn after the first frost comes, and set in the west soon after evening dusk around the time of the last frost of spring. When the hunters saw the Pleiades directly overhead when night fell, they knew that the time of frost was half over, and the Midwinter Ceremony would be held four nights (five days) after the next new moon.[7]

The Iroquois nations had several stories about the Pleiades. In one the stars were once children, in another more specifically sisters, in a third boys. Often they are said to have been hungry, and to have danced their way into the sky. Indeed, the theme of hungry children seems always present in stories related to this constellation of the lean months.

The Midwinter Ceremony falls just after the first new moon of the annual cycle. It was a time when hunters returned from the fall hunt to refresh themselves, bring news to the village, and equip themselves for renewed hunting in the deep snows of winter. The ceremony was observed but not very well understood by Jesuit missionaries and other seventeenth-century acquaintances of the Iroquois. It was not until the middle of the twentieth century that anyone carried out a comprehensive study of the ceremony in all of its surviving variations. Even now the basic structure remains consistent.

During the moons of winter the Iroquois have always enjoyed a game called snow snakes. Players make snakes from hickory poles

## The Midwinter Ceremony

The ceremony begins in late January or early February, depending upon the occurrence of the midwinter new moon, and it lasts at least a week. At the beginning, special medicine mask messengers, "Big Heads" or "Our Uncles," go through the houses, stirring the ashes of cold fires and announcing the beginning of the ceremony. The following days are spent in the first segment of the ceremony, fulfilling or renewing dreams, dancing, and playing games. The second (now third) segment was originally spent in a performance of the Our Life Supporter dances. These sacred dances included the Women's Dance, the Corn Dance, the Stomp Dance, the Hand-in-Hand Dance, the Striking-the-Pole Dance, and the War Dance. Social dances are also included, often in the evenings, and the Thanksgiving Speech is recited many times, before and after the events of each day.[8]

Dream guessing has long been an essential part of the protracted ceremony. People guess the content of each other's dreams on the basis of subtle hints, and offer suggestions as to how the dreams might be fulfilled. Dreams are regarded as supernatural messages, and fulfillment of the dreamers' desires is necessary for their continued health.

The general tone of the ceremony is one of contentment and thanksgiving. The traditional Iroquois ask the supernatural for nothing, but are grateful for what they get as a matter of course. It is an appropriate time to announce names. It may be that a child has been born, or is adopting an adult name, or an adult is assuming a faithkeeper name. In any case the name will be drawn from a pool of currently unused names owned by the individual's clan.

Almost two hundred years ago, the Seneca prophet Handsome Lake added four sacred rituals as a second segment of the Midwinter Ceremony. These are the Feather Dance, the Thanksgiving Dance, the Rite of Personal Chant, and the Bowl Game, which added as many as four days to the ceremony. In the nineteenth century the ceremony still called for the strangulation and later the burning of one or two white dogs, whose deaths and immolation carried accumulated evil up and away from the community. Modern sensitivities put an end to the practice, although many insisted that the problem was that the breed of white dogs had died out. Some substituted white baskets for the sacrificial dogs, and at least one Iroquois artist still paints white dogs on modern shopping bags as a continuation of the tradition.[9]

*Figure 1.2   Modern snow snakes*
*Source: photograph courtesy of the Iroquois Indian Museum,*
*Howes Cave, New York.*

that are about as long as a man's height. Since the seventeenth century
the hickory snakes have had heads weighted with lead, and the poles
are tapered towards the opposite end. Players throw the snakes on
packed snow, the winner being that which travels the farthest.

## Language Origins

The family of Northern Iroquoian languages has three subdivisions.
The first of these is made up of the languages of the Five Nations of
the Iroquois proper plus Susquehannock. The Mohawk and Oneida
languages are somewhat more closely related to one another than
they are to the other four languages in this group, Onondaga, Cayuga,
Seneca, and Susquehannock. The second group is Huronian, com-
prising Neutral and Huron-Petun. The latter became further sub-
divided between the Huron of Lorette and Wyandot after the dispersal
of the Hurons around 1650. The third group is the poorly understood Laurentian language recorded by Cartier on the St Lawrence
in the early sixteenth century.

The Tuscarora and Nottaway languages represent an early off-shoot of Northern Iroquoian. They were spoken in North Carolina until the remnants of these people moved north to join the Five Nations in the early eighteenth century. Although classified with the other Northern Iroquoian languages, these are more remotely related to the other Northern Iroquoian languages than the latter are to each other. They probably broke away even before the main body of Northern Iroquoians moved into what are now New York and Ontario.

The only surviving representative of Southern Iroquoian is Cherokee. The split between ancestral Cherokee and Northern Iroquoian is deep, having occurred 3,500–4,000 years ago. The breakup of the languages of the Iroquois probably took place within the last 1,000–1,500 years. This means that the Iroquois languages relate to each other in about the same way that the Romance languages relate to each other. The Romance languages diverged as local expressions of Latin at about the same time, and they differ from each other to about the same degree that the Iroquois languages differ from each other.[10]

Linguists can reconstruct portions of proto-languages from the vocabularies of surviving descendant languages. Thus key vocabulary items can be reconstructed for Proto-Five-Nations, Proto-Northern-Iroquoian, and Proto-Iroquoian. No horticultural terms have been reconstructed for Proto-Iroquoian, but several can be reconstructed for Proto-Northern-Iroquoian, including Tuscarora. This means that Northern Iroquoians all had maize horticulture when they began to break up into separate language groups a millennium ago. It was not acquired by them gradually or separately after that time. However, it was acquired after the split between Northern and Southern Iroquoian.

Proto-language reconstruction also assumes a relatively small and localized speech community. None of this is consistent with the idea of a gradual evolution of Iroquoian societies out of a general and widespread cultural base. The older Proto-Iroquoian language contained words for the key plant and animal species of the Appalachian highlands. Their reconstructed vocabulary suggests that they were skilled hunters and gatherers who had not yet adopted cultivation. The later Proto-Northern-Iroquoian languages contained all of these elements and more, including a term for tobacco. By the time that the Proto-Five-Nations language was spoken, perhaps a thousand years ago, domesticated plants (particularly maize) had been added to the vocabulary. They had words for mortars and pestles, as well as grain, dough, winnow, flour, and mush, all terms related to the preparation of food from domesticated crops. Stone mortars and pestles are known archaeologically. Large wooden mortars and dumbbell-shaped wooden pestles were used at least as early as the eighteenth century, but none has been preserved in the archaeological record.[11] There were also terms for barrels, spoons, rattles, pails, and mats, all things that one would expect to find in a seventeenth-century Iroquois longhouse. In other words, the basic elements of Iroquois culture were probably in place even before the Five Nations diverged from their common ancestor.[12]

One of the most significant discoveries of historical Iroquoian linguistics is the antiquity of the Midwinter Ceremony. Terms that refer to major parts of or activities in the Midwinter Ceremony are unanalyzable in Seneca. Such words are usually inferred to be very ancient. In English, words like "railroad" and "airplane" are analyzable, while more ancient words like "arrow" and "spear" are not. Thus the Iroquois Midwinter Ceremony and the vocabulary that pertains to it must be ancient in Iroquois culture. This is the most important of all Iroquois calendrical ceremonies, and apparently the model upon which all others were based. It is a ceremony of renewal, with elements of shamanism that seem to hark back to a hunting tradition that predated the horticultural lifeway of the more recent Iroquois.[13]

### Archaeological Origins

Nineteenth-century speculation by Euro-Americans about the origins of various American Indian nations usually focused on migration. This seemed consistent with European experience, for much of the history of the middle ages there was characterized by the dramatic movements of named tribes across the landscape. Unlike biologists, early anthropologists did not concern themselves much with the underlying forces that propelled population movements, and supposed migrations came to be explanations in and of themselves. Archaeologists, who did not yet appreciate the great antiquity of American Indian cultures, were content to move them about the map like chess pieces, explaining change over time by the replacement of one piece by another. Migration stories also preserved the notion that American Indian cultures were not only footloose but culturally static, not subject to cultural change except through loss by attrition. The drive by early anthropologists to record what they perceived to be mere remnants of Indian cultures was well intended, but as we shall see it carried with it some unfortunate consequences for twentieth-century Indians.

Lewis Henry Morgan, writing in the middle of the nineteenth

century, was among those who used migration to propose a recent origin for the Iroquois. Cartier had encountered Northern Iroquoians along the St Lawrence River during his voyages of 1534, 1535, and 1541. They had disappeared by the time French and Basque fishermen returned to the St Lawrence later in that century. Morgan and others imagined that these were the Iroquois proper, who had moved to what is now New York in the middle of the sixteenth century, fragmenting into five nations in the process.

In 1916, Arthur Parker proposed that the Iroquoians had originated around the mouth of the Ohio River. He imagined an elaborate scenario according to which some groups crossed the Detroit River and pushed northeastward through southern Ontario. Those that moved farthest eastward to the vicinity of Montreal were the Mohawks. Ancestral Onondagas soon moved across the St Lawrence to take up residence in Jefferson County, New York. The remainder became the ancestors of the Huron, Petun, and Neutral nations. He supposed that at the same time the ancestors of the Eries, Senecas, Cayugas, and Susquehannocks had moved along the southern shore of Lake Erie to their historic locations.[14]

Parker's hypotheses might seem almost foolish in retrospect, but it is important to realize that the scenario he concocted was consistent with contemporary Euro-American concepts of cultural development, with the details of historic Indian migrations, and with at least some of the details of Iroquois myth. Parker's error was in assuming that working backwards in time from the perceived realities of recorded history would reveal an accurate portrait of prehistory. This error has sometimes been repeated by others who have inappropriately projected backwards what may be only recently evolved traits in order to explain some archaeological phenomenon. Thus many modern students of the Northern Iroquoians are reluctant to use national terms like "Seneca" or "Mohawk" for periods prior to AD 1500. It is unlikely that these individual Iroquois nations yet existed then, even in incipient form, although the ancestral Iroquois certainly did exist at that time in some form.

Archaeological views changed by mid-century, and the reaction to the excesses of the migration scenarios led archaeologists to prefer explanations that centered on the in-place evolution of prehistoric cultures. Richard MacNeish used the evidence of pottery designs to argue that the Iroquoians had evolved *in situ* from ancestors who had lived in the same region a thousand years or more earlier. The *in situ* hypothesis put no starting point on the process, and archaeologists soon convinced themselves that the Iroquoians had been in place for thousands of years.[15]

William Ritchie carried out most of the archaeological fieldwork that first defined the history of the Iroquois culture prior to their contact with Europeans. Ritchie had worked for Parker in Rochester during the early part of his career. Like Parker, he was aware of the large and clearly Iroquoian village sites that could be found in the traditional homelands of the Iroquois nations. He was also aware of similar sites clustered in Jefferson County and other areas that had clearly not been lived in by any known Iroquois nations. However, they all seemed similar enough to deserve classification as Iroquois culture.

Ritchie also found evidence across New York State for an earlier cultural tradition, which he called "Owasco." The tradition was named for the lake at Auburn, New York, on the shore of which was found the Emerson site. Owasco culture seemed clearly ancestral to later Iroquois culture, and therefore clearly Iroquoian. He named three century-long archaeological phases for the Owasco cultural tradition, and two more for the Iroquois cultural tradition.[16]

At first, Ritchie did not propose pushing the origins of the Iroquois back any further than the beginnings of the Owasco culture, about AD 1000. However, MacNeish's new *in situ* hypothesis was quickly becoming a controlling model in Iroquois archaeology during the same period. Ritchie's last major joint publication with Robert Funk reflected the shift in general archaeological opinion toward MacNeish's view: "The unbroken continuity of material culture and settlement patterns, from Early Point Peninsula into the earliest Owasco expressions, persisted into the early historic period."[17] This pushed the in-place development of the Iroquois back another thousand years. Instead of seeking evidence of breaks in sequences, archaeologists now sought evidence of gradual change over time. Instead of change involving migration, they emphasized evolutionary processes. Archaeologists almost everywhere in the region sought continuity over time, and we found it; we did not find what we did not seek.[18]

The Point Peninsula cultural tradition covered nearly all of Northern Iroquoia and much more. Point Peninsula sites are scattered across southern Ontario and Quebec, sometimes north of the southern edge of the Canadian Shield, but never farther north than the 47th parallel. The culture fades into the related Saugeen culture to the west of Toronto. The southern limits of Point Peninsula do not extend into Pennsylvania or New Jersey. However, closely related ceramics occur throughout New England. It was really only a ceramic tradition as originally defined, but more recent usage has elevated Point Peninsula to the status of a long-lived cultural tradition.

Early Point Peninsula pottery exhibits pseudo-scallop shell, dentate, and rocker stamp decoration, all of them common for the time in the northeastern woodlands. Later Point Peninsula pottery differs from earlier forms in several ways. Later vessels are larger, and lips are more rounded to slightly flattened. Most later vessels have cord-malleated surfaces, and corded decorations come to predominate. These were presumably made with the edges and flat surfaces of core-wrapped paddles. Dentate stamping, pseudo-scallop shell decoration, and rocker stamping all disappeared. There are appliquéd collars on some vessels, but although they are superficially similar to the collars that appear on later Owasco and Iroquois vessels, they are technologically different from the latter. All Point Peninsula vessels tend to be elongated, with conical rather than rounded bases. Interior surfaces are often channeled. Sherds often show fracture planes that indicate that the vessels were constructed from layers of coils and fillets.[19]

In contrast to Point Peninsula ceramics, Owasco vessels made by Iroquoian potters were modeled by a paddle-and-anvil method, had more rounded bottoms, and lacked body decoration and the fracture planes that would suggest coil manufacture. Interior surfaces were smoothed, not channeled like Point Peninsula pots, and exterior surfaces were finished by cord, fabric, or later on check-stamp malleation. Rims were flat, not rounded, and thick, and later on were splayed outward. Pronounced Owasco collars on later vessels were technically new and different from the appliquéd collars occasionally seen on earlier Point Peninsula vessels. Perhaps most significantly, Owasco vessels were generally much larger than Point Peninsula ones, and this probably indicates communal dining by relatively larger family units.[20]

The motor habits implied by Owasco ceramics were still obvious to seventeenth-century observers of Iroquoian potters. Gabriel Sagard, a Recollect missionary, described in 1632 the process used by the Huron:

> But the Hurons and other sedentary tribes and nations used and knew how to make earthenware pots, as they still do, firing them in their ovens. These are very good and do not break when set on the fire even though they may not have water in them. But they cannot stand moisture and cold water for long, but become soft and break at the least blow given them; otherwise they last for a long time. The women savages make them, taking suitable earth which they sift and pulverize very thoroughly, mixing with it a little sandstone. Then when the lump has been shaped like a ball they put a hole in it with their fist, and this they keep enlarging, scraping it inside with a little wooden paddle as much and as long as is necessary to complete the work. These pots are made without feet and without handles, quite round like a ball, except of the mouth which projects a little.[21]

*Figure 1.3   Small Owasco vessel from the Bates site, 16.5 cm tall*
*Source: photograph courtesy of the New York State Museum.*

The subsistence systems of the people responsible for Point Peninsula culture appear to have been broadly based on hunting, foraging,
and fishing. Scheduled movements probably took them to a succession of regularly used camps, mainly on the shores of lakes and
streams. Cultivation would have been restricted to the tending of
tobacco and a few native food plants like pigweed (*Chenopodium*).
Point Peninsula sites are usually small camps that were sited at strategic places near where fish runs, waterfowl, passenger pigeons, or
other resources were concentrated.[22]
   In short, as seen by archaeologists, Point Peninsula culture does
not really look much like later Iroquoian culture. Two factors that
prevent us from inferring an easy *in situ* evolution from one to the
other have already been mentioned. First, analysis of language origins
has convinced many linguists that the breakup of Northern Iroquoian
languages from a single Proto-Northern-Iroquoian language began
only about a thousand years ago. Second, several horticultural terms
can be reconstructed for Proto-Northern-Iroquoian. This means that
Northern Iroquoians all had maize horticulture when they began to

break up into separate language groups a millennium ago: It was not acquired by them either gradually or separately after that time. This second point is very important, for it means that the Northern Iroquoians had horticulture when they were still a relatively small local culture and before they broke up into several isolated clusters scattered across the region. The proto-language must have been spoken by a relatively small and localized speech community, nothing as widespread as Point Peninsula culture.

There is a third line of new evidence that has to do with matrilocal residence and its origins. Matrilocal residence, wherein a young newly married couple takes up residence with the woman's family, was strongly developed among the Iroquoians. Matrilocality typically arises in dominant societies that expand into territories at the expense of hostile but subordinate societies already there. It is a form of social organization confined to societies operating at a tribal level of development. The matrilineage, a basic unit of Iroquois society five centuries ago, is a successful predatory organization in conflicts with other tribes, although perhaps unnecessary against bands and ineffective against chiefdoms and states.[23]

Anthropologists have traditionally tended to assume a gradual development of matrilocal residence and to attribute it to the advent of dependence on female activities in subsistence.[24] Archaeologists have also tended to assume that it was a gradual process that paralleled the gradual development of plant domesticates and the role of women in food production. But the evidence now indicates that multifamily (probably matrilocal) residence, horticulture, and compact villages appeared suddenly, not gradually, in Iroquoia.

There is additional evidence from historical linguistics. The word for "mother" is basically the same in four of the five Iroquois languages, Seneca, Cayuga, Onondaga, and Oneida. The Mohawks appear to have made a separate and more recent change. However, in all cases the terms referred to mother's sisters as well, an extension that anthropologists expect when people live in extended matrilocal households. If all of the Iroquois languages had this term and its meaning in their vocabularies, it must have been present with the same meaning a thousand years ago when there was only one ancestral language.[25]

It now seems clear that early Iroquoians arrived in the region with their matrilineages and their subsistence practices already developed. These traits were not only already present, but crucial to Iroquoian dominance over the people that they were displacing. Further, they must have arrived on the order of a thousand years ago, not earlier.

The displaced peoples were probably speakers of Algonquian

languages who had expanded southward through southern Ontario, New York, and New England at some earlier date. These were the carriers of Point Peninsula culture, whose own expansion may well have been made possible by their acquisition of the bow and arrow from other cultures to the northwest of them. Yet they remained mainly hunters and gatherers, and they lived at a low regional population density. Although with the bow and arrow they were dominant over those they had displaced earlier, they were culturally subordinate to the Northern Iroquoians expanding northward after AD 900. By that time the Iroquoians also had the bow and arrow, but they also had much more, and their expansion could not be stopped.

We should expect to find archaeological evidence of a swift appearance of Northern Iroquoians in the northeast. There should be clear evidence of discontinuity with respect to earlier culture(s) in such things as ceramic styles and settlement patterns, and there should be evidence of a source for the intruders.

These predictions necessarily focus attention on the advent of the Owasco culture. This tradition appeared after AD 900, and it is almost universally acknowledged to have been produced by Iroquoians. Looking at it again from a new perspective, there is a clear discontinuity between it and the last phase of the Point Peninsula cultural tradition.

Ritchie defined the Hunter's Home phase on the basis of five sites: Hunter's Home, White, Turnbull, Willow Tree, and Kipp Island No. 4. His interpretation of the sites is based upon his assumption that Point Peninsula culture evolved into early Owasco culture. He assumed that the materials found at the five sites should document the gradual processes implied by a smooth *in situ* development. However, the evidence puts great strain on the model, and there are certain data that Ritchie admits cannot be explained in those terms. Nonetheless, all of the data *can* be explained by a hypothesis that provides for the replacement of a late Point Peninsula population by an intrusive Owasco population.

The type site is the half-acre Hunter's Home site on the edge of Montezuma Marsh near Savannah, New York. The site has two components, an Early Owasco level and a late Point Peninsula level just below it. Ritchie used the late Point Peninsula level to define the Hunter's Home phase.

The largest known component currently assigned to the Hunter's Home phase is the White site near Norwich. Ritchie originally assigned this site to the Early Owasco culture. Later, when a radiocarbon date of AD 905±250 became available, he decided that it was very early Owasco and transitional from Point Peninsula. Finally, by

1965, he defined the late Point Peninsula Hunter's Home phase and put the White site into it. Despite careful searching, no maize remains were found by the avocational archaeologists who excavated the site, and this too encouraged Ritchie to conclude that it was really a pre-Owasco site.

Ritchie illustrates pottery sherds from the White site, but he does not type them or provide any other relevant data. We have only his general observation that in the Hunter's Home phase cord decoration and cord-malleated surface treatment rapidly replaced the older dentate, rocker-stamped, and other styles.[26]

The White site lies on the top of a high ridge that divides the Unadilla and Chenango rivers, an unusual setting for a Point Peninsula village, but one that is common for Early Owasco villages. The radiocarbon date calibrates to AD 992, so it is easy to argue that the White site is really an Early Owasco component, just as Ritchie believed in 1944. But what then of all the Late Point Peninsula ceramics found there mixed with Owasco styles? These, I suggest, were made by women from the earlier population who were absorbed by the intrusive Owasco community. This explanation is consistent with both the archaeological evidence and anthropological theory regarding the process of intrusion and replacement of one population at the expense of another. Specifically, it is consistent with what is known about tribal warfare, in which the capture and incorporation of women by expanding dominant societies is one of the most common features.

The Turnbull site near Schenectady is Ritchie's third Hunter's Home component. The projectile points from the Turnbull site are of the triangular form common to Owasco sites, but unlike the Jack's Reef forms common to the Point Peninsula cultural tradition. About 80 percent of the Turnbull ceramics are Point Peninsula types, while the remaining 20 percent are Owasco types. Ritchie and others could not explain this strange mix in terms of the *in situ* model, and they let it stand as an enigma.[27]

Maize kernels were recovered at the site, and these have been dated to AD 1457. They apparently come from a small later component present at the site, and the date does not help us solve the puzzle. However, the puzzle disappears if we take a new view of the Turnbull site and what was probably going on there. It seems likely now that this was an Early Owasco site that was occupied by an intrusive community that included a substantial number of adopted non-Iroquoian women. In this way, Owasco triangular points and Point Peninsula potsherds are simultaneously accounted for. The only possible problem with this interpretation is that the site is a riverside camp site, not a typical Owasco hilltop village. I suspect that a contemporary base village can probably be found among the many Owasco sites known for the Mohawk Valley.

The Willow Tree site near St Johnsville contains Ritchie's fourth Hunter's Home component. This component has a calibrated radio-carbon date of 955 BP (AD 995). The radiocarbon date calibrates to three calendar dates, AD 1031, 1144, and 1146. Ritchie probably put the site into the Hunter's Home phase only because of the age of the uncalibrated date, for 97 percent of the ceramics are Owasco types, and only 3 percent of the sherds are assignable to Point Peninsula. Clearly the Willow Tree component is simply an Early Owasco site, not Late Point Peninsula.

Kipp Island No. 4 is Ritchie's fifth Hunter's Home component. The four-component site lies in the town of Tyre, Seneca County. The component appears to have been identified as separate from Kipp Island No. 3 mainly on the strength of a single radiocarbon date. Kipp Island No. 4 is a cemetery component in which grave offerings were very rare and not diagnostic of anything but Point Peninsula. Kipp Island No. 3 is a habitation area of the site that yielded another radiocarbon date that was almost indistinguishable from that of Kipp Island No. 4. Kipp Island ceramics include speci-mens of 11 Point Peninsula types. None of the types present appears to indicate an early Owasco connection. Thus Kipp Island No. 4, and for that matter No. 3 as well, appears to be a pure Late Point Peninsula site that probably dates somewhere between AD 770 and 900, just before the arrival of intrusive Northern Iroquoians carrying Owasco culture.

Overall, the Hunter's Home phase seems now to be an unfortunate hybrid. Ritchie had it right the first time, and had it not been for the powerful influence of the *in situ* hypothesis he may well have never conceived the Hunter's Home phase as an artificial transitional one from Point Peninsula to Owasco. Both the Hunter's Home type site and the Kipp Island site are clearly Late Point Peninsula sites. The White site seems to clearly be what Ritchie thought it was in 1944, an intrusive Early Owasco site. The Turnbull site is similar in kind if not in size or location. It is an Owasco site with some Late Point Peninsula ceramics mixed in. The Willow Tree component is later and even more clearly Owasco.

Whether or not the Hunter's Home phase is retained as a conven-ient category, the advent of Owasco is more economically explained as an intrusion than by the older *in situ* alternative. This explains evidence at the Turnbull and White sites that cannot be accommo-dated by the gradual changes assumed by the *in situ* hypothesis. It is time not to abandon the *in situ* hypothesis, but to conclude that Northern Iroquoian development had a clear beginning in New York and Ontario.[28]

There were sharp and fundamental differences between the Point Peninsula and Owasco ceramic traditions, the best evidence archaeologists have to assess ethnicity. The contrast between coil construction and paddle-and-anvil modeling, basic construction techniques, indicates very different procedures and perhaps very different sets of motor habits. One should not expect to find profound shifts within a slowly evolving technology.

Of course, not all of the characteristics of later Iroquois pottery appear full-blown in AD 1150. Early Owasco pots are elongated when compared to more globular late vessels. Collars are rare at first and become more common later on. The most common Owasco decorative technique was cord impression, a trait that is also found on Late Point Peninsula vessels. Nevertheless, the change from Point Peninsula to Owasco styles amounts to a major break in the archaeological sequence.

An excellent test of discontinuity might be a new comparative examination of Point Peninsula and Owasco skeletal remains to see if the two peoples looked different physically. Although there are some indications that there might have been significant biological differences between the Point Peninsula and Owasco populations, the detailed analysis necessary to resolve the question remains to be done. What is required is a new osteological study using modern techniques to directly test a hypothesis favoring discontinuity. However, this kind of research might well be frustrated by the probable nature of Iroquoian growth and expansion. Non-Iroquoians, particularly women, were probably absorbed in large numbers, and their absorption would make later Iroquois look less like their Iroquoian ancestors. If such a study is ever undertaken, it should concentrate on the earliest Owasco people, whom we should expect to look least like the Point Peninsula people they were both displacing and absorbing.[29]

### Ethnic Origins

Proto-Northern-Iroquoian vocabulary suggests very general Appalachian origins. Clemson's Island culture is the best candidate for the source of Owasco immigrants to what is now New York around AD 900. Clemson's Island sites cluster along the Junista and West Branch tributaries of the Susquehanna River in central Pennsylvania. Radiocarbon dates indicate that Clemson's Island culture flourished from

AD 775 to 1300. Its origins remain obscure, but its significance for Iroquois history does not. Clemson's Island sites first appear over a century before Iroquoian sites begin to appear farther north. Maize, squash, and other cultigens are present from the beginning, and Clemson's Island ceramics are very similar to Owasco ceramics. The collared rims that are characteristic of most later Iroquoian ceramic types could have easily developed out of Clemson's Island rim styles. The same is true of burial practices and bone technology.

Clemson's Island settlements were farming hamlets that were occupied during at least the summer and fall seasons. Some hamlets are apparently associated with burial mounds, but mound construction did not move north with migrating communities. Their settlements were not palisaded, and Clemson's Island culture disappeared with the spread of warfare around AD 1300.[30]

A combination of related cultural and environmental factors produced the conditions favorable to the Northern Iroquoian expansion. They had maize horticulture and lived in compact hamlets by at least AD 750. This preadaptation made them dominant over the smaller, less compact, and less sedentary Point Peninsula communities that they were about to displace. By adopting an aggressive matrilocal settlement system, they were equipped to settle anywhere they wanted in the thinly populated region to the north, even if they were initially outnumbered on a regional scale.

It is probably not merely coincidental that the northward incursion occurred around the beginning of the medieval warm epoch.[31] Longer growing seasons and the availability of maize that was adapted to the region must have made the loamy soils of what are now New York and southern Ontario very attractive. Once established on rich soils along an east–west axis south of Lake Ontario, the Iroquoians were positioned for later expansion around the lake, down the St Lawrence, and to the eastern shore of Lake Huron.[32] But it is the history of just those whose descendants were known as the Iroquois proper that concerns us here. We must leave aside the Iroquoians who pushed on past what is now New York, and focus on the Owasco.

# 2

## Owasco, 1150–1350:
## The Sugar Moon

The Northern Iroquoians of a millennium ago moved northward along the upper tributaries of the Susquehanna River. Most took up residence on the rich flatlands around Lake Ontario and eastward down the Mohawk Valley. They moved north of the Appalachian highlands, but stayed south of the unfertile Canadian Shield. It was and still is a region dominated by maple, beech, elm, and birch trees. Pine and hemlock trees mix with these and give way to fir and spruce in the north. Walnut and butternut trees were there too, but the maples, pines, and elms were the species most crucial to Iroquoian technology. They are still venerated, and they still appear as Iroquoian political metaphors.[1]

These forests were populated by large numbers of deer and turkeys. Swans, geese, and ducks were both resident here and swept through in large migrations in the spring and fall. But none of these migrations was as spectacular as the March flight of passenger pigeons. They came in clouds of millions to roost together in huge beech trees. Harvesting them was a straightforward matter of using long poles to knock down nests from trees full of squabs still too young to fly away.

In the lakes and streams were trout, pike, perch, bass, turtle, and other resident species. Eels and salmon migrated up the St Lawrence and into most of the streams flowing out of Iroquoia into Lake Ontario. The great waterfall at Cohoes kept the migratory fish out of the Mohawk River, so the easternmost of the Owasco villages had to trade for them.

It was then also a time of global warming. During this episode, often called the Medieval Optimum, the climate north of their earlier homeland was attractive. The same warm spell drew the Norse westward out of Scandinavia to homestead what were before and since much harsher places in Iceland and Greenland. The climatic episode,

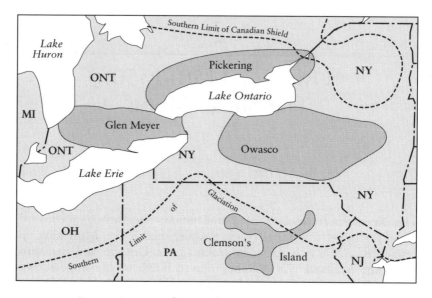

*Figure 2.1    Early Northern Iroquoian cultures*

which lasted until the onset of the Little Ice Age around AD 1300, must have had similar effects in many parts of the world.

The Iroquoian expansion could not have been a single migration, but must rather have been several branching and sequential ones. Major migratory leaps by communities hiving off from older ones produced clusters of sites on the regional landscape. With each migration, a group of Iroquoians established itself in a new area, displacing any older population and perhaps absorbing largely female portions of it in the course of sporadic warfare. The Northern Iroquoians were also growing in numbers as new communities budded off from old ones.[2] Even older communities found it necessary to move from time to time, as local firewood supplies ran out and the unfertilized fields wore out and became less productive. Often the new daughter communities moved only a short distance from the older ones, and the sites that they all left behind form clusters on the archaeological landscape. Sometimes, however, a community would move greater distances, leaping perhaps 100 kilometers or more in a single move. We can only guess at the causes of these giant leaps, but similar societies in modern times have often undertaken them as a result of conflict or a scarcity of critically important resources. Whatever the cause, the relatively rare leaps established new village centers across Northern Iroquoia. Some of the major moves failed.

For the successful major moves, subsequent village multiplication through smaller-scale village relocations led to the creation of clusters of sites around the initial destination points. By AD 1600 there were many such clusters, all separated by spaces in which one finds no Iroquoian village sites at all. But in Owasco times there was still a fairly even spatial distribution of founder villages that had yet to either succeed or fail to establish clusters.

The Northern Iroquoians found themselves owners of a new homeland. Their Algonquian predecessors there were dead, displaced, or adopted. It was the springtime of their cultural life in this new land. They brought with them the memory of the midwinter new moon, and they kept the practice of its ceremony. The springtime brought the maple moon, when the branches of the maple tree begin to drip with sweet sap. The gathering of the maple sap prompted another seasonal ceremony, which followed the basic structure of the midwinter ritual. Once again they asked for nothing, but gave sincere thanks for the bounty of the forest in a season when game was scarce and the winter stores were nearly gone.

Over time, people in different clusters came to speak different dialects as local patterns of speech drifted off in their own directions. Common ritual also took on varying forms, and the details of traditional ceremony came to be slightly different from one village cluster to another. By the nineteenth century, the Maple Ceremony was not one ritual, but a variety of similar ceremonies practiced a bit differently in each of the communities that still observed it. But one finds only the germs of these later divergences in the largely uniform Owasco culture of AD 1000.

Ritchie based his definition of Owasco on the Emerson type site on Owasco Lake at Auburn, New York, and 23 others across the state. Figure 2.2 maps the distribution of those Owasco sites that are named and have been studied sufficiently to allow them to be dated to one of the three Owasco phases.

Had the Iroquoians developed out of the Point Peninsula cultural tradition, we should expect to see an emergent culture having three broad characteristics. First, there should be continuity from earlier to later culture. Second, the evolution should occur everywhere within the range of the Point Peninsula where the new adaptation was viable and superior to the old adaptation. Third, there should be local stylistic diversity across the whole range of the evolving cultural tradition as related but distinct groups each adopted specific new forms within the more general evolution of Point Peninsula culture.

If, on the other hand, northern Iroquoian culture arose from an intrusive migration of founders, we should expect to see three very

## The Maple Ceremony

The Maple Ceremony was and is one of the major calendrical ceremonies. Despite its variations across Northern Iroquoia, it has enduring themes at its core. These also characterize the Midwinter Ceremony, which was the model for all the other calendrical ceremonies that apparently developed after it. Those themes include a formality of speech and behavior. It is important to use the native language, especially today, when English is overwhelming the Iroquois languages. There is always balance and reciprocity between men and women, and between the two moieties into which the clans are grouped. Feasting, singing, and dancing must always be part of the ceremony. The interpretation or acting out of dreams and confession of sins are important for cleansing of minds, and tobacco is always burned to carry the message to the creator above. Masks, wampum, and other powerful and symbolic artifacts are used in the ceremony. Almost always the Thanksgiving Speech marks both the opening and the closing of the ceremony.

The Thanksgiving Speech is a speech that begins and ends all important Iroquois ceremonies. Its theme is gratitude for things received, and this pervades traditional Iroquois thought. The speaker may adjust the length of the speech to fit the occasion, and the order in which phenomena are recognized and thanked varies. But the general structure of the address is the same. Things of the earth are mentioned first, from those closest to the earth upwards to those nearer the sky. In a repetitive cadence that is soon picked up even by those unfamiliar with the language, the speaker thanks first the earth itself, then the springs, streams, rivers, and lakes. Next are thanked the plants, bushes, and saplings, sometimes very specifically. Food plants, particularly maize, beans, and squash might be singled out. These are followed by the trees, animals, and birds.

The second portion of the address is devoted to the sky. The wind and the thunderers are thanked, followed by thanks to the sun, moon, and stars. In the last two hundred years the address has often climaxed with thanks to the four messengers sent to the prophet Handsome Lake by the Creator, thanks to Handsome Lake himself, and finally thanks to the Creator.[3]

different broad characteristics. First, we should expect to see discontinuity rather than continuity, as described in Chapter 1. Second, the new culture should appear across an area different from and at least initially smaller than Point Peninsula culture. Third, the intrusive culture should be initially quite uniform across its area.

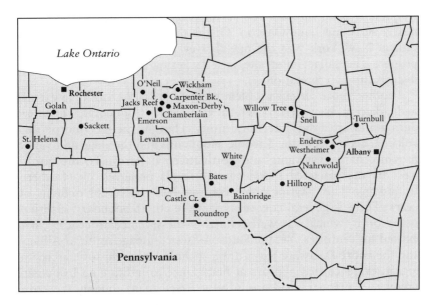

*Figure 2.2   Owasco sites found in New York*

Owasco culture, which replaced Point Peninsula culture in New York, was initially quite uniform across an area that was substantially smaller than the range of Point Peninsula. Owasco sites occur from Schenectady on the east to just west of Geneseo. They are frequent in the Susquehanna Valley and in the Finger Lakes region, but seem not to occur in northern, southeastern, or western New York.[4] If Owasco culture had developed out of Point Peninsula culture, one would have to account for why the evolution failed to take place in these areas, where Point Peninsula sites are known and the local environments were conducive to farming. The answer, of course, is that Owasco culture did not develop out of Point Peninsula, but rather expanded and radiated up the northern tributaries of the Susquehanna River.

There are some possible difficulties with this new scenario. One is that some have counted the Pillar Point site in northern New York as an Owasco site. However, Ritchie has observed that the artifacts from Pillar Point are more closely related to Pickering culture in Ontario than to Owasco.[5] Pickering and Glen Meyer are two early branches of Ontario Iroquoian culture, and it is likely that they were established north and west of Lake Ontario at about the same time and through mechanisms similar to those through which Owasco became established in New York. Indeed, the history of the Northern

Iroquoians following AD 900 is focused on these three areas that nearly surround Lake Ontario. Of the three, the Owasco culture of central New York was the one that eventually led to the Iroquois proper. The Pillar Point site is a Pickering outlier that does not disturb this interpretation.

Another, more serious problem is found in southeastern New York and adjacent New Jersey, which was clearly Algonquian territory during and after the sixteenth century. Here lie the metamorphosed volcanic bedrocks of the Taconic Mountains and the ridge and valley province of Pennsylvania and northern New Jersey. To the north-west lie the glaciated sedimentary uplands preferred by Northern Iroquoians. This physiographic contrast has existed for millions of years. There is general consensus that the ethnic boundary superimposed on it, which was well defined in the seventeenth century, has existed for centuries. Yet the Hudson River drainage south of Albany and the entire Delaware River drainage hold late prehistoric archaeological evidence that appears at first glance to indicate an Iroquoian presence. Pahaquarra culture in New Jersey spans roughly the same centuries as Owasco and its ceramics are similar to Owasco types. But there the similarities seem to end. Pahaquarra sites were occupied by small groups for long periods, like Point Peninsula but unlike Owasco. Furthermore, their houses were relatively small, elongated wigwams with side entrances, as compared to Owasco larger longhouses with their end entrances. The Pahaquarra houses probably also lacked central aisles and compartments, and were not clustered in villages or palisaded. Thus the culture seems non-Iroquoian in all respects other than pottery styles. The appearance of Iroquoian pottery at the Menands Bridge site on the Hudson near Albany is a very similar case.[6]

It is possible that Pahaquarra potters and others along the Hudson simply adopted the styles of their dominant Owasco neighbors to the northwest. It is also possible that Iroquoian women were incorporated into these Algonquian communities, bringing at least their pottery-making ideas with them. Specific hypotheses have yet to be tested. It is unlikely that trade had much to do with the spread of Owasco pottery types southeastward. Kuhn has shown that although later Iroquoian pipes traveled far and wide in the northeast, bulky and fragile pots did not.[7]

### Phases of the Owasco Cultural Tradition

The Owasco cultural tradition is divided into three phases named Carpenter Brook, Canandaigua, and Castle Creek, in that order.

Earlier estimates defined them as three century-long phases falling between AD 1000 and 1300. However, recent calibration of radiocarbon dates pushes all of them forward in time. Thus calibration opens an apparent gap between the dates associated with the last phase of the Point Peninsula cultural tradition and the first Owasco dates. But as shown in Chapter 1, the poorly dated Hunter's Home phase, the last of the Point Peninsula cultural tradition, is in fact an artificial hybrid, designed to give the appearance of continuity. Its components are a mix of Early Owasco villages that contain a few Point Peninsula sherds, and Late Point Peninsula sites having the remains of still later Owasco camps superimposed.[8]

If these cases are ignored, the calendrical date for the beginning of the Early Owasco or Carpenter Brook phase falls around AD 1150 rather than AD 1000, and the Carpenter Brook phase itself is made to be improbably short. However, the White site produced a radiocarbon date that calibrates to AD 992. Thus the apparent gap between the last Point Peninsula dates and the first Owasco dates does not exist. The small sample of Early Owasco dates currently lacks more cases from the AD 800–1150 period during which the first Owasco villages were established.

Early Owasco (Carpenter Brook) sites occur across the entire range shown in Figure 2.2. St Helena, Turnbull, Wickham, and Roundtop are all Early Owasco components. There are more components known for this earliest phase than from the two later and shorter phases combined. This pattern is what one should expect to see after the initial establishment of a successful and uniform culture in a new area. There is little local stylistic variation at first, and the adaptation is persistent.

Radiocarbon dates from Middle Owasco (Canandaigua) sites indicate that the Early Owasco phase was replaced by AD 1200. Middle Owasco was replaced quickly, for Late Owasco (Castle Creek) sites have produced dates that cluster in the period AD 1275–1350. However, the ceramic styles that we regard as late in the Owasco sequence might really be regional variants more than time markers. Castle Creek ceramics are found in the eastern two-thirds of Owasco territory, but not in the western third.

Calibration indicates that the whole Owasco cultural tradition came and went in about four centuries between AD 950 and 1350. Both later phases, which together probably lasted a century less than Early Owasco, reflect growing diversity as Owasco villagers adapted to local conditions and diverged from their common origins.

While earlier Point Peninsula people lived and traveled along rivers and streams, the Iroquoians preferred living near their fields and

*Figure 2.3   Longhouse floor plan at the Roundtop site*
*Source: photograph courtesy of the New York State Museum.*

traveling overland. Owasco sites occur as camps, hamlets, and villages. Some Early Owasco sites were large villages, ranging in size from 2,500 to 8,000 square meters, but they lacked palisades or earthworks. Middle and Late Owasco villages were protected by earth rings, palisades, or both. Camps were located at the edges of marshes and streams, but hamlets and villages were horticultural communities, and they were more often built on well-drained knolls or terraces, away from major streams. One of the large Owasco villages of the Susquehanna Valley, a place called Roundtop, still has the earliest dates for maize in New York. These dates come to AD 1161 and 1185 when they are calibrated.

There was variation in Owasco house form, but it was not inconsistent over time. Seven houses were found at the Maxon–Derby site, and they look like multifamily residences. The smallest of them was only six by seven meters in size, but it contained partitions and four hearths. Another house was eight by eighteen meters, oblong, with end doors and a line of hearths. This must have been a multifamily dwelling, for it hinted at later larger matrilocal longhouses.[9] The longhouse at the Roundtop site was 27 meters long and looked even more like later Iroquois longhouses. The variation suggests that the form was still new and unstandardized, but clearly multifamily residences were present from the beginning of Owasco. Similar houses are not documented for earlier Point Peninsula sites.[10]

Middle Owasco village and hamlet sites exhibit a pattern of lengthening longhouses. Overlapping patterns also indicate that these communities were rebuilding in place over long occupation periods, rather than moving frequently. Frequent moves later became characteristic of larger historic Iroquois villages.

Owasco population appears to have grown rapidly, and most Owasco villages were palisaded by AD 1350. The Chamberlain site had an earthen ring that was still visible in the nineteenth century. Two houses there were about seven meters wide and 15 and 26 meters long respectively. It is clear that by this time longhouses were being built to varying lengths in order to accommodate matrilineages that chance dictated would be of varying sizes. Thus the basic form and function of the later Iroquois longhouse was fully developed by AD 1350. Refinements would continue to be made, but one of the most potent symbols of Iroquois culture was put in place during the course of the Owasco cultural tradition.

Like the historic Iroquois, the Owasco people paid little attention to major drainage boundaries. Owasco sites occur in the upper Susquehanna Valley and as far south as the junction of the main river with the West Branch in central Pennsylvania. Late Owasco pottery types are apparently even rarer than earlier ones in central Pennsylvania. This indicates that Late Owasco gave rise to the Susquehannock nation of the upper Susquehanna Valley as well as to the five Iroquois nations.[11]

### Owasco Artifacts

Early Owasco pots were more elongated and more globular than later vessels. Collars were rare at first, but became more common later on. The most common decorative technique was cord impression, a trait that is also found on late Point Peninsula vessels. But paddle-and-anvil construction techniques and castellated collars were Owasco innovations.

Owasco smokers made obtuse elbow pipes (Figure 2.4). These became progressively more elaborate in form and decoration through the period. By AD 1300 there were pipes with human effigy faces and a variety of animal effigy forms.

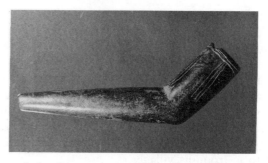

*Figure 2.4   Owasco pipe from the Mohawk Valley*

The common Owasco triangular point is called the Levanna type and contrasts sharply with the pentagonal and notched types of earlier periods. The triangular form remained virtually the sole arrow point form used by Iroquoians from this time forward, surviving even the conversion to copper and brass after European contact. Later specimens were generally smaller, and have been typed separately as Madison points by archaeologists.

### Owasco Villages

The standard Iroquois longhouse emerged slowly through Owasco times from an early unstandardized multifamily form. However, even the earliest Owasco villages had longhouses up to 18 meters long, large enough for three pairs of nuclear families. Moreover, even the earliest Owasco villages could be very large when compared to earlier Point Peninsula camps, up to 8,000 square meters in size. At densities common later on, such a village could have held 400 people. Villages built after AD 1200 were palisaded.

The debris around Owasco villages indicates that, while farmers, these early Iroquoians still engaged in much hunting and gathering. The charred remains of acorns, hickory nuts, butternuts, walnuts, hazelnuts, hawthorn seeds, cherries, and plums all point to a well-balanced diet that went beyond their staple of maize. All of this was stored in cylindrical or bell-shaped pits when the soil depths permitted it. Some of them were large and they were often dug inside the longhouses. They were used until fouled by mold or pests, after which they became graves or trash pits.

The races of maize grown by the Iroquois at this time can only be guessed from information recorded in later centuries. There were by then varieties having black, variegated blue and purple, yellow, or white kernels. The darker forms were probably hominy or flint maize. The lighter varieties were probably common flour maize.[12]

Seeds of all kinds, whether from wild or domesticated plants, could be parched and made into a kind of gruel. Alternatively they could be ground into flour and made into cakes, which were baked in hot ashes. Berries were sometimes added for extra flavor.[13]

## Owasco Warfare

Two principal inferences can be drawn from the evolving Owasco settlement pattern. First, there was continuing elaboration of settlement on a matrilocal base. Second, there was increasing warfare through the course of at least two centuries.[14]

Archaeology can do little more than tell us whether or not warfare was common. To understand the forms it probably took requires examination of records regarding conflict in pre-state societies and the development of generalizations that are basically theoretical in nature. States support standing armies and engage in prolonged warfare, annihilation, and conquest. Modern concepts of warfare are often based on these characteristics, but they do not apply to pre-state conflicts of the sort the early Iroquoians engaged in. Some of the characteristics of Owasco warfare have already been alluded to in Chapter 1. The general description provided by Quincy Wright covers the Iroquois case very well.

> Warriors consist of all men of the tribe trained in the war moves from youth. Tactics involve little group formation or cooperation but consist of night raids, individual duels in formal pitched battles, or small head-hunting or blood-revenge parties. War is initiated and ended by formalities, often quite elaborate. Its purpose is blood revenge, religious duty, individual prestige, sport, or other social objective. It may on occasion involve considerable casualties in proportion to the population of the group and is characterized as cruel or bloody by some writers because prisoners are not taken. Land or booty of economic value is not taken either. The object is slaughter of the enemy or acquisition of trophies, such as heads or scalps, of symbolic significance.[15]

We can distinguish between feuding, raiding, and open pitched battles. Feuding is organized violence between families, lineages, bands, or other groups *within* societies. If two or more villages are politically linked, then fighting between them amounts to feuding, whereas if they are not so linked fighting amounts to warfare.

Warfare can be either internal or external. Internal warfare is warfare conducted between communities of the same society, as would be the case if one Iroquois group fought another. External warfare is warfare conducted between culturally dissimilar communities, as would be the case in a conflict between a Northern Iroquoian community and neighboring Algonquian hunter-gatherers. Of course the distinction becomes blurred if the conflict is between two Northern Iroquoian nations that had been separated long enough to be considered different societies.

The raid was the most common form of warfare. Typically, 10–100 men would cautiously approach an enemy village, either attacking it directly or, more commonly, ambushing its residents as they left on their daily business. The raiders typically killed as many men as they could, took scalps and captive women, and fled homeward until they were sure they were not being chased. Treachery, such as an invitation to a celebration that culminated in a slaughter of the guests, might have been common.

Pitched battles were common among tribal societies. They usually involved 200–2,000 warriors on each side. Each army might be composed of men related by marriage from several villages. The pitched battle was disorganized, with few casualties as individuals dueled and dodged arrows.

The motivations for warfare included revenge and the perceived need to counter encroachment on some critical resource. Females were taken captive, and men were sometimes brought back to be tortured and on occasion eaten.

Matrilocal societies are generally more successful at suppressing both feuding and internal warfare, while patrilocal societies engage in both more feuding and more internal warfare. Polygyny is also associated with patrilocal societies and consequently with wife-capture in the context of internal warfare.

A matrilocal residence pattern breaks up groups of fraternal males, which in turn suppresses both feuding and internal warfare. At the same time, it facilitates the organization of external warfare, allowing the intrusive society to deal effectively with violent resistance from the people being displaced.

Most Owasco warfare was probably with non-Owasco groups, although by AD 1350 Owasco culture was developed so widely in the region that some internal warfare might have been going on as well. Where we see the best archaeological evidence of external warfare is on the margins of Owasco territory, in western New York, the Hudson Valley, and northern Pennsylvania. Here there are occasional Owasco pottery types found together with local types that have often been assumed to be earlier. But the very different types have sometimes been found together in the same refuse pits, indicating that they were made and discarded simultaneously. Rather than being evidence of the phasing in of one set of types and the phasing out of an older set, these cases are evidence of Owasco females being incorporated into non-Owasco communities.[16]

### End of the Period

There appears to be little doubt about continuity from the Owasco cultural tradition to the Iroquois cultural tradition. As Ritchie and Funk have put it, "In nearly every respect, the material expressions of Owasco culture foreshadowed the patterns of the later Iroquois in New York. This is true of ceramic trends, house types, subsistence bases, burial customs, etc. Indeed, continuity from Late Owasco into the Early Iroquois Oak Hill phase has been amply demonstrated in central and eastern New York."[17]

But the transition was not without significant culture change. The warm Medieval Optimum drew to a close after AD 1300. What followed it has been referred to as the Little Ice Age. This prolonged period of lower temperatures persisted until after the arrival of Europeans in Iroquoia. Its onset in the fourteenth century must have shortened the growing season and made some portions of Owasco territory subject to more frequent crop failures. Critical resources were probably even more restricted in their availability than they had been earlier. The climatic shift accelerated the clustering of villages as unproductive areas were abandoned and communities congregated in areas where farming was still viable. It may be that they found further comfort in being closer to kindred communities among which food could be redistributed in lean months. Regardless of the degree to which Late Owasco villages remained self-sufficient, the village clustering laid the foundations of the later Iroquois village clusters. Those that survived became the Iroquois nations of the sixteenth century and later times.

# 3

## The Development of Northern Iroquoian Culture, 1350–1525: The Fishing Moon

The brief period AD 1350–1400 is called the Oak Hill phase, based on a cluster of sites on and around Oak Hill in the Mohawk Valley. The fifteenth-century Chance phase was named for the type site located in the valley of the Schoharie, a tributary of the Mohawk.[1] There can be no doubt that Late Owasco culture foreshadowed Oak Hill culture, and that Oak Hill led into Chance in a smooth developmental continuum. Together they constitute the Iroquois cultural tradition, which ultimately leads into the five separate village sequences of the Iroquois nations.

Although some archaeologists have applied these phase names to sequences in central New York, they were devised for the Mohawk sequence and are not truly applicable elsewhere in Iroquoia. By AD 1275 Owasco culture had become so variable that the diagnostic markers for the Late Owasco (Castle Creek) phase do not appear at all in the Genesee Valley, where the Seneca nation later emerged. Archaeologists have long used ceramic types as time markers, necessary perhaps before the discovery of radiocarbon dating, but a form of self-deception if applied dogmatically. The breakup of Owasco culture into regional variants should be expected to put an end to widespread common pottery types, however inconvenient that may be to archaeological cross-dating.

Pottery types of the Oak Hill phase do appear in and around the Genesee Valley, but the full range of Oak Hill artifacts appears to be missing there. The Chance phase is still less evident in the west, further evidence that the descendants of Owasco culture were going their own ways. Both Oak Hill and Chance sites are detectable in the sequence found southwest of Oneida Lake, the homeland of the later Onondaga nation.[2]

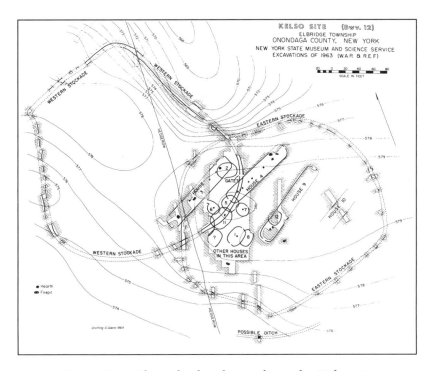

*Figure 3.1 Plan of a longhouse from the Kelso site*
*Source: drawing courtesy of the New York State Museum.*

## AD 1350–1400

Population growth produced more and larger villages. The eastern village at the Kelso site west of Syracuse, which dates to this time, probably had a population of about 330. There were three or four longhouses, ranging from 34 to 39 meters (112–128 feet) in length (Figure 3.1). There were also smaller oblong houses, but the classic Iroquois longhouse was clearly the dominant form. The Furnace Brook site, also near Syracuse, contained about a hectare (2.5 acres) of ground inside its palisade. None of the sites of the period in the Mohawk Valley yields such statistics, but it is probably safe to say that Furnace Brook was a large village for its time, housing perhaps 500 people. The longhouse had by now become fully developed, and some excavated examples show evidence of repairing and expansion. A longhouse excavated on the Howlett Hill site was found to be an almost incredible 102 meters (334 feet) long.

*Figure 3.2   Iroquois triangular arrow point*
*Source: drawing courtesy of the New York State Museum.*

Most villages had double or triple palisades, and they were occupied for long periods, perhaps up to a century. Farming played an even greater economic role than it had previously. Fish provided a large portion of the villagers' animal protein, but large game animals, particularly deer, were also still important.

Oak Hill ceramics are frequently decorated with cord-stamped collars and check-stamped bodies, both attributes that faded after AD 1400. While Owasco smoking pipes were made with their bowls attached to stems at obtuse angles, Oak Hill pipes had more nearly right angles and a variety of novel styles. Many have straight, flaring, or barrel-shaped bowls with incised decorations. They contrast with cord-impressed Owasco pipes.

Stone work continued much as it had in Owasco times. The distinctive triangular arrow points were generally a bit smaller, as the large Levanna type (Figure 3.2) evolved towards the much smaller Madison type of the later Iroquois. Bone work was not elaborate, and appears mainly in the form of awls, fishing gear, and a few beads.

Cordage twisted from Indian hemp fiber was woven into nets and lines. The hollow dried galls of goldenrod served as floats, while flat pebbles were notched to make sinkers.[3] Iroquois families moved in the spring of the year to falls and rapids where the migrating fish were forced to slow down, and there they harvested them by the thousands. The middle moon of springtime brought with it the fish runs and the first echoes of thunder. This in turn prompted another of the seasonal ceremonies.

---

*The Thunder Ceremony*

As in all Iroquois ceremonies, the principal rites of the Thunder Ceremony fall between opening and closing recitations of the Thanksgiving Speech. After the opening speech, there is a tobacco invocation, during which the speaker throws loose tobacco on the fire from time to time. The tobacco smoke greets the Thunderers, who live at a distance. There is usually also a performance of the War Dance, and in some places a lacrosse game is played. Other variations occur as well.

Traditionally, the Thunder Ceremony has been held when the first sounds of thunder are heard in the spring. It is thus typical of calendrical ceremonies, which emphasize thanks for gifts received rather than requests for favors withheld. The Iroquois still object to glib references to rain dances or any suggestion that they might conduct ceremonies of supplication.

---

It is likely that this was a period in which population increased and internal stability promoted widespread interaction within the broad interior of New York, even as local clusters of villages were diverging from each other as cultural variants on a common theme. The two simultaneous trends have long been confusing to archaeologists, and their contradictions are still being sorted out.

Sites of this period are found scattered thinly and broadly from the Mohawk Valley westward through the Finger Lakes region of New York. Another cluster of sites sometimes known as the Oakfield phase lies just north of Batavia in western New York. These, however, appear to have derived from the Ontario Iroquoian cultural tradition. The Oakfield communities probably influenced Seneca development in a variety of ways, but they probably moved later to the vicinity of modern Buffalo, where they became the Erie nation of the seventeenth century.[4]

### Significance of the Period

Iroquoian pipes were often discarded far from their places of manufacture. This is in contrast to ceramic vessels, which despite the spread of decorative motifs over time and space tended to be made and discarded locally. Pipes, but not pots, traveled far and wide in Iroquoia. Generally, pots were made by women and pipes were made by men. The pattern suggests that the historic male Iroquois habit of long trips and gift exchange was well established by this time. The meaning of the widespread distribution of common motifs on pots, despite the tendency for individual vessels to stay home, is less obvious. Increasing regional homogeneity of ceramic styles can be explained as resulting either from widespread intermarriage and post-marital relocation, or from widespread internal warfare and wife capture (or both). Most probably there were several different specific forces at work. In any event, there were increasing contacts between communities during AD 1350–1400. This may well have been stimulated by or at least accompanied by trade, which had languished in the northeast for seven centuries. The occurrence of Onondaga chert in sites far removed from New York quarry sources presages the later appearance of marine shell in several later prehistoric Iroquoian sites. Whatever the specific cause(s), there was an increasing number of contacts between Iroquoian communities in this era.[5]

There is also evidence that the overall population was growing rapidly. Both average village size and average longhouse length doubled from what they had been only two centuries earlier. The evidence suggests that this was a time of internal population growth, and that the increase in average village size was not just the result of two or more previously independent villages coming together. While earlier villages showed evidence of abandonment and reoccupation over comparatively long periods, these appear to have been continuously occupied over shorter periods. Special-purpose hamlets, camps, and cabins provided shelter for occasional or seasonal use by parts of the population away from the main villages. The full economic potential of Iroquoian horticulture was realized by this time. Maize, beans, squash, and sunflower remains have all been found in village middens.[6]

Some, but not all, sites were palisaded, but there is little other evidence of intense warfare until the late fifteenth century. Randomly discarded human bones indicating prisoner torture and cannibalism do not appear this early in Iroquoia, although they seem to appear on related sites in Ontario soon after AD 1300. It is likely that the dramatic growth of some but not all longhouses reflects the emergence of dominant lineages. This could easily have resulted from simple random birth factors in household growth. One residential unit could have grown more than another merely because of a small random difference in the ratio of female to male births in this strongly matrilocal society.[7]

We have yet to fully explore the social, economic, and political dynamics of the vigorous regional culture that emerged in this brief period. It may well have been a modest golden age for Northern

Iroquoian culture, which followed the triumph of their regional adaptation but preceded the emergence of widespread internal warfare.

One point of considerable interest to anthropologists is the absence of an expected cultural form. Theory based on similar systems elsewhere in the world predicts that we should find evidence of both increasing house floor areas and men's houses in matrilocal Iroquoian communities. Certainly we have clear evidence of the former. But men's houses have never been identified in either documentary or archaeological sources pertaining to Iroquoia. Where they exist elsewhere, men's houses function to socialize young adult males who later marry into exogamous matrilocal households. They also serve as places for scattered clan brothers to gather. In the American southwest they take the form of kivas. But enlarged residential house areas can provide the same function, and it appears that the Iroquoian longhouse was sufficient for this purpose. Clan brothers could gather in their childhood homes so long as they had married within the village or a close neighboring village.

Iroquoians usually practiced lineage exogamy that did not entail village exogamy. Although some scholars have used a sixteenth-century source to argue that at least the Mohawks lived in clan villages, closer analysis shows that this would have been socially impossible given the sizes and numbers of the villages. All villages must have had men and women of all three Mohawk clans, albeit in varying numbers. So long as men relocated only to their wives' houses and not to different villages, they could continue to associate with their sisters and other kinsmen, and the need for men's houses remained low.[8]

It is also the case that historic Iroquois villages are often paired. If this tendency for communities to occur in pairs existed prehistorically, they could have both sustained village exogamy and escaped the need for men's houses. This is an especially likely (but unproven) possibility for the centuries before AD 1350, when villages were small but close to others in their clusters.

Yet despite all these considerations, the absence of men's houses would remain troublesome but for one unusual feature of Iroquois life: Iroquois men were frequently absent from their homes. The village was the domain of women, while men owned the forests, in which they often engaged in trade, diplomacy, or warfare for months on end. Men's houses are retreats for males in the most sedentary matrilocal communities, but they are unnecessary if clan brothers can find equivalent shared refuge outside the village. Like the Jesuits who would come to live with them in the seventeenth century, Iroquois men had no need of bark cloisters, for their domain was a lodge turned inside out.

## The Longhouse

After centuries of experimentation and development, the Iroquois longhouse design reached its classic form by AD 1400. The form changed little between then and the seventeenth century, when written descriptions fill gaps in archaeological knowledge. The first description was written by Samuel de Champlain in 1616. Gabriel Sagard and various Jesuit missionaries later wrote their own descriptions. Joseph Lafitau wrote the most detailed description in 1724. Historians have often treated these as independent sources, but careful reading of Sagard reveals that he cribbed from Champlain, and Lafitau cribbed from both of them. Worse than that, true meanings have often been distorted and confused by translators.

> Their cabins [*cabannes*] are in the shape of tunnels [*tonnelles*] or arbors, and are covered with the bark of trees. They are from twenty-five to thirty fathoms long, more or less, and six [*sic*] wide, having a passage-way through the middle from ten to twelve feet wide, which extends from one end to the other. On the sides there is a kind of bench, four feet high, where they sleep in summer, in order to avoid the annoyance of the fleas, of which there were great numbers. In winter they sleep on the ground on mats near the fire, so as to be warmer than they would be on the platform. They lay up a stock of dry wood, with which they fill their cabins, to burn in winter. At the extremity of the cabins there is a space, where they preserve their Indian corn, which they put into great casks made of the bark of trees and placed in the middle of their encampment [*au milieu de leur logement*]. They have pieces of wood suspended, on which they put their clothes, provisions, and other things, for fear of the mice, of which there are great numbers. In one of these cabins there may be twelve fires, and twenty-four families. It smokes excessively, from which it follows that many receive serious injury to the eyes, so that they lose their sight towards the close of life. There is no window nor any opening, except that in the upper part of their cabins for the smoke to escape.[9]

Longhouses were consistently built in the shape of an arbor, with compartments down each side and hearths in the center aisle, spaced so that two families shared each fire. Modern reconstructions often assume that long poles were stuck in the ground and then bent and joined at the top such that the arbor began at ground level and the house had a parabolic cross-section. This, however, is clearly not the case according to Joseph Lafitau, who wrote in the eighteenth century. Instead, poles were set vertically to form the walls of the house.

These extended straight upwards to a height equal to 60 percent of the width of the house.[10]

Houses were commonly 6 meters wide, so the indicated height of the outer wall would be 3.6 meters. Horizontal poles and interior vertical supports along the aisle completed the basic framework of elements consistently intersecting at 90 degree angles. A typical aisle would be 2 meters wide, leaving compartments 2 meters deep along each side of the longhouse. The roof arbor began at the top of the outer wall, being arched from side to side as shown in a 1743 sketch of an Onondaga longhouse by John Bartram. Interior vertical supports along the aisle probably extended beyond 4 meters so that they could be used to support the roof arch as well.

Most translations of Champlain are accurate (or at least not misleading) except at one crucial point. The translation of *logement* is critical, for one source translates it as "lodge" but another translates it as "encampment," making the passage seem to mean that the Indians kept their casks of corn outside their houses in the middle of the village. Further, most translators err in translating *milieu* as "middle" rather than "midst." Champlain intended the reader to grasp that bark casks were used to store corn within the houses, but not necessarily in their middles.

Sagard apparently copied and embellished Champlain's description, which Champlain published after his 1616 voyage. Sagard repeats Champlain's phrases in the original French word for word, inserting additional detail here and there. Sagard's estimate of 200–300 households (by which he means family units consisting of a couple and their children) in 30–40 longhouses implies a minimum of five and a maximum of ten households per longhouse. We know that households came in pairs, each pair sharing a hearth and occupying facing longhouse compartments. Consequently the real range of family units per longhouse must be stated in even numbers. Sagard's figures thus lead to a range of six to ten compartments and families, or three to five hearths per house. Later he says that some longhouses might have as many as eight, ten, or twelve hearths, figures he cribbed from Champlain.

Lafitau also depends upon earlier sources, but organizes and expands upon the information. It is unfortunate that the word "platform" is used by his translator, because it makes his description seem garbled. If the word "cubicle" is substituted the confusion disappears: a critical clarification, for Lafitau describes the most important of interior longhouse structures. The cubicles are clearly elongated boxes walled on three sides, open only toward the fire. Each is about 4 meters long, leaving space totaling 2 meters at one or both ends

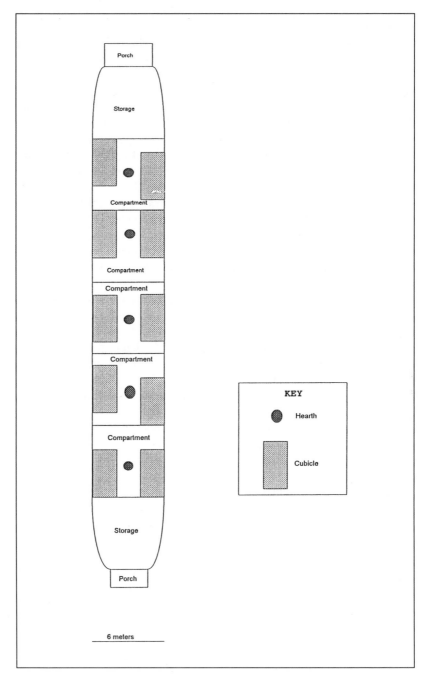

*Figure 3.3  A typical Iroquois longhouse with five compartments and two end storage rooms*

within the compartment for cabinets and casks for storing corn. Thus there was an important difference between the cubicles, which took up two-thirds of the lengths of the compartments, and the compartments themselves, which were house segments measuring 6 meters by 6 meters.

The cubicles were about 4 meters long and 2 meters deep, with ceilings 2 meters high and bottoms raised about 40 centimeters above the earthen floor of the compartment. We know from various sources that the Indians kept firewood under the cubicles and household belongings on top of them. The cubicles did not abut one another end to end because they were shorter than the distances between the fires that warmed them. Thus there were open spaces between the cubicle ends and the partition walls separating compartments, and in these were located storage casks and other items.

Bartram and some other later sources have indicated (or seem to indicate) that nuclear family compartments were about as long as they were deep, each being around 2 meters square. However, archaeological research has supported Lafitau's description of the standard house segment as being about as long as the whole house was wide (6 meters). Thus each nuclear family area was about 2 meters by 6 meters. Each pair of nuclear families shared a main fire in the center of the common aisle. Six meters farther along would be the common fire of the next pair of families, and so on to the far end of the house. Each house was as long as it needed to be to accommodate all the parts of a large extended family.

Although Bartram's drawing suggests that four smaller compartments shared a common fire, he might have been only showing a further special partitioning of the longhouse in the middle of the eighteenth century. The houses of the Onondaga of 1743 were generally small dispersed cabins, unlike the houses we know to have been used everywhere in Iroquoia a century earlier. The house described by Bartram was probably a traditional longhouse kept as a hotel for visitors, so the inconsistency of compartment size is not a matter for serious concern.

Several sources and the archaeological evidence point to the use of rounded end compartments as storage areas. Archaeologists have recently tried to standardize the name for this area to "vestibule," particularly when translating from French, but published translations are variable, and words like "lobby" and "porch" are also used.

Thus we should expect that a 42 meter longhouse had 6 meter storage compartments at both ends, leaving room for five residential compartments and five hearths in between. What remains is to estimate the average number of people per family (or per hearth) in

order to determine the size of the household. Most researchers assume that pre-epidemic nuclear families were made up of four to five
individuals. Fortunately, we have some later data to confirm this
estimate. In three well-documented 1730s longhouse villages outside
Detroit there were actually two or three families per hearth, apparently depending upon the sizes of the families. Smaller nuclear families were apparently joined to make more efficient use of longhouse
compartments. The sources provide data on the numbers of hearths,
and population figures for the same three villages indicate a range of
1.5–3.2 warriors per hearth. The figures indicate no fewer than six
and no more than 13 people per hearth when the convention of 25
per cent warriors is applied. When aggregated, the Detroit data yield
9.3 people per hearth, or 4.7 per compartment. The figures are based
on estimates, but are strong enough to justify adopting a more precise standard of five individuals per family.[11]

Put the other way, a house large enough to accommodate 50 people would require ten cubicles, five compartments, five hearths, and
a total length of 42 meters, not including porches. Actual measurements varied, but this can be used as an average.

Many longhouses were rounded at the corners, unless a storage
compartment was not built and a flat end wall was left in anticipa-
tion of extending the rafters to incorporate another compartment.
The walls here were carried straight up to the eaves. Small sloping
porch roofs were often constructed over the outer doors leading into
the end storage compartments. These, unfortunately, are sometimes
called "vestibules" or "outer vestibules" in published translations.

Each house contained nuclear families of women belonging to the
same clan segment. Harmen van den Bogaert described houses with
painted totems on wooden ends, or at least boards with painted
totems over the doors, in 1635. It appears from our archaeological
evidence that the houses were most substantially built where there
were living compartments, but that the end storage areas were rather
lightly framed. The almost temporary ends would have been easily
rebuilt into more substantial compartments if houses had to be expanded to accommodate more people. In the meanwhile, they kept
stores safe and dry, and provided buffers between residential areas
and winter winds.

There was a tendency for houses to be oriented northwest–southeast unless there were compelling topographic reasons to do otherwise. All houses were covered with large shingles of elm bark. Elm
bark was also used for canoes, for canoe birches of sufficient size do
not grow in most of Iroquoia. Elm bark was peeled in the spring and
stacked to flatten. Trees girdled to make fields around new villages

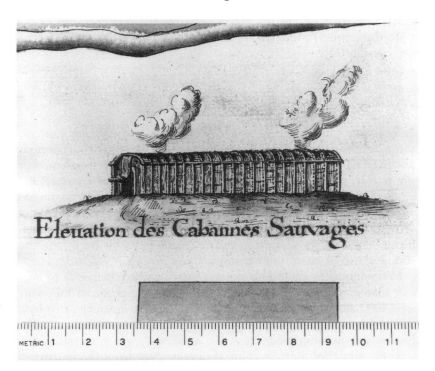

*Figure 3.4    Fort Frontenac longhouse*
*Source: photograph courtesy of the Newberry Library.*

thus provided the materials for new houses and the firewood to warm them in the winter. The walls and roofs of the houses were sheathed in shingles that might have averaged 1 by 2 meters in size. A hole was left in the roof over each hearth, and there was probably a flap of bark to pull over the hole in heavy weather.

The drawing of the early eighteenth-century longhouse at Fort Frontenac (Kingston, Ontario) indicates that light poles were lashed vertically over the outsides of the shingles to hold them in place (Figure 3.4). These extended across the roof as well. This would have given the impression of a second house frame, this one over rather than under the bark sheathing. The scale on this drawing indicates that the house was 10 *toises* (fathoms) long, or about 20 meters. The vertical poles over the bark were set at half *toise* (1 meter) intervals.

Measurements on several completely excavated villages, historic census data, and maps of Iroquois villages have enabled a standard ratio of people to village area to be established. Where a village population can be independently determined and the village size measured, it is found that except for the densely packed fortified sites of the sixteenth century, Mohawk villages contained about 20 square meters per person.

## AD *1400–1525*

Period names and their dates are particularly confused for the centuries following AD 1400. This is in part because some short periods are given names based on phase names that are in turn based on type site names, while others are given temporally descriptive names. Examples of the former case are the Chance and Chautauqua phases and the periods they are supposed to occupy. Examples of the latter are the Late Prehistoric and Protohistoric periods. The situation is further confused by disagreements about the probable beginning and ending dates of these brief periods.[12]

My solution to these and other contradictory schemes is to suggest that we reference mainly the calendar for the centuries following AD 1400, and avoid the difficulties and hidden meanings of phase and/or period names. I use AD 1525 and 1600 as convenient chapter breaks, but nothing more.

There was continuity in cultural development from the fourteenth through the fifteenth century AD. The time boundary at AD 1400, which has been traditionally used to separate the Oak Hill phase from the later Chance phase in eastern New York, is marked mainly by a shift in styles of ceramic decoration and projectile point size. Corded decorations waned as incised decorations became more popular. The decorative motifs remained much the same, as did overall vessel forms. Pottery was particularly well made at this time, and it has been said that this was the era when Iroquois pottery attained its artistic zenith. At the same time, the large triangular Levanna projectile point type gave way to smaller Madison forms. New forms of smoking pipes appeared after AD 1400. Innovations included animal and human effigies, some of them quite beautiful to the modern eye.[13]

There is a general increase in the numbers of villages, in village sizes, and in longhouse lengths after AD 1400. Furthermore, the villages by now clearly tended to cluster in areas that would later be known as the homelands of individual Northern Iroquoian nations. The Getman and Elwood sites, each of which probably housed around 200 people, are the best known of a score of fifteenth-century sites in the Mohawk area.[14] By late in the period, such communities were coming together to form larger villages, often located on defensible terrain and/or surrounded by new and improved palisades. If one

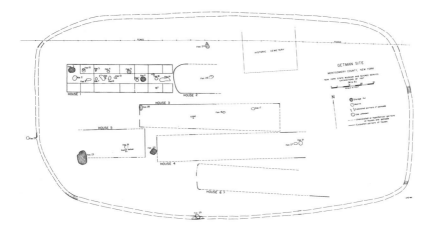

*Figure 3.5    Plan of the Getman site
Source: drawing courtesy of the New York State Museum.*

counts sites without regard to the size change, one gets a false impression of decline. In fact, the population appears to have been still growing steadily, even as villagers came together in larger but fewer communities. Average longhouse lengths increased, probably as lineage segments grew, and the average amount of village area per person shrank from 20 square meters to 12 square meters. All evidence points to defense against increasing warfare as the inspiration for these trends. Villages became both larger and more dense, and as they periodically relocated they moved into ever tighter clusters. By the end of the period the Mohawks emerged as a distinct nation, living in perhaps only two large fortified villages. One of these, Otstungo, has recently undergone intensive excavation.

The sequence in Oneida country is less well known. Although attempts were once made to determine whether the Nichols Pond site could have been the Oneida village that was attacked by Champlain in 1615, Pratt's work showed that the site dated to the late fifteenth century. The inhabitants of this village might have moved to the area from the upper Mohawk drainage, which lies only a few kilometers to the east. This is likely because there are few if any clear Oak Hill or Owasco sites in the Oneida area that might have been ancestral to this Iroquois nation. Fifteenth-century ceramics from the Oneida area are very similar to contemporary Mohawk ceramics. Indeed, the Oneida language is linked most closely with Mohawk.[15]

*Figure 3.6    Human effigy pipe from the Otstungo site*

Tuck examined several fifteenth-century sites in the Onondaga area.
One of them, the Schoff site, yielded evidence of a longhouse built
to a record length of 122 meters (400 feet), 20 meters longer than the
house at Howlett Hill. The ends of longhouses are notoriously difficult to define archaeologically, and Tuck's excavations were far
from complete at the Schoff site, so it is possible that he found two
or more structures built in a line. Nevertheless, it is clear that here
too the population was growing and that people were living in ever-
larger communities.

Before AD 1350 there was a widely scattered distribution of Iroquoian villages across the Finger Lakes region of central New York.
During the fifteenth century these communities too drifted into clusters. One such cluster formed along the Genesee River, Honeoye
Creek, and Mud Creek south of Rochester. This would later be
known as the homeland of the Seneca. Another loose cluster formed
around Cayuga Lake. That cluster of communities would later tighten
in the hills just east of the lake and be known historically as the
Cayuga nation.[16]

At the beginning of the period villages were too scattered for nations to have existed as clearly as they did later in the seventeenth century. Divisions above the village level across the region must have been little more than vaguely recognized linguistic units. As the villages began to cluster, some sense of linguistic and political unity must have emerged within each cluster. By the end of the period, large fortified villages were clustered in the homelands of the historic Mohawk, Oneida, Onondaga, Cayuga, and Seneca nations, and it is appropriate to speak of them in those terms. It is also likely that the need for regional defense and the impulse to end strife between them led these five to form the League of the Iroquois at about this time. This political innovation redefined external warfare between the Five Nations, converting it to internal warfare and abolishing it.

During the period 1400–1525 the upper Susquehanna River valley was inhabited by Iroquoians whose descendants would be known as the Susquehannocks. They are best known from a series of around 20 sites in Bradford County, Pennsylvania, and adjacent Tioga County, New York. These were probably all small hamlets, and many more like them might lie still undiscovered in the valleys of the North Branch Susquehanna and its tributaries north of its junction with the West Branch at Northumberland, Pennsylvania. These communities, like other Iroquoian communities in New York, developed out of an Owasco base, but few specifics are known about them. The Iroquoians in this cluster apparently suffered more than most from the effects of warfare in this period, for at or shortly after its close they abandoned the area altogether. There is linguistic evidence that some of them joined the Cayuga. Rapid population growth in proto-Mohawk villages suggests that some might have gone there as well, perhaps as captives, although there is as yet no clear evidence for this. The bulk of them moved south along the Susquehanna River to their postcontact location near Lancaster. This move took them out of the Iroquoia, but it positioned them to take advantage of the European trade that was to begin after 1525.[17]

East of Lake Ontario, the period saw the development of Iroquoian villages in Jefferson County, New York, and along both sides of the St Lawrence where it separates New York and Ontario. William Engelbrecht has documented 55 sites in Jefferson County. The well-known Roebuck, McKeown, and related sites are found on the Ontario side of the river. Settlement patterns and artifacts are indisputably Iroquoian, although there are distinctive styles that allow archaeologists to identify the St Lawrence Iroquoians as distinct from their relatives to the west and south. Some of these communities eventually moved northeastward and settled in two additional clusters around modern Montreal and Quebec, but early in the period there was still no clear Iroquoian presence on the St Lawrence. By 1500 there were Iroquoian sites distributed in three major clusters from Jefferson County to Quebec. These Iroquoians are important here not because they were Iroquois, for they derived from early Ontario Iroquoian groups, but because many of them later became Iroquois. This will be explained in Chapter 4.[18]

### The Chance Phase

Some fifteenth-century ceramics of the Hudson Valley are so similar to Mohawk ceramics that Ritchie used three sites from the Mohawk drainage and one (Kingston) from the Hudson Valley to define the Chance phase. One site from an upper tributary of the Susquehanna, Deowongo Island, was also used, but this lies so close to the Mohawk River that it is actually nearer two of the Mohawk sites (Oak Hill No. 2 and Second Woods) than the type site (Chance) is. Nevertheless, of the 14 pottery types Ritchie used, three were Hudson Valley types that did not appear on any of the sites other than Kingston, and five clearly Iroquoian types of the century did not occur at Kingston. While not disproving that Iroquoian types occurred in substantial amounts on Mahican sites, the ceramics at the Kingston site do suggest that there is some basis for distinguishing them as an assemblage from Mohawk assemblages.

Once again, the evidence seems to indicate that ceramics are not poor ethnic markers, but just the opposite. Iroquois ceramic styles do appear to mark ethnicity, and we are challenged to explain their presence out of place on sites like Kingston. If the ethnic boundary between the Iroquois and the Mahicans on the Hudson persisted since Owasco times, then we should begin to examine the processes that caused Mohawk ceramics to appear on Mahican sites. Once again, the most likely explanation for the small number of Mohawk types at Kingston is probably that Mohawk women were captured and incorporated into the community. Elemental analysis of this pottery would at least determine whether or not it was made of local clay.

A Mahican site on Fish Kill, between Saratoga Lake and the Hudson River, offers a second but equally plausible explanation for what is superficially a similar case. Here again most of the archaeological evidence points to expected Mahican affiliation. But a significant subset of the pottery sample is comprised of Mohawk types. One is tempted to conclude from evidence like this that ceramic types do not serve well to mark ethnicity. However, later Mohawk travelers habitually used the Fish Kill to bypass Mahican settlements farther south along the Hudson when going to and from Canada by way of the upper Hudson, Lake George, and Lake Champlain. In this case the pottery might have been made of Mohawk clays and carried to the site, although we know that pots did not usually travel far from their places of manufacture.[19]

# 4

## The Rise of the League, 1525–1600: The Planting Moon

By 1525 a series of major demographic and political changes was underway in Iroquoia. These set the stage for the formation of the League of the Iroquois and the tentative interactions with Europeans that followed over the next hundred years. Even before 1525 Iroquois villages had begun combining into ever larger communities. Periodic relocations now often involved the fusion of two or more previously separate small villages. The larger villages seem to have become magnets that gained still more population as they incorporated smaller communities by accretion. These larger villages were often located on more isolated hilltops, away from major routes of travel. Defensible hills with steep slopes, sometimes embraced in the meander loop of a stream, were deliberately sought out, even at the cost of moving away from prime farming land.[1]

The new settlement pattern was clearly adopted for defensive reasons. The villages were larger and more heavily fortified than before, either by ravines or by artificial earthworks and multiple palisades. The larger village populations concentrated warriors and provided more manpower for work on systems of common defense. Simple arithmetic shows that by doubling the length of a village defensive perimeter, they could increase village area four times. A village that doubled its perimeter quadrupled not only its area but also, consequently, its population. This economy of scale reduced the amount of perimeter that had to be maintained and defended by each warrior.

The Iroquois did not stop with just changes in village size and location. Village population densities were also increased so that more people were squeezed into the available space. Houses were positioned closer to each other, despite the risk of fire.[2] The standard of 20 square meters of village area per person had dropped to as little as 12 square meters by 1525. The Mohawk site of Garoga was completely excavated to reveal nine longhouses, arranged in three

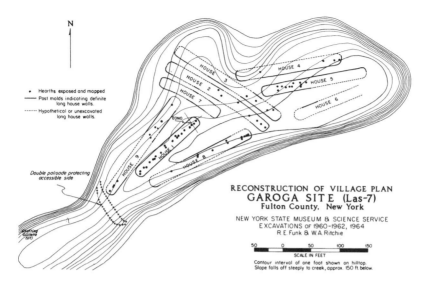

*Figure 4.1  Plan of the Garoga site*
*Source: drawing courtesy of the New York State Museum.*

sets of three (Figure 4.1). The placement of hearths and other internal features indicate that there were no end storage compartments but 82 active hearths at the height of village occupation. Figures from several sources indicate that on average a hearth served ten people, five in each of two nuclear family units. Thus Garoga must have had a population of about 820. The area of the site is only 9,876 square meters, so the area per person on the site was only 12 square meters.[3]

## Warfare and Death

The sixteenth century was a time of violence, when villages were turned into what the Dutch and English would later call "castles." This was the time of troubles that is still preserved in Iroquois oral tradition. Severed finger bones and other evidence of torture and cannibalism turn up in village refuse middens from this time forward. General anthropological research has shown that such extreme behavior arises only under specific circumstances. Feuding or warfare must be truly prominent, and the taking of prisoners must be an important objective. Further, there must be a strong ethic of conformity and generosity within the society, as well as the shared belief that even the most mundane events are controlled by super-natural forces. Religious practices always involve sacrifice in these cases, and there is always intense competition for limited resources. The existence of all six of these features in the sixteenth-century world of the Iroquois set the scene for interpersonal violence that did not abate until near the end of the eighteenth century.[4] It was indeed a time of troubles for the Iroquois and their neighbors.

Feuding and warfare, both internal and external, were rampant, whether it was the little warfare of young hotheads or the larger warfare sanctioned by councils of chiefs. The Iroquois believed that no death or injury was accidental or natural. Good and evil existed in everyone, just as the good and evil twins had been borne by the same mother of all real people. When the evil side ascended, a person's mind became crooked and prone to witchcraft. The irony was that all people saw the world by their own lights, and evil existed mostly in the eye of the beholder. In this relative universe bad things could be done by good people. Yet no evil could be allowed to pass unavenged. It is little wonder that competition for resources led the Iroquois into endless cycles of feuding, where every death led to an act of revenge that would in turn require its own vengeance.

Yet the ritual that surrounded warfare was subtle. Chiefs maneuvered for allies, and they manipulated both the parties of young men who wanted war and the factions that opposed it. There was no wish to hurry matters, for the achievement of consensus at home and surprise at the village of the enemy was most easily accomplished through delay. Setting the war kettle (or pot) of dog meat on the fire would at last initiate action. Speakers appealed to the sun for victory and captives, and asked for illumination of the path to and from the enemy. They promised to kill and eat their captives as sacrifices to the sun, or if nothing else to at least offer up a bear. Painted men sang furious songs, night after night until the time of departure. They left the village in their finest clothes, moving to the edge of the woods where they met the women carrying provisions and their travel clothes. After they left they would not be seen again until they returned and the leader made a thanksgiving feast.[5]

War parties traveled carefully in single file, the last man covering the tracks. They traveled at night and rested by day, avoiding fires and sniffing the air for the smoke of enemies who were not as careful. To return with captives or the heads of enemies (scalps were more portable but less impressive) was glorious; to lose even a single man was disgraceful. The residents of the village awaited the return, preparing themselves for the moment when captives would be forced to run the gauntlet outside the village. If men had been lost on the

*Table 4.1  Clans of the Iroquois nations (moieties are unnamed and are listed here as A and B for convenience only)*

| Mohawk | Oneida | Onondaga | Cayuga | Seneca |
|--------|--------|----------|--------|--------|
| | | *Moiety A* | | |
| Turtle | Turtle | Turtle | Turtle[a] | Turtle |
| Bear | Bear | | Bear[a] | Bear |
| | | Wolf[a] | | Wolf |
| | | Beaver | | Beaver |
| | | | Deer | |
| | | Ball | | Ball |
| | | *Moiety B* | | |
| Wolf | Wolf | Wolf[a] | Wolf | |
| | | Deer | | Deer |
| | | | Heron | Heron |
| | | Eel | | |
| | | | Snipe[a] | Snipe |
| | | Bear | | |
| | | Hawk | | Hawk |

[a] There is no clear consensus regarding the number and/or moiety assignments of these clans.

*Source:* Tooker (1978b: 426–8).

raid, this was announced first by a runner, so that the bereaved could be condoled before the main party returned for the celebration. They were greeted at the woods' edge by women, some of whom wept for their lost sons and brothers. The captives were tortured while the heads and scalps of their less (or perhaps more) fortunate comrades were hoisted on poles above the village palisade.[6]

Huddled sets of Northern Iroquoian villages by now existed in two dozen clusters. For the most part people directed their hostilities outside their local villages. Within villages and sets of adjacent villages that customarily intermarried, all Iroquoians followed conventions to minimize conflict. Clans were grouped into moieties, as shown in Table 4.1, so that for any function there was a natural division of people into two sides. These engaged in friendly competition and provided services for each other. The most important of those services was occasioned by death. Upon the death of any individual,

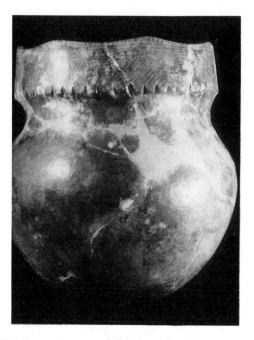

*Figure 4.2   Iroquois vessel from Lake Pleasant, 34 cm tall*
*Source: Walter Elwood Museum, Amsterdam.*

that person's moiety immediately assumed the role of the grieving
and the opposite moiety took on the role of condolence while attending to the practical matter of burying the deceased. The elaborate
funeral rite ensured that everyone was either grieving or condoling,
and that no one could be blamed for causing the death. The process
effectively shifted blame outside the close-knit immediate community, whether it comprised one village or several allied villages. It also
unified the rage of the survivors, and turned grief into grievance
against unknown and unknowing perpetrators elsewhere.

The death of a close relative caused people to fall into the most
profound grief. Faces and clothing were covered with ashes, and the
bereaved were unable to perform daily tasks. Members of the condoling side, necessarily from the opposite moiety in the village, washed,
greased, and dressed the corpse, thus preparing it for burial. Women
wept and forgot to prepare food for themselves or their families;
their opposites condoled them. Usually the body was buried on the
third day, although important individuals who might be mourned by
people having to travel a great distance were sometimes not buried

for over a week. Food and other necessities were often buried with the dead. A man might take along his favorite pipe, while a woman was sent off with the small bowl she had always eaten from while menstruating. Because of their vulnerability and the love parents had for them, children's burials were particularly lavish. The name of the deceased was set aside and not reused until the sting of loss had left the bereaved, sometimes a matter of many years.[7]

### Iroquois Clans

Although it was and is still appropriate to marry someone from outside one's own clan, regulation of marriage was not the primary function of clans (see Table 4.1). Clans probably arose to facilitate trade and exchange between residential groups, only later taking on the local reciprocal duties already described. A clan identification provided fictive kinship for men traveling away from home; a turtle was always welcome in the home of another turtle, regardless of distance and language barriers. Such long-distance trade had been highly developed in the eastern woodlands a thousand years earlier, and the reappearance of marine shell beads in Iroquoia in the late fifteenth century tells us that contacts had been revived with the southern Atlantic coast.

### The League of the Iroquois

Adjacent and closely allied villages probably cooperated in raiding villages of other Iroquoian and non-Iroquoian groups. Supposed wrongful deaths were avenged, and captives taken to replace lost loved ones. A raiding party could bring back both men and women, but men were more often tortured and killed. Some, especially women, were adopted to take the places of recently lost relatives. This bestowal of citizenship entailed renaming the adoptees from a set of traditional names owned by the clan. The adoptee might even be given the name of the person (s)he was to replace, thus completing the change in identity. Indeed, all people abandoned their names and identities upon their deaths, and even children who were given the same names when they were old enough were thought of as assuming those identities.

The violence of the time was by definition external warfare, for anyone beyond the pale of the community was an enemy beyond the protection of society. But a few leaders took a broader view, and to them the endless feuding was clearly internal warfare between nations that ought to have been brothers. As internecine violence swirled into a regional maelstrom, these few began to seek a way out.

From this time of perpetual warfare came the innovation now known as the League of the Iroquois. The story of how it came about has come down in several versions, a few of them more complete than the others. Unlike the origin myth, the story of the origin of the League reads like history with only a patina of myth. The figures in the story have the personalities of real people rather than supernaturals. Yet, like King Arthur of England, they have been made partly mythical with time.

The most extensive version of the legend of the League is the one dictated by John Gibson on the Six Nations Reserve in 1912, of which more is said later. There exist two other lengthy versions of slightly earlier age, and a shorter but readable gloss published as the *White Roots of Peace*. The version reproduced here is a very abbreviated one derived mainly from the last of these.[8]

### Legend of the Peacemaker

*It was a time when war was the normal state of things. North of Lake Ontario there was a young Huron woman who lived apart from her mother. Although still a virgin, the young woman became pregnant. Her mother dreamed that the child was destined to do great things. In due course the child, a boy, was born. The child was named Deganawida and accepted by his mother and grandmother as a truly gifted child.*

*Deganawida grew quickly to become a handsome young man. He had a natural gift for speaking, and preached to the children of his community. Eventually he clarified his message of peace through power and law. But he came up against the doubt and jealousy faced by all prophets in their own countries. After announcing his intention to depart, he built a stone canoe, and launched it with the help of his mother and grandmother. He came to the country of the five Iroquois nations, who were then fighting each other as vigorously as they fought other nations.*

*He passed from west to east through Iroquoia, urging the hunters he met along the way to take his message of peace back to their chiefs. Eventually he met a woman, who lived in a small house along the trail, where she fed hunters who passed by. She was the first to accept his news of peace and power, and he renamed her Jigonhsasee, "New Face."*

*The Peacemaker moved on, stopping among the Onondagas and gazing through a smoke hole into the house of Ayonhwathah (Hiawatha).[9] He quickly converted Ayonhwathah from cannibalism,* and charged him with converting Thadodaho (Adodarhonh), a particularly malevolent Onondaga shaman with snakes in his hair. Leaving Ayonhwathah to convert Thadodaho by combing the snakes from his hair, the Peacemaker left to travel to Mohawk country.

He went to the place of the great Cohoes Falls near the mouth of the Mohawk River. There he climbed a tree over the gorge and waited. The Mohawks felled the tree into the torrent, but the next morning they found the Peacemaker sitting by his fire. The feat convinced the Mohawks of his power. They accepted his message and became the founders of the League.

Meanwhile, Ayonhwathah's efforts to convert Thadodaho had met with failure. Worse, the shaman had killed each of Ayonhwathah's three daughters. Devastated by grief, Ayonhwathah left his village, following the trail eastward toward Mohawk country. Along the way he came to a lake. A flock of ducks flew up to allow him to pass dry shod, carrying the water with them and revealing a lake bottom strewn with shell beads. These Ayonhwathah collected and put in a buckskin bag. Some he strung on three strings as symbols of his grief. Wandering aimlessly, he eventually encountered the Peacemaker. Deganawida took the strings of shell beads and made more strings from the beads collected by Ayonhwathah. Laying the strings out one at a time, he uttered the words of the Requickening Address for the first time. With fifteen strings he wiped away the tears, removed obstructions from the ears, cleared the throat, dispelled the darkness, and dealt with the other eleven essential matters of condolence. The ritual cleared Ayonhwathah's mind of grief, and together they sang the Peace Hymn, the Hai Hai.

The Peacemaker and Ayonhwathah taught the ritual to the Mohawks, and accepted adoption into the Mohawk nation. With the essential ritual now in hand, they traveled westward, accompanied by Mohawk chiefs. The Oneidas joined the League quickly, and were called younger brothers by the Mohawks. Beyond the Oneidas were the Onondagas and the evil Thadodaho. They bypassed this obstacle to approach the Cayuga, who joined as easily as the Oneida had done. They also took the side of the younger brothers. The three nations then returned to the Onondagas, all of whom save Thadodaho also joined, but as older brothers on the side of the Mohawks. Then, with the chiefs of the four nations, they went to the Senecas, who also joined as older brothers, completing the League.

With the power of the chiefs of Five Nations behind them, the Peacemaker and Ayonhwathah returned to the lodge of Thadodaho. There, with the greatest difficulty, his mind was made straight, and Ayonhwathah combed the snakes from his hair. The Peacemaker made Thadodaho first among equals in the role of the fifty League Chiefs, placed antlers on all their heads as signs of their authority, and taught them the words of the Great Law.

The Deganawida legend has basic elements that appear in all of its complete oral versions, although sometimes in different orders. The scene always opens on villages of male hunters and female farmers that are scattered and disrupted by chronic warfare. There are a few reasonable but marginalized people who cannot stop the violence. Deganawida lives north of Lake Ontario in a community of displaced people. Like most prophets he is an outsider, fatherless, and capable of making miracles. Ayonhwathah (Hiawatha) is a recidivist Onondaga cannibal. He dreams of better life, but loses his daughters, wanders, and is eventually cured by the protocol of greeting strangers in Mohawk country. A "mother of nations" who has fed passing war parties accepts the message of peace. She is a symbol of the maternal role. Atotarho (Thadodaho) is magically cured by song, and he gives up excessive sex, cannibalism, and violence. Deganawida's code rests on three points: the good word (righteousness), power (civil authority), and peace (health of society). Hiawatha is concerned about condolence for the dead. Together they conceive requickening and the short-circuiting of blood feuds. The joint mission of Deganawida and Hiawatha is to get the code accepted among the nations, who eventually come together as two moieties.

The confederation of the five Iroquois nations, the Mohawks, Oneidas, Onondagas, Cayugas, and Senecas, was probably complete by around 1525. Both Iroquois oral tradition and archaeological evidence for endemic warfare suggest that the League could not have formed prior to around 1450. However, neither is there any convincing evidence that it formed as a consequence of contact with Europeans.[10]

There is some weak evidence from Seneca oral tradition that points to 1536 as the specific year they joined the League of the Iroquois, although 1451 is a less likely possibility. The specific reference may be to an eclipse of the sun that took place around the time of the second hoeing of the fields. The only two eclipses falling between 1450 and 1600 that approached totality in Seneca country in that season occurred in 1451 and 1536. The latter was an annular eclipse, but would have been nearly as impressive as a total eclipse.[11]

### Operation of the League

The structure of the League divides the nations into younger and older brothers. This device mimics clan moieties at the League level. The League members still refer to themselves as the People of the Longhouse, the *Hodenosaunee*. The metaphorical longhouse of the

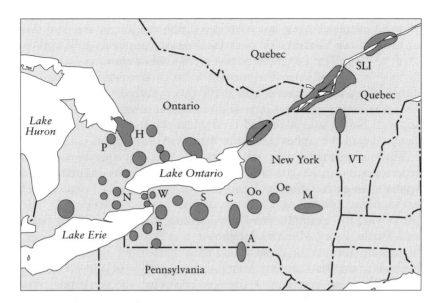

*Figure 4.3   Northern Iroquoian site clusters in the fifteenth and sixteenth centuries. Those persisting into the seventeenth century were the Saint Lawrence Iroquoian, Petun, Huron, Neutral, Wenro, Erie, Seneca, Cayuga, Onondaga, Oneida, Mohawk, and (A) Susquehannock*

League stretches across Iroquoia. The Mohawks guard the eastern door and the Senecas guard the western door. The Onondagas keep the fire at the center. Above them all soars the Tree of Peace, atop which sits an eagle that watches over the peace. Each League Chief (sometimes called a "sachem" in recent centuries) is like a tree or a support pole of the great longhouse. Together the chiefs link arms and act as one.

Iroquois custom requires unanimity in League decisions. Concepts of quorum and majority rule were not acceptable. Achievement of unanimity was often facilitated by having the most senior chiefs speak last, so that they could incorporate the wisdom and diversity of opinions expressed by more junior men. Orators often spoke for the chiefs, appealing repeatedly to the audience for confirmation that the message was being well received. Elaborate procedures evolved for passing matters for discussion from one side to the other until either consensus was reached or the matter was dropped. If the nations could not agree, they could act individually so long as their actions did not harm another League member. Thus the basis of the League was more a mutual nonaggression pact than a political union. It allowed persuasion but not coercion within the longhouse, and this in turn allowed nations or even factions of nations to follow their own policies. The League was put at risk when those policies conflicted, for its consensual/segmented form of government tended to dither when circumstances called for quick authoritarian decisions. This weakness sometimes later allowed brothers within the League to come to blows, and it proved fatal when the Iroquois later became caught up in the upheaval of the American Revolution.

Without majority rule, there was no need to equalize national representation in League affairs. Senior women from dominant clan segments in each nation each chose a man to serve as a League Chief or sachem, known as *royá:ner* in the Mohawk language. The Mohawks, for example, were divided into three clans: Wolf, Bear, and Turtle. Every Mohawk longhouse was inhabited by the women of one or another of these clans, their unmarried sons, and their husbands, the last coming from one or another of the other two clans. The clan segment or lineage, excluding the husbands, was called *ohwachira* by the Mohawks.[12] At the time the League was formed, Mohawk politics were such that nine clan segments, three from each clan, had the power to insist that they each contribute a League Chief. Ayonhwathah was adopted by the Mohawks, but Deganawida's role as Peacemaker set him above the others. His name was retired and his position never filled after his death. Ayonhwathah, on the other hand, was adopted by the Turtle clan and made one of three League Chiefs from that clan. However, out of respect his position has also remained unfilled since his death.

The village now known as Garoga was probably the dominant Mohawk community in the second quarter of the sixteenth century (Figure 4.1). Longhouses there are grouped in three sets of three, and it is possible that these were the residences of the *ohwachira* that sent the first delegation of nine chiefs to the other nations with the Peacemaker.

The Oneidas also designated nine League Chiefs, but the Cayugas named ten. The Onondagas contributed 14, including Thadodaho, who was styled first among equals. Finally, the Senecas contributed eight. Each nation devised its own internal mechanisms for selecting and organizing its League Chiefs (Table 4.2). The Senecas paired chiefs from different clans, giving three positions to the Snipe clan and two to the Turtle clan, while giving no positions at all to the Beaver, Deer, or Heron clans. The last three might have appeared among the Seneca only later, during the wholesale adoptions of the seventeenth century. Similarly, the Cayuga did not appoint chiefs

## Table 4.2  Iroquois League Chiefs

| Name | Clan | Moiety[a] | Function |
|---|---|---|---|
| **Mohawks – Older Brothers** | | | |
| 1 Dekarihokenh | Turtle | A | Firekeeper |
| 2 Ayonhwathah | Turtle | A | Firekeeper |
| 3 Shadekariwadeh | Turtle | A | Firekeeper |
| 4 Sharenhowaneh | Wolf | A | Sibling |
| 5 Deyoenhegwenh | Wolf | A | Sibling |
| 6 Orenregowah | Wolf | A | Sibling |
| 7 Dehennakarineh | Bear | B | Cousin |
| 8 Rastawenseronthah | Bear | B | Cousin |
| 9 Shoskoarowaneh | Bear | B | Cousin |
| **Oneidas – Younger Brothers** | | | |
| 10 Odatshedeh | Wolf | A | Firekeeper |
| 11 Kanongweniyah | Wolf | A | Firekeeper |
| 12 Dayohagwendeh | Wolf | A | Firekeeper |
| 13 Shononses | Turtle | A | Sibling |
| 14 Dehonareken | Turtle | A | Sibling |
| 15 Adyadonneatha | Turtle | A | Sibling |
| 16 Adahondeayenh | Bear | B | Cousin |
| 17 Ronyadashayouh | Bear | B | Cousin |
| 18 Ronwatshadonhonh | Bear | B | Cousin |
| **Onondagas – Older Brothers** | | | |
| 19 Thadodaho | Bear | B | Thadodaho[b] |
| 20 Awennisera | Beaver | A | Cousin[b] |
| 21 Dehatkadons | Beaver | A | Cousin[b] |
| 22 Yadajiwakenh | Snipe | A | Cousin[b] |
| 23 Awekenyat | Hawk | B | Sibling[b] |
| 24 Dehayatgwareh | Turtle | A | Cousin[b] |
| 25 Ononwirehtonh | Wolf | A | Wampum keeper |
| 26 Oewenniseronni | Deer | B | Sibling |
| 27 Arirhonh | Deer | B | Sibling |
| 28 Oewayonhnyeanih | Eel | B | Sibling |
| 29 Sadegwaseh | Eel | B | Sibling |
| 30 Sakokeaeh | Eel | B | Sibling |
| 31 Seawi | Turtle | A | Cousin |
| 32 Skanaawadi | Turtle | A | Cousin |

Table 4.2   (cont.)

| Name | Clan | Moiety[a] | Function |
|------|------|--------|----------|
| *Cayugas – Younger Brothers* | | | |
| 33 Dekaeayough | Deer | Turtle | Firekeeper |
| 34 Tsinondawerhon | Deer | Turtle | Firekeeper |
| 35 Kadagwarasonh | Turtle | Turtle | |
| 36 Soyouwes | Turtle | Turtle | |
| 37 Watyaseronneh | Turtle | Turtle | |
| 38 Dayohronyonkah | Wolf | Wolf | |
| 39 Deyothorehgwen | Wolf | Wolf | |
| 40 Dawenhethon | Wolf | Wolf | |
| 41 Wadondaherha | Snipe | Wolf | Doorkeeper |
| 42 Deskae | Snipe | Wolf | Doorkeeper |
| *Senecas – Older Brothers* | | | |
| 43 Skanyadariyoh | Turtle | A | 1st Pair[c] |
| 44 Shadekaronyes | Snipe | B | 1st Pair |
| 45 Shakenjohwaneh | Hawk | B | 2nd Pair |
| 46 Kanokareh | Turtle | A | 2nd Pair |
| 47 Deshayenah | Snipe | B | 3rd Pair |
| 48 Shodyenawat | Bear | A | 3rd Pair |
| 49 Karonkerihdawih | Snipe | B | 4th Pair |
| 50 Deyohninhohhakarawenh | Wolf | A | 4th Pair |

[a] Moieties are usually unnamed "sides" that are identified here as A and B.
[b] At the Six Nations Reserve, these now function as Firekeepers.
[c] Seneca League Chiefs are paired.

from the Bear, Ball, or Heron clans, and might not have had them in the sixteenth century. The Onondagas left out only the Ball clan.

The complete roll of Iroquois League Chiefs is shown in Table 4.2. The 50 names became a permanent roster, although only 49, excluding Ayonhwathah, could be filled. As chiefs died, the senior women of their clan segments chose new ones to raise up in their places, each assuming the name and identity of his predecessor. If he did not serve his *ohwachira* well, the women could remove his antlers and replace him. If a suitable man was not available in the *ohwachira* that held the chiefly name, then a man might be borrowed to serve from another clan segment. This practice sometimes alienated a title from its original *ohwachira* and led to later disputes about its proper ownership.[13]

## The Role of Women in the League

The central role of Iroquois women in food production and in the appointment of sachems has long attracted both popular attention and scholarly research. It has also been used to support arguments that would have mystified the Iroquois of four centuries ago. Iroquois matriliny was used by nineteenth-century advocates for women's suffrage to support their demands for equality, and has attracted the attention of modern feminists as well. Unfortunately, the cultural biases and political motivations of men and women alike have tended to misrepresent Iroquois matriliny as often as not. Iroquois women were not matriarchs, or Amazons, or drudges. They were Iroquois women, who lived in a nonhierarchical society in which their role as food producers was properly appreciated and in which the elevation of some aspects of kinship to political significance gave them influence that they might not otherwise have had.[14]

## Chiefs and the Condolence Council

The Great Law of the League (*Kaianerekowa*), which the Peacemaker gave to the Five Nations and which was preserved for generations through oral tradition, provided for the rights, duties, and symbols of chiefs, clans, and nations. The office of Pine Tree Chief was defined to accommodate men of ability who did not happen to come from clan segments that held League titles. The office of War Chief was also defined, and it was provided that a League Chief had to temporarily leave his office if he took on that role. Laws of adoption and emigration were also laid out, as were the elements of the Requickening Address and the songs that accompanied League ceremonies. All of this was committed to memory by the leading orators of the League, and preserved by constant repetition for generations.[15]

The League was founded upon two important pre-existing structures, the clan and the Condolence Ceremony. Later formal meetings of the League were typically begun with the Condolence Ceremony, to wipe away the grief of those who had lost chiefs since the previous meeting, and to raise up new chiefs in their places. The ritual constantly renewed the League and gave it life. In a world where war was the normal state of affairs, one could not take peace for granted.

*Table 4.3   The matters of the Requickening Address*

1 To wipe away the tears
2 To unplug the ears
3 To unstop the throat
4 To restore disturbed organs of the body and remove the yellow spots
5 To wipe the blood from the mat
6 To dispel the darkness and bring daylight
7 To make the sky beautiful
8 To replace the sun in the sky
9 To level the earth over the grave
10 To bind the bones together by the 20 strings of wampum given for murder (not returned but used reciprocally at a later condolence)
11 To gather together the scattered firebrands and rekindle the fire
12 To raise up the minds of women and warriors
13 To dispel the insanity of grief
14 To restore the torch to its place (which has been carried through the longhouse of the League to notify people of the death)
15 To restore the chief by raising him up again

The Condolence Council, also known as the Hai Hai, begins at the edge of the woods. The clear-minded approach the bereaved at the fire. The four major parts of the council begin with the roll-call of the chiefs (Eulogy) or Journeying on the Trail. This is followed by the Condoling Song, the second major part. Third comes a recitation of the laws of the Confederacy. The fourth and final major section is the Requickening Address. This varies in content. At the modern Six Nations Reserve there are fifteen "matters," each associated with a particular string of wampum. These are listed in Table 4.3.

### Marine Shell Symbols

Shell beads became the tokens of League activity. Marine shell had been making its way into Iroquois villages for several decades, and its symbolic significance was already established. The whiteness of durable marine shell connoted the positive harmony of right-mindedness, socially positive and constructive. Black or purple connoted the reverse: the negative, the destructive, and death itself. The strings of shell beads that symbolized the fifteen matters of the condolence combined white and dark beads, just as life itself was characterized by the contending forces of good and evil, light and dark, life and death (Figure 4.4). Significantly, the last string was comprised entirely of white beads, for with it a chief was raised up again and named.[16]

Much of the marine shell appears to have been whelk (*Busycon*) from the Atlantic coast, probably from somewhere around Chesapeake Bay. Oyster and quahog shell, which also occurs, could have come from closer sources, perhaps even from the lower Hudson. These earliest beads would not have been the small tubular wampum of the seventeenth century, for this later form required iron tools for its crafting, but they had the same powerful significance.[17] The Susquehannocks were probably a conduit for much of the trade in shell in the sixteenth century. Shell, and later spirals made of European brass, moved from them northwestward to the Senecas, Neutrals, and Hurons. But only the Senecas came into the League, and although the Susquehannocks continued to supply the Neutrals and Hurons later on, by 1600 the Senecas were cut off from this trade, and turned eastward toward their Iroquois allies.[18]

The Susquehannocks were close relatives of the five Iroquois nations, having like them descended directly from Owasco antecedents. Yet the Susquehannocks were not drawn into the League. Moreover, the Iroquois nations soon turned their combined power against the Susquehannocks. At some time in the second half of the sixteenth century they were forced to abandon their villages in the area where the New York–Pennsylvania border now crosses the Susquehanna River, and they relocated nearer the mouth of the river, in Lancaster County. Some of them doubtless found their way as captured adoptees into Iroquois society.

### Horticulture and New Towns

Earlier smaller villages might have been occupied for decades. But those of the sixteenth century were larger, and because they were chosen for their defensive positions, they were often surrounded by poorer soils. The nature of their adaptation forced the Iroquois to move more frequently than they had before. Iroquois farmers practiced a form of shifting or swidden horticulture. Men opened up fields around new villages by girdling the trees of the forest. In the spring

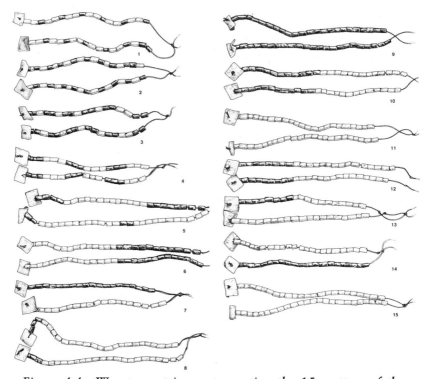

*Figure 4.4 Wampum strings representing the 15 matters of the Requickening Address of the Iroquois Condolence Ceremony*
Source: drawing from the Handbook of North American Indians, *vol. 15, p. 439, reproduced courtesy of the Smithsonian Institution.*

of the year they burned the lower shrubs and brush to clear the soil so that the women could scrape it into small hills among the skeletal trees. For this they used only hoes made of wood and bone. Only the heaviest work was done by men, who would have been ridiculed by other men and women alike had they engaged in women's work. When the leaves of the white oaks of the unburned forest were the size of a red squirrel's foot, it was time to plant. Women did the rest: planting, hoeing, and harvesting. Women also did the collecting of roots, maple syrup, berries, greens, nuts, and small animals.

Maize was planted in hills of dirt, nearly a meter in diameter, that were scraped up from the exposed forest floor. Beans and squash were also planted in some, but not all, of the hills. The beans climbed the maize stalks, using them as natural poles, and the squash spread out between the hills, choking out unwanted plants with the shade of its large leaves. The fields were hoed twice after planting, once when the maize was a span high and again when it was knee high. Just as the fruits of the three sisters, maize, beans, and squash, would later combine to provide a balanced diet for the Iroquois, the plants themselves combined to provide each other with support, shade, and cover while they grew.

Like maize, beans and squash could be boiled, roasted, or baked in various preparations. There were no set times for meals. People ate when they were hungry, and guests were offered food whenever they happened to arrive. While the day was largely unscheduled, the year was carefully scheduled by the natural seasonal round. The planting moon was a time when one gave little thought to the activities of other seasons and concentrated on the demands of the moment.

While the ground was being prepared, seed maize was soaked in a warm decoction made from the ground root of arrowhead lily or may apple. The water softened the hulls and stimulated germination. The ground roots, called "corn medicine," were believed to intoxicate any crows that might eat the seedlings, causing them to flutter about and scaring off others of their kind.

A society of women existed in each village to take charge of ritual surrounding the spring planting. They maintained the ceremonies needed to propitiate the spirits of the three sisters. Women worked in family units in fields cleared by their clan brothers. So long as each did her share of the labor, she also shared in the communal harvest. Individual women might also keep private plots, but they shared in the communal harvest only if they also did their parts in the fields of the *ohwachira*. An *ad hoc* mutual aid society was sometimes formed by these women so that they could bring collective effort even to fields not supervised by clan matrons.[19]

When they were not out on raids or attending councils, men spent much of their time hunting. All three activities required great energy and endurance, and took them away from home for long periods. They rested while at home, the place where women did most of the work, leading later European visitors to conclude that Iroquois men were lazy compared to their industrious wives. They hunted deer with the bow and arrow or by catching them in snares. Large groups of men might drive deer over a large area and into enclosures. Bears and some smaller animals were killed in deadfalls. Pigeons and beaver were delicacies, but almost any meat was eaten. It was considered manly to eat everything, even entrails. Men raised a strong tobacco (*Nicotiana rustica*) by simply scattering the seeds in the spring and

## The Planting Ceremony

Planting time is traditionally loaded with hope and uncertainty. There is an edge to prayers of thanksgiving in the Planting Ceremony, for no one can be sure that the summer will produce a successful crop. The Creator is urged to provide as he always has, as the participants skirt the shame of outright supplication. Yet if the rains fail to come, desperate planters might hold another Thunder Ceremony.

The structure of the ceremony replicates the basic forms of the prototypical Midwinter Ceremony. Sacrifices of tobacco and marine shell beads are made to the spirits of growth as well as to the little people of the forest. The smoke of the burning tobacco carries the message skyward to the Creator.

Our Life Supporters dances form the major rites of the Planting Ceremony. Gourd rattles called pumpkin shakes, which are also used in some medicine society meetings, are used to beat out the rhythms of the songs. As is customary in all Iroquois ceremonies, this one begins and ends with the Thanksgiving Speech. Tobacco would be burned in an invocation near the beginning were the life supporters not so close by, but their proximity makes this unnecessary. Our Life Supporters dances include the Women's Dance, the Corn Dance, the Stomp Dance, the Hand-in-Hand Dance, the Striking-the-Pole Dance, and the War Dance.

drying the leaves over the fire in the fall.

The Iroquois practiced an extensive (as opposed to intensive) form of horticulture. Aboriginal America was not well stocked with animals suitable for domestication, so the rise of farming and settled life had to proceed without the benefit of animals that might have provided hides, wool, meat, draft power, and manure. Without draft animals, neither plows nor wheeled transport were possible. The Iroquois thus had neither a ready supply of fertilizer nor the means to move it to their fields. Like all American Indians, they relied on crops that provided high yields from the planting and tending of a small number of seeds. Without the plow, domestication of grasses similar to the wheat and barley of Eurasia was out of the question.[20]

As time went on fields lost fertility and became infested with pests. New fields were opened farther from the village to make up for the poorer crops. After a decade or so the older fields had to be abandoned altogether, and women had to walk farther to the active fields.

When village populations were fewer than 200 it took 50 years for the process to force hikes of up to one kilometer. By that time the old abandoned fields near the village had grown up into new forest, had recovered their fertility, and could be cleared as new fields once again. Only the accumulation of waste and the deterioration of structures would prompt the inhabitants of one of these smaller villages to relocate. However, the residents of the larger villages of the sixteenth century had fewer options. After a few decades one of these villages would have been surrounded by deep middens of garbage and vast tracts of abandoned fields. They had little choice but to move the village, if only two or three kilometers to the other side of the most active and productive fields.[21]

The three sisters were supplemented by game, mostly venison, but the diet centered on plant foods. A wide range of edible wild plants was also gathered. After a winter of living on stored carbohydrates and lean meat, fresh greens and tubers from the forest were a welcome change. But gathered plants were also used for medicinal purposes. Hundreds of plant species were used as medicines according to specific recipes. Many of these were focused on fertility; love (and antilove) potions and abortion medicines account for a large fraction of native medicines. Others had more practical uses. While many apparently provided only psychological comfort, some had real biochemical value. The sap of the touch-me-not was used to treat poison ivy, and snakeroot leaves were an instant poultice for bee stings.[22] In all cases such remedies were regarded as medicines that served to restore order, balance, and harmony in situations of disorder and imbalance. A sick person was a person whose system was out of order. By extension a witch was also a person whose system was out of order. A talented herbalist had the ability to put either condition right. In the case of the witch, however, the victim might be too far gone to be salvaged. In such a case the witch might have to be killed lest (s)he continue to harm others. Through another extension of this logic, many things could be medicine. Indeed, anything that contributed to order and harmony was in some sense good medicine.

## Iroquois Society

There was more to the expansion of villages than mere numbers. Longhouses were now commonly up to a dozen compartments long, large enough to house 120 people or more. Nuclear families were small, largely a consequence of careful family planning. A woman with primary responsibility for farming could not afford to care for

*Figure 4.5    Traditional Iroquois cradleboard*
*Source: courtesy of the Iroquois Indian Museum, Howes Cave,*
*New York.*

children that were spaced too closely together. An infant and a tod-
dler, both still nursing, would have taxed any woman beyond her
ability to provide. Abortion medicines abounded in the Iroquois
pharmacopeia. Only one of a pair of twins was normally allowed to
survive, a choice justified by the precedent of the origin myth. A child
born too soon after an older sibling had little chance of survival.[23]

An unwanted child would not be kept long, but once accepted
children were loved beyond all else. Like most American Indians, the
ancient Iroquois swaddled their babies to cradle boards. Surviving
examples are often wooden and elaborately carved and decorated
(Figure 4.5). Europeans regarded Iroquois parents as very permissive,
a repeated observation that says as much about the Europeans as it
does about the Iroquois. Children were never struck, yet they were
well socialized, and so sensitive to criticism that a strong rebuke
could drive a youth to suicide. Small children ran naked as much as
possible in their early years, a practice that toughened them and
made diapers unnecessary. Both discipline and clothing appeared as
children neared puberty.

Children were much desired so long as they came at appropriate
intervals. Children who were lost through death or capture were

replaced quickly. This could be accomplished by attempting to conceive a new baby as quickly as possible, or by adopting a captive of about the same age and gender. There was apparently some preference for daughters, for they helped to increase the size and power of the household.

In ancient times an Iroquois woman gave birth kneeling on a deer hide and hanging on to a house post. She delivered her child alone or with the help of a female relative. Once the child was born the mother buried the placenta and got back to her work as quickly as possible. The newborn child was bathed in the nearest stream or with snow.[24]

From time to time a child would be born under an ominous cloud. Perhaps its head would be covered by caul (fetal membrane), or some other sign would indicate that the child possessed unusual powers of clairvoyance. Such a child was valued for its purity and would be "down-fended," secluded in the care of a single guardian until puberty. Until then the child would live under corn husks in a corner of the longhouse, coming out only at night. A line of cattail down, which would betray any disturbance, ensured that the child remained isolated.[25]

Puberty probably brought fasting, isolation, and induced dreaming for boys under the supervision of a shaman. Girls were supervised in their own seclusion by matrons, for people avoided eating with or even being in the same house with menstruating women.

In the traditional longhouse young people looked mainly to their matrilineal relatives for guidance. Boys were close to their mothers' brothers, with whom they shared clan membership. Although Euro-Americans have long been most fascinated by matriliny, the Iroquois also reckoned a unit called *athonni* in Mohawk. This was the lineage of one's father, to which one also had some obligation.

Adolescent boys often formed close formal friendships. These bound them by mutual obligation through the rest of their lives. Such friends exchanged gifts, shared booty, traveled, fought, and often died together. Whereas male partners were once war buddies, changes in the ways in which Iroquois men have gone to war altered this important institution into a curative association. Later formal male friendships were formed and renewed by ritual. Dream fulfillment and curing have remained important aspects of these partnerships.

Adolescents assumed adult names that were more than just names in the Euro-American sense. Specific names were held by the clans, and an adolescent was given an appropriate name from the available pool. He or she then became the reincarnation of the previous holders of the same name.

Three children spaced well apart was the ideal. Later European writers would be amazed by the small sizes of Iroquois families, "so that it is a wonder when a woman has three or four children."[26] For their part, the Europeans had long since adapted to the lethal endemic diseases of plague and smallpox by spawning as many children as possible, a practice made easier by their permanent housing and division of agricultural labor. Iroquois women had no such option. However, an Iroquois woman would attempt to replace a lost child promptly, either by new pregnancy or by adoption. Thus, even though families might seem to be small, steady population growth was easily maintained.

Perhaps more important to Iroquois society was the growth in the size of the longhouse. A longhouse having 12 living compartments would have housed about 120 people, about 96 of them related women and their children. The remaining 24 would have been husbands whose blood ties were with women in other longhouses. Given the small sizes of Iroquois nuclear families, it would have taken at least five generations, or about a century, for the *ohwachira* of one woman, her descendants, and their husbands to require such a large longhouse. That means that it is very unlikely that a longhouse of 12 fires was presided over by a single senior woman, for the founder of such a large *ohwachira* would have been long dead by the time it reached that size. Iroquois women of the sixteenth century must have achieved new political understandings for such households to evolve, and for the houses to be packed so tightly together in large villages. Some senior women must have been content to defer to a sister or a cousin as household matron.

The members of many households had to look back as many as seven generations to find their common ancestor. This number remains significant even today. Iroquois orators still talk of drawing upon the wisdom of seven generations, and of their responsibility to seven generations yet to come.

The sixteenth century might have been the time during which Iroquois terms for close kin went through some important changes. Previously, Iroquois children called their aunts by the same word they used for their biological mothers. This was true in all five of the Iroquois languages, although the exact terms differed. However, at some time prior to 1635 they all found it necessary to distinguish once again between a biological mother and other women in the household of the mother's generation. Each language found its own solution to the problem. Mohawks began referring to "female parents" in order to distinguish them from other women called "mothers." It may be that the growth of the *ohwachira* matrilineages simply generated too many mothers.[27]

*Figure 4.6 European trade axes from a Mohawk village site*

European goods began to appear in increasing quantities during this period, turning up in ever larger but still modest amounts in eastern village sites. The Mohawks probably obtained most of these goods from the French at Tadoussac and elsewhere along the St Lawrence River. This contrasted with the situation among the western Iroquois. A substantial amount of material reached the Onondagas and Senecas from Chesapeake Bay by way of the Susquehanna River.[28]

As early as 1580 the Indians knew that they wanted iron axes and knives, and that the French wanted pelts, particularly beaver pelts, in exchange. The problem for the Mohawks was that St Lawrence Iroquoians and Algonquians stood between them and the French traders on the lower St Lawrence. The St Lawrence Iroquoians were eliminated by the Mohawks, Hurons, and others, leaving only the Algonquians to interfere with Mohawk traders after 1580.

### Iroquois Demography

Little is known about the demography of the other four Iroquois nations at this time, but Mohawk demography is better understood.

Mohawk population began to surge in the late sixteenth century, rising steadily to around 1,700 people by 1580. By the second decade of the next century it had nearly doubled. The increase was too rapid to be explained by internal growth alone; there must have been some immigration as well.

Some of the new Mohawks might have been adopted Susquehannocks, people captured when the main body of Susquehannocks were driven southward to the lower Susquehanna River around 1580. A more likely explanation for the sudden increase is that Jefferson County Iroquoians abandoning their villages around the same time made their way to the Mohawk Valley and elsewhere in Iroquoia. Analysis of Jefferson County ceramics has shown that they resemble most closely the ceramics found on late sixteenth-century Mohawk sites.[29] We know that the St Lawrence Iroquoians who were encountered by Cartier earlier in the century had also disappeared by 1580. Those people were apparently attacked and then largely absorbed by the confederacy that would later be called Huron. The Jefferson County Iroquoians, who were closely related to those farther down the St Lawrence, were probably attacked mainly by the Iroquois, and appear to have preferred moving to the Iroquois nations.

# 5

# The Coming of Europeans, 1600–1634: The Strawberry Moon

### *The First Trade Goods*

European goods had been trickling into Iroquoia since the middle of the sixteenth century. At first they were limited to a few items, mainly iron axes, glass beads, and copper kettles. Many of the early kettles supplied by Basque fishermen in the Gulf of St Lawrence were large and heavy compared to later ones. These receptacles were valued not just as containers, but also for the sheet copper they provided for other things once they wore out. Sheet copper cut from kettles was rolled into tiny tubes then bent into spirals, perhaps symbolic of the panther's tail. Larger tubes were bent into hoops that could have served as neck ornaments. Straps of copper kettles were bent into bracelets. Conical tinklers made from sheet copper and imported hawks' bells began to replace the bone phalanges of deer on dancing costumes. Chipped stone arrow points were slowly replaced by cut copper ones. At first the copper points were supplied with stems, but later they came to mimic the triangular chert points more closely. Iroquois men found that they could haft the copper points more easily by sharpening their arrow shafts and bending the softened tips through holes in the copper points before lashing them.[1]

By the end of the sixteenth century, Basque, French, and other northern European fishing boats were arriving with increasing frequency on the Grand Banks, in the Gulf of St Lawrence, and elsewhere along the Atlantic coastline. Salt was an expensive commodity in northern Europe, so the fishermen from this region were more likely than southern Europeans to use shore stations in America to dry fish rather than salting them down at sea. Their landings brought them into more frequent contact with the Indians than was the case for Portuguese fishermen, and they soon learned what was in demand in the new American market. Beaver felt hats were all the rage in

Europe and the fishermen found that they could make a little money on the side by trading for beaver pelts, which they could later sell to the felt makers. Both the Indians and the Europeans thought that they were getting valuable goods at low cost.[2]

Later traders added iron needles and long-bladed iron knives to their stocks. There was steady demand for copper kettles. Traders soon found that they could increase demand by supplying thinner brass kettles that would wear out faster. Finally, large numbers of round glass beads began to appear, most of them solid white or light blue in color. These were popular with the Iroquois, for clear, white, or light blue things had very positive symbolic value. By 1600 there were also tubular beads in white or indigo, as well as round or oval black beads. Black still had a negative symbolic connotation for the Iroquois.[3] Some of these items came from the Gulf of St Lawrence, where the Iroquois, the feared "killer people," were already making their presence felt. Others of them came up from the middle Atlantic coast by way of Susquehannock country.

Much is often made of this process and its presumed lethal character. Certainly, the Iroquois valued the goods they were able to obtain from the Europeans, and the fur trade drew them into a worldwide economic system. However, they were not utterly dependent upon those goods, and would not be for another two centuries. So long as they had the land, they could always revert to their earlier way of life. That they did not was a matter of preference rather than necessity.

### Direct Contacts

Even for the Indians of Newfoundland, who had encountered Europeans six centuries earlier, the failed Norse colony of AD 1000 was nothing more than a bad dream. The explorers who followed Columbus touched the coast and explored the American continent throughout the sixteenth century, but rarely approached Iroquoia. Cartier's voyages of 1534, 1535–6, and 1541–2 penetrated the St Lawrence to the site of modern Montreal, bringing the French into direct contact with the St Lawrence Iroquoians. But the Iroquois proper remained largely out of contact, behind the wall of the Adirondack Mountains and the great lake above the rapids.

Finally, in 1609, Iroquoia was approached more closely by both French and Dutch explorers. Having established a settlement at Quebec in the previous year, Champlain explored south and west, up the lake that would later bear his name, in July. Around the place now called

Crown Point, Champlain and his Algonquian allies encountered an army of Iroquois, mostly Mohawks. As mentioned in Chapter 2, up to this time pitched battles usually involved large numbers of warriors on each side. Each army might be composed of men related by marriage from several villages. The pitched battle was disorganized, with few casualties as individuals dueled and dodged arrows. Champlain's shocking use of firearms and the prompt deaths of the Mohawk chiefs put an end to this form of warfare in Iroquoia, but traditional raiding remained. Later Iroquois raiding matched the needs of French and English frontier tactics, for set-piece battles were not possible on a vast landscape having only a few strategic forts, whereas Indian raiding fitted well with the need to focus on attacks on remote forts. It also presaged later guerrilla tactics. Yet too much has been made in recent years of this battle, which has often been described as the defining moment in which the French became permanently allied with the Algonquians and the Mohawks became enemies of them both. In fact, the Mohawks had already been trading with the French and fighting with the Algonquians for decades. They had probably made and broken treaties with both for years, and they would make and break many more in the century that followed this event.

In September 1609, Henry Hudson ascended the river that now bears his name to within sight of modern Albany. Hudson was an Englishman, in the employ of the Dutch and looking for a passage to the Pacific. His interaction with Indians was much more peaceful than that of Champlain. He visited with Algonquian-speaking Mahican Indians who lived along the river, and judged that although a river and not a strait, the place was a suitable location for a trading post.

Soon the French were established on the St Lawrence and the Dutch had permanent bases on the Hudson. Explorers, traders, and missionaries operating from these European outposts left behind the documents that ended the long twilight of Northern Iroquoian protohistory and brought them all into the realm of documentary history. Despite the importance of those documents, much of what we know about Northern Iroquoians from 1525 to 1700 derives from archaeological research. Very often the two lines of evidence work together to tell us much more than we could know from either of them alone.

Champlain had explored Canada since 1604 under the Sieur de Monts, who had a French monopoly in the region. In 1612 Louis XIII, ignoring an earlier grant to de Monts from Henry IV, gave all of North America from Florida to the St Lawrence to Mme de Guercheville and the Jesuits. This move, along with several others, weakened Champlain's position at Quebec. The Jesuits established a small colony on the eastern site of Mt Desert Island, Maine, in 1613, and plans were made for greater things.[4]

The Dutch followed up on Hudson's explorations in 1614, establishing Fort Nassau on an island on the southern side of what is now Albany. The trading post provided almost immediate access to European goods for the local Mahicans and the Mohawks living just to the west. Unfortunately, the Mohawks and Mahicans were already enemies, and the latter resisted Mohawk efforts to gain easy direct access to the Dutch traders. Nonetheless, almost straight away Dutch goods began to appear in Mohawk villages in much larger numbers than earlier. One Dutchman was so impressed by this that he described the Mohawks as owning the west side of the Hudson while their enemies the Mahicans owned only the east side. The Mohawks clearly got into the habit of hiking overland from what is now Schenectady to Castle Island in order to trade with Dutch ships there.[5]

The arrival of the Dutch was a windfall to the Mohawks. A century earlier they were the farthest removed of all the Iroquois from the center of things, which at the time was in the Mississippi and Ohio valleys. Even after the European trade began, much of it came up the Susquehanna, bypassing the eastern Iroquois and benefiting their western neighbors, including the Eries, Senecas, and Neutrals. Fort Nassau turned the back door of Iroquoia into the front door, and the keepers of that door realized immediate benefits.

### Iroquois Demography

Champlain led the Hurons and Andastes in an attack on the Iroquois in 1615. His opponents were either the Onondagas or the Oneidas: it is not certain which, for he referred to all the eastern Iroquois as *Antouhonorons.* The following year he gave us our first description of Iroquois village movements.

> This is all that I have been able to learn about their mode of life; and I have described to you fully the kind of dwelling of these people, as far as I have been able to learn it, which is the same as that of all the tribes living in these regions. They sometimes change their villages at intervals of ten, twenty, or thirty years, and transfer them to a distance of one, two, or three leagues from the preceding situation, except when compelled by their enemies to dislodge, in which case they retire to a greater distance, as the Antouhonorons, who went some forty to fifty leagues. This is the form of their dwellings, which are separated

from each other some three or four paces, for fear of fire, of which they are in great dread.[6]

Hidden in this passage is an important clue to a sudden population increase among the Mohawks at this time. A village of 1,500 people suddenly appeared amid other Mohawk villages, and the pottery found in it was mainly of an Oneida type.[7] Champlain explains this anomaly, simultaneously accounting for the sudden surge in population, the appearance of a foreign pottery type, and an unexpectedly small number of people in Oneida country at around the same time. This sudden infusion of new immigrants swelled the Mohawk population even more than it had been increased by the arrival of people from Jefferson County. Overall, the Mohawk population shot up from around 4,000 at the turn of the century to over 7,700 by 1634.[8]

The partial solution of the Mohawk demographic puzzle reveals some of the difficulties inherent in any attempt to assess Iroquois populations. Migration of individuals and of groups both large and small was a constant feature of the Iroquois landscape. Local populations fluctuated as people came and went, and population estimates must somehow take this fluidity into account.

The attractiveness of the Mohawk Valley around 1615 is easy to understand. The Dutch had opened the equivalent of a modern megamall on the eastern edge of Iroquoia, and the Mohawks were closest to the new riches. The initial arrangement lasted only two years, for Fort Nassau was wiped out by spring flooding in early 1617. However, the Dutch continued to come up seasonally from their permanent post on Manhattan Island to trade on the same spot. The Mohawks took advantage of these sporadic opportunities, pushing past Mahican opposition to trade directly with the Dutch on Castle Island, now the port of Albany. They anticipated the Dutch demand for beaver pelts, carrying them overland from the site of modern Schenectady to the rendezvous point. But the trade was only intermittent, for the Mohawks could not remain permanently in hostile Mahican territory along the Hudson, and the Dutch traders were not regular in their visits.

The new trade brought more of the goods the Iroquois already desired, but it brought new items as well. Now there were mouth harps (sometimes called jaws or Jews harps), glass bottles, and European salt glaze pottery. This included Weserware, whch was made in northern Europe from 1570 to 1620. Another new item was multicolored glass beads, many of them with red stripes or layers. Unlike white, black, or blue, red was an ambiguous color to the Iroquois. It was the color of blood, positive when it connoted life, negative when it marked the consequences of war. Thus later red medicine masks were invested with the power to cure disorders in which blood was predominant, while later wampum belts and tomahawks would be painted red to signal war.[9] Red glass beads had the same symbolic power as copper, the red metal, and the Iroquois prized it above all other colors. Chevron beads with interior red layers were sometimes ground down to expose the red as much as possible.

The Dutch trade caused the Senecas and the other western Iroquois to turn their backs on their former trading partners and solidified the League of the Iroquois as never before.

### The Approaching Scourge

A major epidemic began in southeastern New England in 1616. This first regional epidemic did not spread west of the Connecticut River, so the Iroquois were spared. It involved some form of hepatic failure, but its exact identification remains unknown. In Iroquoia it was an unheard warning of things to come.[10] Contacts with the Dutch and sporadically with other Europeans continued, but lethal diseases remained at a safe distance for the time being.

By 1620 English pilgrims had founded Plymouth Plantation in what is now Massachusetts. By 1624 the Dutch decided to attempt a new permanent outpost on the upper Hudson, and constructed Fort Orange (Figure 5.1). This time the river did not carry the post away, and the settlement that would later be known as Albany was permanently established. The new fort renewed Mohawk demands for direct access to the Dutch trade. Mahican resistance to this idea led to the outbreak in the same year of the Mohawk–Mahican War, which raged for four years.

Meanwhile, the Jesuits finally arrived in Quebec in 1625. Although the Jesuits had been promised a free hand in Canada, missionaries of the Recollect order had arrived in Canada in 1615, and had led attempts to convert Indians for a few years. In 1628 the Mohawk–Mahican War ended, and at the same time the English decided to blockade Quebec. Canada fell to the English the following year. Champlain had only sixteen fighting men with him when David Kirke took Quebec. The Recollects and Jesuits were forced to leave and return to France. The Mohawks saw an opening and used it to destroy the Indian settlement at Trois Rivières on the St Lawrence.

The 1630s began with the Dutch patroon Killiaen van Rensselaer sending settlers to occupy Rensselaerswyck, the patroonship

*Figure 5.1   Fort Orange around 1630, painted by L. F. Tantillo*

surrounding Fort Orange. The first settlers, including families with small children, began arriving the following year. In 1632 Canada was returned to France under the Treaty of Saint-Germain-en-Laye. Only Jesuit missionaries were allowed to return by the French government. The Indians would later blame the Jesuits for what was about to befall them, but it was the little Dutch children that would unknowingly bring the worst disaster.

The Jesuits turned their attention first to the Hurons, but they saw potential in Iroquois country as well. The English were out of the picture for the time being, but the Dutch were well established. Unlike the French, the Dutch were businessmen who had little interest in traveling into Indian country. They were content to remain at Fort Orange and wait for the Indians to bring in furs to trade. Ten years after the founding of Fort Orange, the Dutch had still not set foot in Iroquoia. But an invisible army of deadly microbes borne by their children was about to change all of that.

### The State of the Nations

The Mohawks lived in fortified hilltop villages for much of the sixteenth century, moving to less defensible sites closer to the Mohawk River as League security improved and the flow of European trade goods increased. By 1634 they were living in four large villages overlooking the river. They were known to themselves and to the

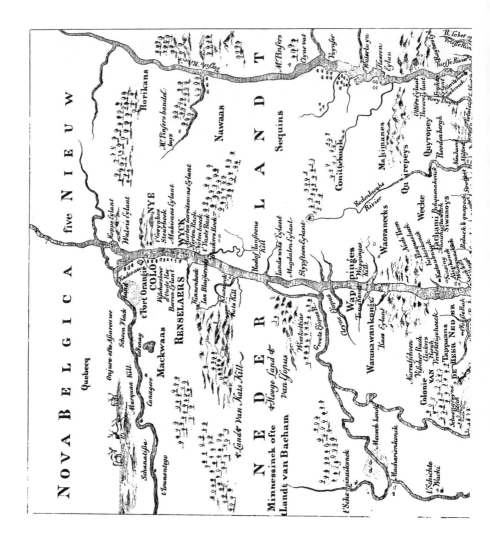

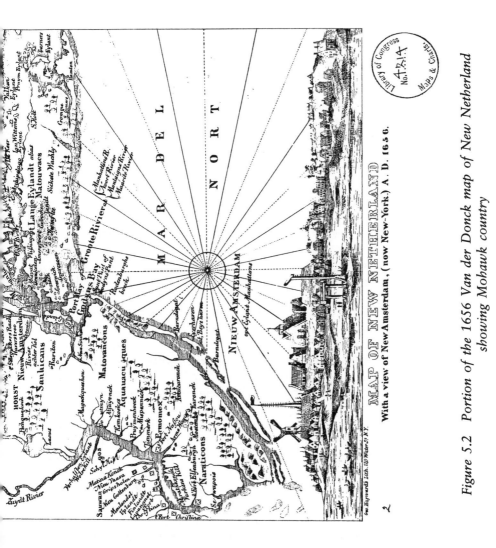

MAP OF NEW NETHERLAND

With a view of New Amsterdam, (now New-York.) A. D. 1656.

Figure 5.2 Portion of the 1656 Van der Donck map of New Netherland showing Mohawk country

other Iroquois nations as the *Kanyenkehaka*, the people of *Kanyenke* (also spelled *Ganienkeh*). This has usually been translated "Place of the Flint," but the flint (or more properly chert) sources in Mohawk country were not particularly sought after. More important were the clear quartz crystals now called Herkimer diamonds, which could be quarried in a few local mines and abound on Mohawk village sites. These were highly valued by Iroquois and other nations. *Kanyenke* was more likely "Place of the Crystals." Crystals were symbolically important as amulets of success, health, and long life, artifacts more likely to inspire a name than second-rate chert.[11] The Mohawks were the main suppliers of quartz crystals up to 1614. After that they became primary middlemen for the Dutch glass beads that replaced them.

"Mohawk" derives from a word meaning "man-eaters" in the language of the Massachusett or perhaps Narragansett people of southern New England. The Dutch followed the Mahicans in calling them by the cognate term *Maquas*, while the French called them *Agnié* or *Agniehronnons*. The last was a Huron cognate for "People of the Place of Crystals." All of these terms of reference were spelled variously, but "Mohawk" eventually prevailed.[12]

The Oneidas, who appear to have been closely related to the Mohawks, were living in a single principal village in 1634. Their name derived from their own word for their village name: *Oneyote*, "Place of the Erected Stone." This refers to a large syenite boulder, reputedly the one now standing next to the community center on the small New York Oneida reservation. Thus they called themselves *Oneyoteaka* "People of the Erected Stone." To the French they were the *Onoiochrhonons* (spelled variously), a name they borrowed from the Huron cognate for *Oneyoteaka*. "Oneida" emerged as the preferred spelling by the middle of the eighteenth century.

Some Oneidas had moved to the Mohawk Valley around 1615, and some of the survivors from that move might have moved back to Oneida country after 1634. Oneida village sites cluster mainly in northeastern Madison County. There are few if any local Iroquoian sites dating to the fifteenth century or earlier. The Oneida language is closely linked to Mohawk, suggesting a recent split between the two. Thus the ancestral Oneidas probably lived in the upper (western) Mohawk Valley until the fifteenth century, when they shifted westward toward the emerging Onondagas.[13]

The Onondagas are also known mainly by their own name, variations on *Onontakeka*, "People of the Hill." Their principal town was *Onontake*, "On the Hill," and their modern reservation near

Syracuse preserves that name. The French called them by variants of
*Onontagueronon*, with the usual suffix of Huron origin.[14]

During the fifteenth century, the Onondagas gradually congregated
into two major communities that moved periodically within the area
lying between modern Syracuse and Cazenovia in Onondaga County.
Here we find a complete sequence from Early Owasco on. There was
an eastward drift of villages as they relocated through the centuries,
culminating by the fifteenth century in two large villages located in
the Pompey Hills. There they continued to evolve through a twin
sequence of village locations.[15]

The Cayuga name for themselves is *Kayohkhono*, a name whose
exact meaning is no longer known despite some plausible guesses.
The modern spelling of "Cayuga" is one of many approximations
made by speakers of English and various other Iroquois languages.
As usual, the French borrowed the Huron word for the Cayuga,
calling them *Oniouenhronons*, spelled variously. As with the
Mohawks, the French later settled on a shortened name, in this case
*Oiogouens*, based on the name of the principal Cayuga town at the
time. In League affairs they have been often referred to as the "People
of the Great Pipe."[16]

The Cayuga nation formed in a cluster of villages located largely
between Cayuga and Owasco Lakes. Some additional village sites lie
north of the main cluster. Others dating to the fifteenth and sixteenth
centuries lie just southwest of Cayuga Lake. There is linguistic evidence internal to the Cayuga language to suggest that the Cayuga
absorbed some Susquehannocks in the sixteenth century. This probably occurred around the time that the Susquehannocks were forced
out of their lands just south of modern Binghamton.[17]

The Dutch traveler Harmen van den Bogaert initially referred to all
Iroquois west of the Mohawks as *Sinnekens*, and this name was
picked up by later cartographers. This name later settled on the
Seneca proper, who call themselves *Onontowaka*, "People of the Big
Hill." This term, of course, caused them to be sometimes confused
with the Onondaga. The Huron name for them, which was used by
the French, was based on various spellings and pronunciations of
*Sonontoerrhonons*.[18]

As in the case of the Onondagas, the Senecas settled into two
primary villages by the sixteenth century. These relocated from time
to time in the vicinities of Honeoye Creek and Mud Creek, south of
modern Rochester. Here too the emphasis is on two major communities moving through parallel sequences of village relocations from
at least 1560 on. Recent work suggests that the Seneca sequence is

also more complex than once thought, for there are additional small villages not accounted for in the two primary sequences.[19]

## Iroquois Populations

By the first part of the seventeenth century, several of the village clusters around those of the five Iroquois nations had been abandoned. The Jefferson County Iroquoians had disappeared, probably absorbed by the Iroquois. The St Lawrence Iroquoians had been incorporated into the Huron confederacy, as had people from other clusters around modern Toronto, the Trent River valley, and elsewhere just north of Lake Ontario. The five nations of the Huron confederacy lived in a compact area between Lake Simcoe and Lake Huron by 1600.

The Neutral confederacy, which probably had five nations of its own, was congregated around the western end of Lake Ontario and eastward to the Niagara River. The Erie were scattered in three related nations along the southeastern side of Lake Erie. Finally, there were three surviving independent nations of Northern Iroquoians, the Wenro nation west of the Senecas, the Petun (Tobacco) nation west of the Hurons, and the Susquehannocks, who by 1600 were living in southern Pennsylvania. Together the Northern Iroquoians numbered almost 95,000 people.

The League of the Iroquois share of the larger Northern Iroquoian population came to about 21,740. The Mohawks were most numerous, swollen to over 7,700 by infusions of immigrants from elsewhere. Table 5.1 summarizes the probable population sizes for the Five Nations.

Iroquois villages had grown dramatically in the sixteenth century,

*Table 5.1   Iroquois nations and their populations in 1634*

| Nation | Villages | Population |
| --- | --- | --- |
| Mohawk | 4 | 7,740 |
| Oneida | 1 | 2,000 |
| Onondaga | 2 | 4,000 |
| Cayuga | 2 | 4,000 |
| Seneca | 2 | 4,000 |
| Total | 11 | 21,740 |

but their form of government limited their sizes. Villages were governed by consensus. Although men appointed by each *ohwachira* probably met as a village council, they had little authority beyond the force of their personalities. This in turn meant that face-to-face persuasion was the rule, a serious problem when the number of faces multiply beyond the ability of even the most skilled politician to remember them all. Most human beings manage only about 500 regular face-to-face interactions, and there were that many adult men alone in a village of 2,000. Even though the largest villages could occasionally be larger for brief periods, they became politically unstable when numbers approached 2,000. This instability usually resulted in a fissioning of a large village on the occasion of the next relocation. This probably explains why the number of Mohawk villages grew to four by 1634.[20]

### Summer in Iroquoia

The years between 1614 and 1634 were exhilarating ones for the Iroquois. The Dutch trade enriched their lives and drew them together as a League as never before. Threats from other nations abated in the face of their combined strength. Villages remained large, but defenses were relaxed. Relocations led to the construction of new villages on more open hilltops and closer to main trails.

---

### The Strawberry Ceremony

The month of June brings a new crop of wild strawberries, which abound in Iroquoia. Even today a strawberry drink is one of the favorites at Iroquois festivals. Little wonder that the coming of summer brings a sense of well-being to the community and prompts one of the happiest of the seasonal ceremonies of thanksgiving. The Strawberry Ceremony begins with the Thanksgiving Speech, as do all the calendrical ceremonies. However, the tobacco invocation is left out, for the strawberries live close at hand and the special ability of tobacco smoke to reach long distances is not needed. The ceremony ends with a repeat of the Thanksgiving Speech.

---

The Mohawks contended with the Algonquians for access to European trade on the St Lawrence during this period. By 1609 the Mohawks so dominated Lake Champlain and the Richelieu River that Champlain referred to the latter as the "River of the Iroquois."[21]

The construction by the Dutch of Fort Nassau on Castle Island ended the need for long trips to Tadoussac and the constant warfare with the Algonquians that it entailed. The chronic shortage of European goods in Mohawk villages ended. During this period we begin to see large numbers of artifacts, especially European trade items, buried with the dead. In the previous century the dead were often buried well away from village sites, perhaps in central mortuary sites.

The lavish character of burial offerings from 1580 on has made burials of this and later periods prime targets of looters for at least the last century. Various arguments have been advanced to explain the sudden surge in burial offerings, but none is as convincing as the explanation of the Indians themselves. They explained to the Jesuit missionary Le Jeune that European goods were new, and that the dead needed to take them along to the next world, inasmuch as the next world was not yet well supplied with such goods.[22] Traditional crafts, it was argued, already existed in sufficient amounts in the next world. However, the Dutch trade was sporadic before 1614 and again after Fort Nassau was washed away. The Mohawks were not necessarily denied access to the Dutch trade by hostile Mahicans, but Dutch ships showed up to trade only irregularly before 1624, and the Mohawks would not have known when to meet them. After 1624, however, the store at Fort Orange was open almost every day.

Tobacco is an American crop that was smoked in pipes by the Iroquois and most other nations long before Columbus. Europeans took up smoking quickly in the sixteenth century, largely because they believed that it had medicinal benefits in combating the humors of illness. By the time they discovered otherwise, the addictive habit was widespread and socially acceptable. The use of tobacco as snuff was introduced in France and Portugal by the 1550s, and made its way to Spain and Italy a decade later. By the 1570s, the English were smoking tobacco in pipes, and by the last decade of the century it was quite fashionable. English companies were making pipes of white ball clay by the end of the century. The favored clays are often called kaolin, although this is strictly speaking only one kind of white ball clay. Dutch and other continental manufacturers quickly began their own industries. Dutch kaolin smoking pipes appeared on Mohawk sites after 1624, after the establishment of Fort Orange (Figure 5.3).[23]

With the new European pipes came a new species of tobacco (*Nicotiana tabacum*), which the English imported to the eastern woodlands from the West Indies. This quickly replaced the older species grown by the Iroquois for everyday purposes. But the traditional native tobacco was kept for ceremonial purposes, and its smoke still carries Iroquois words skyward.

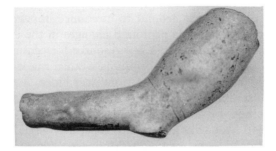

*Figure 5.3   White ball clay pipe from a Mohawk village site*

The Dutch also discovered that the Iroquois were interested in marine shell beads. The distinctive small tubular shell beads we know as wampum appeared after 1624 when the iron tools needed to make them became available. Many of these beads were made by Indian and English craftsmen in southern New England. Dutch entrepreneurs also made wampum at Fort Orange. Wampum quickly replaced the larger and cruder marine shell ornaments and beads that the Indians had made themselves previously. The beads came in two colors favored by the Iroquois: white and purple. White beads were originally made mainly from the columns of whelk shells (*Busycon* sp.). Later both white and purple beads came from quahog shells (*Mercenaria mercenaria*).[24]

The Dutch trade made it unnecessary for the Mohawks and their Oneida relatives to continue their struggle for domination of Lake Champlain and the St Lawrence. During this period, French goods declined and Dutch goods increased on Mohawk sites. By 1622 the Mohawks had agreed to a truce with the Algonquians of the St Lawrence Valley, and by 1624 they had finalized a treaty with them. Now, instead of competing with the Algonquians for the French trade, the Mohawks were serving as middlemen for Dutch goods moving north. The item most desired by the Canadian Indians was wampum, which the Dutch manufactured locally or obtained from other Indians in southern New England and Long Island. The Mohawks could allow the Canadian Indians to come directly to Fort Orange when it pleased them, or they could control the flow of wampum north themselves.[25]

Within a few years the flood of wampum had transformed the symbols of ritual from just a few strings of wampum to these plus large belts containing thousands of individual beads. Belts were exchanged at treaty conferences; matrons spoke through belts to War

Chiefs to goad them into action, or to deter them from it;[26] belts were painted red and sent around to announce impending war.

The European trade made profound changes in the everyday lives of the Iroquois. Deer had been a key resource for centuries, for their hides were critical for survival. Iroquois women made nearly all of the clothing their families required from deer hides. A family of five needed about seventeen hides every year just to clothe itself. The meat was a bonus, for the family could have survived without it. If there were 7,740 Mohawks around this time, they would have needed over 26,000 deer hides per year. The Mohawk River drainage, which is a reasonable estimate of Mohawk hunting territory, covers about 10,000 square kilometers. This area would have supported about 76,000 deer, about a third of which could have been culled every year without endangering the herd. Not surprisingly, the number of Mohawks in the first quarter of the seventeenth century was very close to the maximum that could be sustained by the resident deer population. Had there been more people, either the Mohawks would have had to enlarge their hunting territories at the expense of their neighbors, or some portion would have had to move to a region where deer were more plentiful.[27]

The Dutch trade ended the forced relationship of human and deer populations by allowing the substitution of cloth for hides. Hunters could turn their attention to beavers, which would be hunted rather than trapped in the winter until the introduction of iron traps a century and a half later. As broadcloth replaced deer hides, glass beads and silver brooches began to replace shell beads. Men wore leggings, breechcloths or aprons front and back, along with shirts and moccasins. These were probably decorated with dyed quills and moose hair early on, beads and other trade items later. Still later they would wear fringed pants and calico shirts with attached ribbons. Women wore leggings from the knees down, long skirts, and long overblouses. There are virtually no reliable images of Iroquois clothing from before the time that broadcloth was introduced, so reconstruction of earlier dress is highly speculative. It is likely that earlier skin clothing was less completely tailored than later broadcloth garments.

Iroquois men probably went bareheaded most of the time. Although sachems were said to have worn horns of office, this might have been as much metaphor as actual headdress. Some men shaved one side or the other of their heads, allowing a long lock to hang down. Others shaved both sides, leaving a central roach in the style now called "Mohawk." Women let their hair grow long, usually securing it up or down in the back.

Iroquois men painted their faces. Blue connoted health and well-being. Black was used to signal the imbalance of war or mourning. Red was ambiguous, suggesting either life or violent death depending upon the circumstances. Men also sported permanent tattoos, often geometric designs and clan crests, which had been applied using charcoal and bone awls.[28] Men would also slit their ears, and decorate the openings with down, fur, wampum, or brass on special occasions. All people smeared their bodies and hair with grease to protect themselves against mosquitos, black flies, lice, and other insects.

# 6

## The Year of Death, 1634:
## The Lost Moon

### *The Coming of Smallpox*

The summer of 1633 had brought a lethal fever to the English settlers on the Connecticut River. The disease, perhaps measles, spread through both the English and Indian communities there, probably killing dozens of people. The epidemic coincided with the emergence of a brood of seventeen-year locusts (periodic cicadas), whose deafening buzzing filled the woods with omen. It was a new experience for the pilgrims, who had been in New England for only thirteen years. The English remembered later that the Indians had told them that sickness would follow the cicadas, a prediction that would have no doubt been forgotten had the fever not appeared. It could have as easily been invented after the fact, a trick in which imagination becomes memory in the creation of new oral tradition.[1]

Waves of new diseases washed over Iroquois from this time forward, shredding the social fabric and giving rise to desperate attempts to understand and counter the scourge. Five years later there would be an earthquake felt throughout southern New England and eastern Iroquoia. The earth rumbled and even ships at anchor felt the tremor and its aftershock. It was a cool and moist summer, and the crops did not ripen properly. Both the European colonists and the Indians thought that these phenomena were connected, and they saw bad omens in all of them. Some Narragansetts said that oral tradition recalled previous earthquakes and that terrible epidemics had always followed them. This was more invention after the fact, for epidemics were no more caused by earthquakes than by cicadas, but oral tradition was revised quickly to serve awful new circumstances.[2]

Measles moved on through various Northern Iroquoian communities in 1634 and 1635. The epidemic was severe, and the Hurons and others associated with the Jesuits blamed the French for its introduction.[3] But worse was on the way. Dutch traders introduced smallpox on both the Connecticut and Hudson rivers in 1634. English observers reported that nearly all of the Indians in a fort on the upper Connecticut were infected and that half of them died. The survivors were so ill that they could not bury the dead. Bradford's description reveals a scene that would be repeated over and over in the years that followed.

> Those Indeans . . . fell sick of the small poxe, and dyed most miserably; for a sorer disease cannot befall them; they fear it more then the plague; for usualy they that have this disease have them in abundance, and for wante of bedding and linning and other helps, they fall into a lamentable condition, as they lye on their hard matts, the poxe breaking and mattering, and runing one into another, their skin cleaving (by reason therof) to the matts they lye on; when they turne them, a whole side will flea of at once, (as it were,) and they will be all of a gore blood, most fearfull to behold; and then being very sore, what with could and other distempers, they dye like rotten sheep. The condition of this people was so lamentable, and they fell downe so generally of this diseas, as they were (in the end) not able to help on another; no, not to make a fire, nor to fetch a litle water to drinke, nor any to burie the dead; but would strivie as long as they could, and when they could procure no other means to make fire, they would burne the woden trayes and dishes they ate their meate in, and their very bowes and arrowes; and some would crawle out on all foure to gett a litle water, and some times dye by the way, and not be able to gett in againe. But those of the English house, (though at first they were afraid of the infection,) yet seeing their woefull and sadd condition, and hearing their pitifull cries and lamentations, they had compastion of them, and dayly fetched them wood and water, and made them fires, gott them victualls whilst they lived, and buried them when they dyed. For very few of them excaped, notwithstanding they did what they could for them, to the haszard of them selvs. The cheefe Sachem him selfe now dyed, and allmost all his freinds and kinred. But by the marvelous goodnes and providens of God not one of the English was so much as sicke, or in the least measure tainted with this disease, though they dayly did these offices for them for many weeks togeather. And this mercie which they shewed them was kindly taken, and thankfully acknowledged of all the Indeans that knew or heard of the same; and their m[rs] here did much comend and reward them for the same.[4]

The smallpox epidemic also reached the Mohawks in 1634. Late in the year the Dutch traders at Fort Orange became concerned about the failure of the fur trade. Business had fallen off sharply, and

Table 6.1    Mohawk castles and villages in 1634

| Village | Houses | Hearths | Population 1626–35 | Population 1635–50 |
|---|---|---|---|---|
| Onekagoncka | 36 | 216 | 2,160 | 0 |
| Canawarode | 6 | 36 | 360 | 0 |
| Schatsyerosy | 12 | 72 | 0 | 720 |
| Canagere | 16 | 73 | 0 | 730 |
| Schanidisse | 32 | 192 | 1,920 | 0 |
| Osquage | 9 | 54 | 0 | 540 |
| Cawaoge | 14 | 84 | 0 | 840 |
| Tenotoge | 55 | 330 | 3,300 | 0 |
| Totals | 180 | 1,057 | 7,740 | 2,830 |

Source: Snow and Starna (1989: 145), with adjustments based on more recent research.

they suspected that French traders were diverting the furs that would normally pass through Mohawk country to Fort Orange. They were so worried that they sent a small expedition up the Mohawk River to visit Mohawk and Oneida villages, the first official trip into Iroquois country since the Dutch began trading at Castle Island twenty years earlier. Harmen van den Bogaert, a barber-surgeon at Fort Orange and leader of the expedition, later wrote a journal of the trip, giving us our first documentary glimpse of the Mohawks. His description of the eight Mohawk villages (Table 6.1) clearly indicates that an epidemic had only recently ravaged their populations. He was especially struck by the large number of new graves outside the village of Canagere. He saw eight villages, but he did not fully grasp the enormity of the disaster that had just befallen the Mohawks. There were actually only four Mohawk communities, and the people were in the process of abandoning their four old disease-infested villages and moving to four newer and much smaller ones.

Van den Bogaert talked about a Mohawk chief who was living at a distance from his village because of the presence of smallpox. What van den Bogaert thought was the man's name was actually a description: Adriochten, translated roughly, means "he has caused others to die." The man had been ostracized by the other villagers, who were acting on the traditional Iroquois belief that disease was caused by witchcraft.[5] Cicadas, earthquakes, and other natural causes would

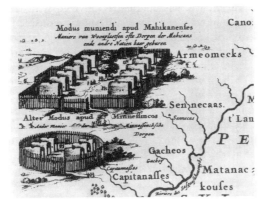

*Figure 6.1   Detail of an Indian village from a Nikolaus Visscher map of 1685,* Novi Belgii Novaeque Angliae nec non Partis Virginiae Tabula

not do for the Iroquois, and the shifting of blame to individuals was ominous.

### Population Collapse

Van den Bogaert also observed curing rituals in both Mohawk and Oneida villages. One of these occurred in the Mohawk village of Cawaoge.

> Since it was Sunday I looked in on a person who was sick. He had invited into his house two of their doctors who were supposed to heal him. They were called SUNACHKOES. As soon as they arrived, they began to sing, and kindled a large fire, sealing the house all around so that no draft could enter. Then both of them put a snake skin around their heads and washed their hands and faces. They then took the sick person and laid him before the large fire. Taking a bucket of water in which they had put some medicine, they washed a stick in it 1/2 ell long. They stuck it down their throats so that the end could not be seen, and vomited on the patient's head and all over his body. Then they performed many farces with shouting and rapid clapping of hands, as is their custom, with much display, first on one thing and then on the other, so that the sweat rolled off them everywhere.

Eleven days later in an Oneida village, van den Bogaert observed another curing ceremony.

The floor of the house was completely covered with tree bark over which the devil-hunters were to walk. They were mostly old men who were all colored or painted with red paint on their faces because they were to perform something strange. Three of them had garlands around their heads upon which were five white crosses. These garlands were made of deer's hair which they dyed with the roots of herbs. In the middle of this house was a very sick person who had been languishing for a long time, and there sat an old woman who had an empty turtle shell in her hands, in which were beads that rattled while she sang. Here they intended to catch the devil and trample him to death, for they stomped all the bark in the house to pieces, so that none remained whole. Wherever there was but a little dust on the corn, they beat at it with great excitement, and then they blew that dust toward one another and were so afraid that each did his best to flee as if he had seen the devil. After much stomping and running, one of them went to the sick person and took an otter from his hand, and for a long time sucked on the sick man's neck and back. Then he spat in the otter and threw it on the ground, running away with great excitement. Other men then ran to the otter and performed such antics that it was a wonder to see; indeed, they threw fire, ate fire, and threw around hot ashes and embers in such a way that I ran out of the house.[6]

Witches, it was believed, could be either male or female. They could turn themselves into animal forms to do their dirty work. Dogs, owls, and snakes were favorite forms for them to assume. The motivation for witchcraft was believed to usually lie in envy, a sin still detested by traditional Iroquois. This perspective on humanity also explains why the Iroquois have traditionally disliked ostentatious display, and why it was so easy for them to consign wealth to the ground as grave offerings. Quartz crystals could be used to magically detect witches. Once identified, a witch was usually executed by clubbing or burning.

The smallpox epidemic had ravaged all four Mohawk villages, playing itself out in perhaps only a hundred days. Only men who were away for the entire period might have escaped infection; the ineffectual quarantine of ostracism was easily breached by the disease. Virtually everyone became desperately ill, and half of them died. Smallpox was hardest on infants and mature adults, selecting both the next generation and the senior men and women who held the vitality of Iroquois culture in their minds. The survivors found themselves forced to reconstitute society without the wisdom of many of the elders on whom they had depended only a few months earlier, and without many of the other individuals who had previously made up their kindred constellation.[7]

The epidemic was severe because it was the first of its kind. European populations had already adjusted to smallpox through repeated epidemic episodes. It was by this time a childhood disease in Europe, because virtually all adults had been infected as children during earlier epidemics and subsequently enjoyed lifelong immunity. Adolescents are better able to survive the disease than infants or adults, and Europeans had responded to the disease load by increasing family sizes. Indeed, so long as the Europeans traveling to Iroquoia were all adults, long passage times and small crew sizes protected the Iroquois from smallpox and the other lethal childhood diseases of Europe. But the arrival of children in New Netherland changed all that, just as the arrival of Spanish children had done in the Caribbean a century earlier. From a few sick children came the seeds of epidemics that would in the end reduce the Iroquois and other American Indian nations from equals to outnumbered remnants in the face of European colonization.[8]

But there was even more to the Indians' misfortune than beginners' bad luck. American Indians had been living in the Americas for perhaps as few as 12,000 years, having been established by a relatively small founding population that came here by way of Beringia.[9] Because of the smallness of the founding population and the short duration of the time since their arrival as compared to the span of human existence in Eurasia and Africa, there was relatively little genetic diversity in America in 1634. Diseases like smallpox are thrown off their stride by heterogeneous populations, for they must adjust to varying immune systems. But their path through Iroquois communities was made smooth by genetic uniformity, with awful consequences. Indian susceptibility and high mortality resulted not from predisposed weakness, but from universal susceptibility.[10]

Roger Williams was impressed that Indian communities "commonly abound with children, and increase mightily; except the plague fall amongst them, or other lesser sicknesses, and then having no means of recovery, they perish wonderfully."[11] This might seem to contradict other evidence that Iroquois women typically had only two or three children, but it does not. Iroquois women spaced births in order to spread out the burden of child rearing, but they also tried to replace lost children as quickly as possible. Even adults could be replaced by adoption so long as there was enough family structure remaining to give the adoptees places within the society. New births, captives, and refugees from even less fortunate nations quickly filled many of the vacant places in Iroquois villages, staving off social collapse.

But the toll was still heavy. Mohawk population dropped from

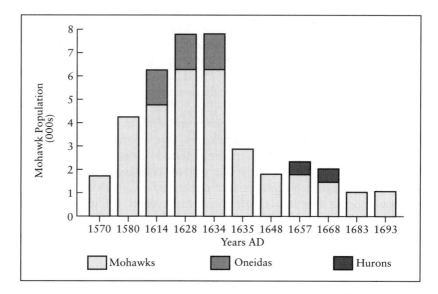

*Figure 6.2   Mohawk population sizes from 1570 to 1693
(some stacked bars include Oneida and Huron immigrants)*

7,740 to 2,830 in a matter of months. Figure 6.2 shows 120 years
of Mohawk population history. The population increased modestly
during most of the sixteenth century, mainly through steady endog-
enous growth. It soared for a half century before 1634, augmented
steadily by captives and immigrants. Chapter 5 has already described
the arrival of 1,500 Oneidas during this period of growth. The
Mohawk population crash of 1634 prompted them to almost immediately move their four communities to new smaller villages. A few
years later they consolidated themselves into only three villages. The
story was much the same among the other four nations. The
populations of the Oneida, Cayuga, and Onondaga were cut in half
during the same brief period. Only the Seneca held their own, apparently by absorbing as many as 2,000 people from outside in order to
maintain their population at around 4,000.

### The Medicine Societies

The catastrophic epidemics of the seventeenth century had profound
effects on Iroquois society, but many of them are alluded to only in
documentary sources. Cultures are remarkably resilient in the face of

*Figure 6.3 'Healing the Sick Woman' by Ernest Smith*
*Source: Rochester Museum and Science Center, Rochester,*
*New York.*

such pervasive shocks, but one should expect to see an intensification of behavior designed to counteract them. Shamanism and ritual curing are very ancient in Iroquois culture, as they are in all American Indian cultures. However, the Iroquois are particularly well known for their elaborated medicine societies, and it is likely that these reached their most complex forms in the context of the seventeenth-century epidemics. It is also likely that the medicine masks, for which the Iroquois are also famous and which are used by some of the medicine societies, reached full development in this period. The horse-hair and brass eye plates of classic wooden medicine masks that are often called "false faces" would not have been available until the late sixteenth century, and archaeological evidence suggests that they became common only in the middle of the seventeenth century.

Shamanism came in a complex of forms. Those possessed of great supernatural power were also known as divine chanters, for the Iroquoian root for "power" is the same as that for "song." The medicine societies to which such people usually belonged were named for their principal songs. In addition, a shaman's ability to communicate with his animal tutelary also gave him status as a spiritual person.

Finally, a shaman was often also a skilled herbalist, and capable of treating wounds and broken bones with skills that surpassed those of the earliest Dutch colonists. As effective as a few of the herbs were, shamans depended more upon sweat baths and magical medicine bundles to drive away illness.[12]

Personal chants belonged to individual men, and were usually sung only by their owners. There were comparable songs that belonged only to individual women. A man might inherit his song from his father, or from someone in his maternal line. Before the nineteenth century, men sang their songs as part of the boasting that went on during war feasts. They also sang them before dying. Captives could often anticipate torture and death at the hands of their enemies, and their songs were essential parts of their protracted ordeals. While some songs belonged to specific medicine societies, others belonged to the people as a whole. Some of them have been linked to sacred dances, and even today they are not performed casually.

Drums and rattles still accompany Iroquois songs. These provide a steady beat against which the sometimes complex rhythms of songs and dances are laid out. The turtle rattle is made from the head and shell of a snapping turtle, or sometimes a box turtle. The head and neck are reinforced by wooden splints so that they can serve as a handle. This rattle is considered sacred by some, for it is used in sacred ceremonies. A gourd rattle is used to accompany the songs of the Company of Mystic Animals. Secular rattles have been made in recent times from sections of cow horns, or even tin cans. In earlier times a folded piece of bark would also serve. Drums are often water drums, which come in several sizes. Water is added to the interior of the drum, and the drum is inverted frequently to keep the head moist. This allows the drummer to regulate the tone of the drum.

Members of a medicine society are recruited by being cured by the society or by dreaming that they should join. One might also in some sense inherit membership or be recommended by a clairvoyant. Thus each society probably began as a single shaman who recruited apprentices by curing them or by being charismatic enough to appear in their dreams. The Medicine Mask Society is the largest and most popular of the medicine societies. Men wearing the medicine masks can handle hot coals without being burned. Masks must be fed by having tobacco burned for them periodically, and they should not be kept in boxes. Members of the society meet at midwinter, and once or twice a year go through the houses to cure illnesses.[13]

There are three orders of medicine societies that use masks: the Medicine Mask, the Husk Face, and the Company of Mystic Animals, the last actually a group of several smaller societies. Each society has officers, but these are variable from community to community. There is often a male leader, and sometimes other men to sing and conduct the ceremonies. Women sometimes serve as cooks or have the duty of oiling the masks with sunflower oil before they are worn. The secrecy of the societies has been emphasized by some writers but played down by others.[14] Members of the Little Water Society do not use masks. They maintain small amounts of medicine made from various parts of animals, and meet three or four times a year in order to renew the medicine. The Little People (Pygmy) Society is another important medicine society. It is also called the Dark Dance because of its practice of meeting and singing its songs in darkness. The Company of Mystic Animals is a set of medicine societies, each with its distinctive songs and distinctive rites in which the tutelary beings are imitated. There is a Bear Society, a Buffalo Society, an Eagle Society, and an Otter Society. The last is for women only. In the case of the Husk Face Society, also known as the "Bushy Heads," the tutelaries are agricultural spirits. The masks of this society are made from braided maize husks. The Husk Faces also meet at midwinter and like the medicine masks they can handle hot coals. The Society of Medicine Men (Shake the Pumpkin) is really the parent of all medicine societies. It owns some masks that do not belong to the Society of Medicine Masks. All members of all specific medicine societies are by definition also members of this one.

Medicine bundles usually contained organic substances: animal hearts, dried snake blood, hair, powders, greases, and the like. There might also be miniature weapons, fossils, crystals, or odd pebbles. Specific rites of medicine societies are interchangeable. The rite chosen to help a sick person is determined by what that person has dreamed. If he cannot remember a dream, then a shaman must be consulted to determine which rite to use. These days such a person is often referred to as a fortune teller, and cards or tea leaves might be consulted to make a determination. The dream, whether or not it is remembered, is thought to express subconscious desires. Failure to act upon those desires is what has made the person sick to begin with. The remedy is thus not so much an effort to cure as an effort to remove the persistent cause of the imbalance caused by suppressed desire.

Medicine masks often have brass eye plates and hair taken from horses' tails. These features make it clear that they could not have reached their fully elaborated forms until European brass and horse-hair became available. The earliest archaeological evidence for eye plates made from brass comes from Seneca sites dating just after the first smallpox epidemics.

Like anything of real importance in a culture, medicine masks have a mythic origin too. There are really two kinds of origin myth for them. One is an epic myth that is tied to the creation of all things. The second is a human adventure that takes many specific forms in the Iroquois repertoire. What follows is a standardized version of the epic myth.

*When the Creator was finishing his work he went around inspecting the earth and banishing evil spirits. He defrocked the stone coats and banished them. He did the same to the little people, but let them stay to help hunters and cure illness. On the western rim of the world he met the great headman of the Faces. When asked where he came from, the stranger said that he came from the western mountains and that he had been around since he made the earth. They argued about who was the true Creator and decided to settle the dispute with a contest. They agreed that the winner would be the one who could make a distant mountain come to them. They both sat with their backs to the west and tried to summon the mountain. The headman of the Faces shook his turtle rattle, but the mountain moved only part way. When the Creator took his turn, the mountain came all the way to him. The headman of Faces became impatient and spun around to see what had happened. His face slammed into the mountain, breaking his nose and distorting his mouth. He had lost the contest, but the Creator realized that the headman had significant power, so he assigned him the role of helping hunters and curing illnesses. The headman agreed that if people would make portrait masks of him, call him "grandfather," and give him offerings of tobacco smoke and corn mush, they too would have the power to cure disease by blowing hot ashes.*[14]

Versions of the human adventure usually focus on the good hunter and his encounter with the medicine mask being in the forest. The epic myth is usually told as a preface to this more variable and mundane story. Important Iroquois themes commonly appear in these versions, and they often serve as origin tales for medicine societies. The hunter may be an orphan who is obliged to overcome adversity in a heroic encounter. There is often an association with trees, particularly basswood, from which medicine masks are supposed to be carved.

There are two main kinds of medicine masks. One, the Door-keeper, is usually painted red or black. The hair is long and the mouth is either twisted or flared to a spoon shape for blowing ashes. The other kind is comprised of the Common Faces, a highly variable range of forms that are likenesses of mythical forest creatures. Some of these have taken the form of pigs in recent times. All wooden masks are united by their craving for corn mush and tobacco, and they must be fed from time to time. Miniature versions of all mask types are sometimes made, and these in turn are sometimes hung on full-sized masks.

Although medicine masks can be carved from maple or more often pine, it is often said that they should properly be carved from living basswood, while the tree still stands. They are never carved of elm, the tree that supplies bark covering for the longhouse. Medicine masks probably began as carvings on living trees or large posts set up within longhouses.[15]

Depictions of masks on ceramic pipes date back at least as far as the fifteenth century. However, these do not depict medicine masks with noses and mouths askew. The use of brass eye plates and horsehair along with this evidence that earlier masks depicted undistorted human faces all combine to place the origins of the classic medicine masks in the seventeenth century. Modern Iroquois sensitivity often opposes the illustration of medicine masks or the turtle shell rattles that are associated with them. Some modern Iroquois, however, make masks for sale and do not oppose their display or illustration, and many Iroquois of earlier generations similarly had few qualms. In some cases museums still display reproduction medicine masks that have never been consecrated for curing purposes. They might also display beggar masks, which are new Common Faces introduced at the Midwinter Ceremony that have not yet accumulated the power associated with masks that are old and have been held by several owners. However, just to be sure no one is offended, many museums have stopped displaying medicine masks and turtle shell rattles altogether.

Iroquois masks are not disguises, but rather representations. The wearer is of no importance as compared to the medicine mask being that is represented. It is interesting that masking tends to be associated with strongly matrilineal societies around the world. The reasons for this remain unclear, but may be related to the ambiguity of male identity in such societies.

### Dealing with Death

Native efforts to stave off or reverse lethal epidemics generally failed. The great mortality of the seventeenth century focused attention on burial practices, which continued to be elaborated except in circumstances so extreme that the dead overwhelmed the living, when practices broke down altogether. The dead were buried with things that relatives could provide for survival in the next world. Young people often needed to be particularly well equipped, and all people needed those new things that came from Europeans and were not yet widely available in the world of the dead. The small human figurines made of bone that anthropologists have dubbed the September Morn effigy are often found with child burials. They are distinctive in having one arm across the chest and the other covering the genitals. We can no longer be sure of their meaning, but it is likely that they were charms meant to protect children from witchcraft.[16]

Members of the opposite moiety arranged things for the bereaved. The deceased was dressed in traditional clothing, his or her "dead clothes." The longhouse was cleaned. Mirrors and other things that might reflect images were covered lest anyone (especially children) be frightened by seeing the ghost in them. Food was set out for the deceased, and at least two people stayed with the body. A wake was held the night before the funeral, at which the moccasin game or a dice game was played.

The soul of the deceased was thought to linger, not leaving until the Tenth Day Feast was held. The possessions of the deceased that were not to be buried were distributed. The feast itself featured the favorite foods of the deceased. Once this took place, the soul could travel along the Milky Way, the Path of the Souls. A year later another feast was held for the deceased, and this marked the end of a year of mourning. No doubt much of this ceremonial was dropped during episodes of widespread mortality.

Once or twice a year there was traditionally a general Feast of the Dead. This featured a speech, tobacco invocation, songs, and a dance. Iroquois dances almost always proceed counterclockwise. However, in this case the dancing was often clockwise, and the dead were believed to join the living in dancing. Food was served after midnight, and there were often presents, especially of cloth. It was important on the death of an individual to redistribute clothing, and the custom was continued during the Feast of the Dead.

The Chanters for the Dead sometimes carried out the Feast of the Dead when someone was being disturbed by a ghost, and the ceremony in this case had some of the features of a medicine society ceremony. This is a culture in which curing and the maintenance of health are not regarded as different things, so it is no surprise that the Chanters of the Dead were often regarded as another medicine society.

### The Cycle of Moons

The Iroquois of 1634 scheduled their lives according to the cycles of the moon. Every three years there will be what Anglo-Americans call a "blue moon," a second full moon within the same calendar month. This much slippage is not a problem when the main purpose is to keep track of ecological time. Fish runs, the ripening of crops, and other seasonal events are apt to vary plus or minus eleven days over the long term.

---

### The Sun and Moon Ceremonies

The Sun Ceremony is not often performed and is variable in its form. It is not performed regularly, but rather depends upon whether or not there has been a long stretch of sunny weather. When such a climatic episode occurs, it is important to thank the sun. Like the Moon Ceremony, this one has traditionally involved shooting at the sun, a tobacco invocation, and the Feather Dance at Newtown and (probably) Tonawanda. The tobacco invocation has been seen as necessary because the sun is too remote to be reached by the ceremony without this medium. At Six Nations it has involved the Feather Dance, the Rite of Personal Chant, and the Thanksgiving Dance.

The Moon Ceremony is only rarely performed. Like the Sun Ceremony, it is variable in its structure. At some reservations, the tobacco invocation is used to reach the moon at its remote location, and the Bowl Game is played. At Six Nations the Bowl Game is combined with the singing of the Women's Planting Song.

---

Later Anglo-Americans borrowed the names of moons from the Iroquoian and Algonquian Indians of the northeast. However, the names are applied to full moons in the European tradition rather than new moons. In recent years the *Farmer's Almanac* has roughly followed a standard list of moons, occasionally inserting a "planting" moon or a "green corn" moon to accommodate blue moons. Table 6.2 compares this Anglo-American tradition with the Iroquois tradition as exemplified by Mohawk moons.[17]

The moons also brought the biological cycle familiar to all women of childbearing age. Menstruation was regarded as unclean, and women were required to seclude themselves from others at this time. Among other things, they were required to eat alone from small pots that held individual servings. Small pots holding about 1.5 liters were often buried with their female owners, but not with males. Larger vessels holding about 7.5 liters were used in common by families for communal dining. The average size of these larger pots is consistent with an average family size of five individuals. Unfortunately, communal dining from a single pot fostered the spread of food-borne

*Table 6.2   Rough correlation of months and moon names*

| Month | Iroquois (Mohawk) New moon | Anglo–American Full Moon |
| --- | --- | --- |
| February | Midwinter | Snow |
| March | Sugar | Sap or Worm |
| April | Fishing | Pink |
| May | Planting | Flower |
| June | Strawberry | Strawberry |
| July | Blueberry | Buck |
| August | Green Corn | Sturgeon |
| September | Freshness | Harvest |
| October | Harvest | Hunter's |
| November | Hunting | Beaver |
| December | Cold | Cold |
| January | Very Cold | Wolf |

diseases, and became one of the Iroquois habits that aggravated already severe epidemics.

Much of the traditional folklore of the Iroquois is concerned with the origins of what were once the common things of their lives. This is true of things as fundamental as female menstruation. The story that follows reveals at once the humanity and the humor of the Iroquois view of the world.

*One day Sapling killed a beaver and took it to his grandmother. They skinned it together and the ancient one threw a clot of blood on her grandson's loins. She told him that now he was menstruating. He said that it was not for men to menstruate, but that women would do so every month. With that he threw clotted blood between his grand-mother's thighs. When she asked how long the condition would last, he told her it would be as many days as there are spots on the fawn. She wept at this, and begged that it be only as many days as there are stripes on the chipmunk. Sapling accepted the compromise and said that the custom would be for women to remain outside the lodge for four days, and return with their clothes freshly washed.*[18]

# The Struggle for Hearts and Minds, 1635–1700: The Green Bean Moon

The Iroquois often say that one must draw upon the wisdom of seven generations, and that one is responsible for the well-being of seven generations to come. From this place in the seventh chapter we can look back to the origins of the Iroquois, as best we can understand them at this time. From here we can also anticipate the next seven generations. But both views were and are still clouded by uncertainties. The Iroquois of 1635, like everyone else in that year, were utterly incapable of anticipating the world of the seventh generation hence. We at least have some general knowledge that allows us to anticipate the last chapter of this book. Yet despite sharing with all humans a profound ignorance of future events, the Iroquois were compelled to adapt promptly to catastrophic events, and to prepare their descendants for the future as best they could.

### More Population Decline

The onset of European epidemics initiated an era of population decline for the Iroquois. This in turn combined with other factors to prompt the regional convulsions now often but inappropriately called the Beaver Wars. Iroquois warriors lashed out at their neighbors for a variety of reasons, only one of which was the desire to acquire furs or control the fur trade by less direct means. More important was the significance of war as the men's traditional path to prestige, influence, and political power. While Europeans tended to think of peace as the natural state of affairs and war as the exception, the Iroquois viewed the world from the opposite perspective. To them war was the natural state of affairs, and peace was the exception to be declared. The League of the Iroquois was a declaration of peace between the

*Table 7.1    Iroquois population decline, 1630–1770*

| Year | Seneca[a] | Cayuga[a] | Onondaga[a] | Oneida[a] | Mohawk[b] |
|------|-----------|-----------|-------------|-----------|-----------|
| 1630 | 4,000 | 4,000 | 4,000 | 2,000 | 7,740 |
| 1640 | 4,000 | 2,000 | 2,000 | 1,000 | 2,835 |
| 1650 | 4,000 | 1,200 | 1,200 | 600 | 1,734 |
| 1660 | 4,000 | 1,200 | 1,200 | 400 | 2,304 |
| 1670 | 4,000 | 1,200 | 1,300 | 600 | 1,985 |
| 1680 | 4,000 | 1,200 | 1,400 | 800 | 1,000 |
| 1690 | 4,000 | 1,280 | 2,000 | 720 | 1,000 |
| 1700 | 2,400 | 800 | 1,000 | 280 | 620 |
| 1710 | 4,000 | 600 | 1,400 | 480 | 620 |
| 1720 | 2,800 | 520 | 1,000 | 800 | 580 |
| 1730 | 1,400 | 480 | 800 | 400 | 580 |
| 1740 | 2,000 | 500 | 800 | 400 | 580 |
| 1750 | 2,000 | 500 | 800 | 800 | 580 |
| 1760 | 4,200 | 504 | 544 | 1,000 | 640 |
| 1770 | 4,000 | 1,040 | 800 | 800 | 640 |

[a] From Tooker (1978b: 421) with adjustments.
[b] From Snow (1993c). Excludes emigrants to Canada.

Five Nations. It was assiduously maintained lest it devolve into conflict, as it surely would do without constant renewal.

The Iroquois perspective was perniciously aggravated by another fundamental belief. This was the view that with the possible exception of drowning there was no such thing as natural death. When a loved one died, someone else was to blame. Whether the death was a violent one or attributable only to subtle witchcraft, someone was to blame and revenge was essential. If the act of revenge occasioned the capture of someone who might serve as an adopted replacement for the lost relative, so much the better.

The horrendous losses of the middle decades of the seventeenth century, shown in Table 7.1, threw the Iroquois into a convulsion of unending retribution against real and imagined enemies. Traditional enemies faced the rage of warriors seeking revenge for the constant loss of friends and family members. Iroquois expeditions attacked Huron, Petun, Susquehannock, and other trading expeditions, partly in order to deny them access to European traders. But booty was not always found, and sometimes was discarded when it was found. Just as important, they seized captives, torturing and killing some and adopting or enslaving others in an effort to replace lost relatives. New epidemics only intensified the mourning wars, and the cycle of loss and revenge sucked the entire region into a maelstrom of violence and death.[1]

Iroquois villages soon became populated by both survivors and increasing numbers of captives. The social changes that were entailed by this had profound effects on Iroquois settlements. Longhouses began to be standardized into three- or four-hearth structures. No longer were they lengthened or shortened to contain the membership of a lineage (clan segment). Surviving lineages were so shattered by premature deaths that they had to merge with others or take in many adoptees in order to remain viable residential units. Fictive kinship facilitated these *ad hoc* arrangements and made it possible for the longhouse to survive as a traditional residential form. But the seeds of longhouse disintegration were sown in these difficult years. As men operating outside the traditional sociopolitical system gained prestige through their war exploits and their connections with European traders, the authority of the traditional chiefs and the matrons who appointed them slowly weakened.[2]

### The New Economy

Trade goods appeared in increasing amounts, with guns and tubular wampum heading the list. Marine shell beads had been symbolically important to League ritual and other formal affairs for many years, but iron tools allowed the manufacture of small tubular wampum beads with small straight bores. White and purple beads were made in large numbers from quahog shells by both southern New England Indians and enterprising colonists from this time forward. Strings and belts of tubular wampum became both currency and the medium needed to cement social and political ties between the Iroquois and their neighbors, whether Indian or European (Figure 7.1).

In the absence of sufficient coinage, wampum beads also became a practical currency for the Dutch and English. In 1637 Massachusetts a fathom of wampum was standardized as a string of 360 beads. By 1640 a white fathom was worth five shillings (60 pence), while a fathom of the more valuable blue wampum beads was worth twice as much. This meant that a penny would buy six white beads or three blue ones in Massachusetts. At around the same time in Connecticut a penny bought only four white beads or two blue ones.[3]

The colonists gradually came to appreciate the additional symbolic significance wampum had for the Iroquois. The primary sources of

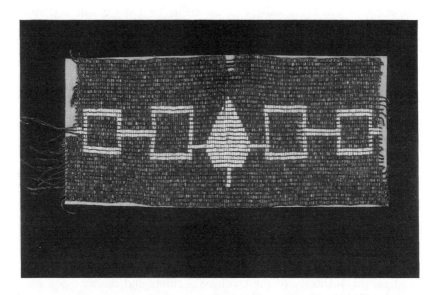

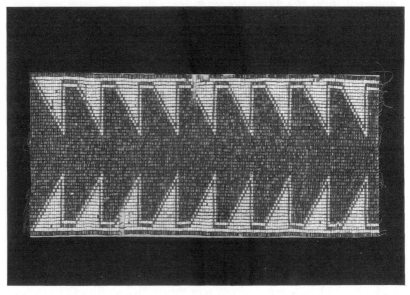

Figure 7.1   Above: The Wing (or Dust Fan) belt;
below: the Hiawatha belt
Source: photographs courtesy of the New York State Museum and
the Iroquois Grand Council

*Figure 7.2   Lock mechanism of a European gun found on an Iroquois site*

wampum were on Long Island and Narragansett Bay. By 1631 the Pequots were already trying to secure a monopoly there, and in doing so they alienated the English, Dutch, and virtually all of the other Indian nations around them. The Pequots were attacked and defeated by the Dutch in 1634. They then had to face the English, who were expanding out of their Massachusetts beachheads with the help of Narragansett and Mohegan allies. The English colonists carried out the Mystic Fort Massacre against the Pequots in 1637. The English killed 700 Pequots in the Pequot War, but Sassacus and some of his followers were able to make their way to Mohawk country. There the Pequots offered the Mohawks a king's ransom of wampum. But the Mohawks had already accepted a gift of wampum from the Narragansetts. They killed about two dozen of the Pequots, and gave their scalps to the English. This ended the power of the Pequots and secured the English in their new Connecticut colony.[4] It also resulted in new Mohawk influence in southern New England, where they had not been a political factor prior to the 1630s. From this time on they were the bogey men of both the English and the Algonquians of that region, the unseen menace that people there used to frighten each other into alliances.

The Dutch tried to outlaw the sale of guns to Indians in 1639, but it was already too late for such measures to succeed. From this time on the Iroquois were well armed, and they could routinely blockade the St Lawrence. Guns replaced the bow and arrow, and in 1648 Peter Stuyvesant reversed Dutch policy and began selling guns directly to the Mohawks. Iron tomahawks of European manufacture replaced the ball-headed war club, changing the older weapon into a status symbol for great men. Slat armor was discarded as useless against the new weapons. Women gradually abandoned making "real" pots in favor of brass ones, and men gave up making "real" pipes in favor of kaolin trade pipes.[5]

The growing strength of the Mohawks, despite wars and epidemics, renewed the antagonism of the Mahicans, who were still proprietary about the Dutch traders living in their midst at Fort Orange. As a result, the Second Mohawk–Mahican War broke out in 1640.

French Jesuit missionaries had been active in Huron country since their return to Canada in 1632, but they avoided the deadly Iroquois for several years. Finally, Isaac Jogues and two other Jesuits went to the Mohawk in 1642. Jogues was mutilated and enslaved, while the others were killed. The following year the Dutch opened their war against the Munsees. But at the same time they also signed their first formal treaty with the Mohawks.[6] Despite this new relationship, Jogues was able to escape from Mohawk country by way of Fort Orange. The Dutch war against the Munsees ended in 1644. The Dutch and the English were increasingly colonial rivals at this time, and the English attempted to cut off wampum deliveries from the Narragansett to the Mohawks around the same time. A year later the Second Mohawk–Mahican War also ended.

In 1646, the persistent Isaac Jogues went back into Mohawk country to take up his mission once again. He was allowed to leave some of his possessions in a Mohawk village while he made a brief trip to Canada. An epidemic occurred during his absence, and the Mohawks blamed it on a locked box that Jogues had left behind. He was consequently tortured and killed when he returned. At the same time, the Narragansetts resumed wampum shipments to the Mohawks, and a third war broke out between the Mahicans and the Mohawks.

### The Internecine Wars

The Iroquois were well supplied by the Dutch at Fort Orange, and they were better armed than their traditional enemies. Stocks of beaver were in decline in Iroquoia because of the fur trade, and some authors have argued that what came next grew out of the Iroquois desire to control the continuing flow of beaver pelts from more remote hunting grounds.[7] However, the Beaver Wars have probably been misnamed. When the Iroquois began to focus their rage on the Hurons, both confederacies were about the same size, with 12,000 people in each. Both had lost nearly half their populations in the epidemics that began in 1634, and the motivation of revenge against the unknown agents of that loss made these at least as much mourning wars as they were beaver wars.[8] But the Hurons could not match the Iroquois in firepower. Driven mainly by the desire for revenge, prestige, and power, along with a desire for captives to replace lost family members, the Iroquois battered the Hurons mercilessly from 1641 on.[9]

The final Iroquois campaign against the Hurons began in 1648. A large Seneca army attacked the Huron village of Teanaostaiaé. The resident Jesuit missionary encouraged the defenders, sprinkling holy water while the battle raged. In the end he urged the Hurons to flee, and faced the Senecas alone. He was killed in a fusillade of bullets and arrows, and his dismembered body was burned in his church, but many of the Hurons escaped. Seven hundred were killed or taken prisoner, and a thousand fled to other villages. In the following autumn Mohawks joined the Senecas in an assault on the Hurons with an army of over 1,000 men. Both of the Iroquois contingents included adopted Hurons who were by now fully integrated into Iroquois society. The large force lived and hunted undetected through the winter in the forests north of Lake Ontario. They attacked the village of Taenhatentaron in the middle of March, when the Huron least expected it. Only three Huron men escaped, while the Iroquois lost only ten. The Iroquois took the nearby village of St Louis almost as easily, capturing the missionaries Brebeuf and Lalemont. While some fell back to Taenhatentaron to torture and eventually kill these captives, others moved on to attack the mission village of Ste-Marie. The Huron defense finally stiffened enough to inflict damage on the advancing Iroquois, and the fighting began to seesaw, with St Louis being retaken by the Hurons. Eventually the Iroquois withdrew, sobered by the loss of almost 100 men, but the Hurons were so disheartened that they began abandoning their country. Some went to live with the Petun nation, others to the Neutral and Erie nations. Still others retreated with their surviving missionaries to Christian Island in Lake Huron, where hundreds later died of famine. Only about 600 left the island alive, and half of those retreated to Quebec with the Jesuits, where their descendants still remain.

The Iroquois returned again in 1649, and by the end of that year they had destroyed or dispersed both the remaining Hurons and the Petuns. By 1651 the surviving Hurons and Petuns had either fled westward or taken refuge with the French at Quebec. Those that went west formed a new nation and would later be known as the Wyandots. They eventually settled around modern Detroit and along the Sandusky River in Ohio country.

Many Hurons were absorbed by the Iroquois. One group of 500 was incorporated by the Seneca nation, where they built their own village. Many were Christians, so their arrival in Iroquoia paved the way for Jesuit missionization here as well.

Thousands of people were killed in European conflicts in this century as well. While these events were not directly related to those in Iroquoia except by the coincidence of timing, they illustrate that the world of the seventeenth century was everywhere a violent place. Torture, slavery, and death were not the special attributes of the Iroquois.

The Wenro had already fled across the Niagara Frontier to take refuge with the Neutral in 1638. They shared in a Neutral defeat at the hands of the Iroquois in 1647. The Senecas pounded the Neutrals again in 1651, forcing the survivors from their homes. By 1653 the Neutral were as scattered as the Hurons, moving first to the vicinity of Saginaw Bay, then possibly southward before disappearing from history. By 1656 the Iroquois had dispersed the Erie as well.

The Mohawks continued to accept wampum from the Narragansetts through the 1640s, subverting the efforts of the English to subordinate them. The Mohegans of Connecticut were more helpful to the English, and the Mohawks consequently sometimes attacked the Mohegans in order to aid their Narragansett suppliers. But the Mohawks and the English did not want to confront each other directly. The Mohawks avoided helping the Narragansetts too much, and the English rejected a reasonable proposal to join with the French in an attack on the Iroquois. Both colonial powers were separately opposed to the Iroquois at the time; however, England was in confusion at home under government by the Protectorate. For their part, English colonists felt isolated in America, and they were at pains to maintain friendly relations with as many Indian nations as possible. There were tensions, but trade was too important to be put at risk by military adventures. The Mohawks were particularly important, for they could bypass the Dutch and supply furs to the English traders at Narragansett Bay and at Springfield on the Connecticut River.[10]

Meanwhile the Dutch encouraged the Mohawks to attack the Susquehannocks and act aggressively elsewhere as well. Peter Stuyvesant named the growing settlement around Fort Orange "Beverwyck" in 1652, and recognized it as separate from the surrounding patroonship of Rensselaerswyck. The First Anglo-Dutch War flared up between 1652 and 1654, but the colonial adversaries did not carry the fight to Iroquoia.

Wampum stopped being used as a currency in New England around this time, so the English dumped their supplies of it in exchange for furs and Dutch goods. The Dutch remained dependent upon it because of a shortage of coins, but the surge in the supply caused severe inflation in New Netherland.

During the 1650s the southern New England Algonquian nations drifted politically away from the Mohawks and toward the more northerly Algonquian nations that were allied with the French. The Third Mohawk–Mahican War, which had been simmering since 1646, finally ended in 1653.

Soon the Iroquois also made peace with the French, and Jesuits were allowed to come into Iroquois country once again. The Iroquois had nothing to lose, having destroyed all significant French allies, and the French were eager to be at peace with the ferocious Iroquois. An agreement was reached with the four western Iroquois nations first, and the Mohawks, alarmed by this development, quickly made a truce with the French as well. The Mohawks competed with the Onondagas to host Jesuit missionaries, both hoping to attract French favors. The friction between them became so serious that in 1657 Mohawk men actually fought with men from the other Iroquois nations, an event that threatened the existence of the League.

Canaqueese of the Mohawks spoke with customary metaphorical eloquence, invoking the metaphorical longhouse and chiding the Jesuits for entering it by way of the central smokehole rather than by way of the eastern door (via the Mohawks), as a proper guest would. Only thieves came in that way, and they risked blinding themselves in the smoke, or burning themselves in the fire below. Nevertheless, the Jesuits built a mission at Onondaga.

However, the arrangement at Onondaga was uneasy, and the Jesuits sometimes felt very threatened. The Jesuits were intolerant of the Midwinter Ceremony and other rituals, which they regarded as superstitious and foolish. They failed to understand the social benefits of activities like dream guessing, which had long served to release tension within the community. For their part, the traditional Onondagas resented the failure of Christian Onondagas to attend to the traditional ceremonies, and they blamed the Jesuits for it, causing them to sometimes fear for their lives. On one occasion in 1655, the Jesuits threw a traditional Iroquois "eat-all" feast in order to stuff the Onondagas into sleepy satiety. After the Indians dozed off, the missionaries slipped away in the night.[11]

The Iroquois rampage against other Northern Iroquoian nations continued even as more peaceful events unfolded with other former enemies. Over the next few years the surviving Eries, along with the Huron and Neutral refugees among them, were in some cases dispersed westward, in other cases absorbed by Seneca, Onondaga, and other Iroquois communities. Those who moved westward became parts of the multinational Indian villages that grew up in Ohio, Michigan, and elsewhere through the rest of the colonial period. By 1657 the Iroquois had eliminated their enemies to the north and west, but, like the victors in most wars, were not content to enjoy the peace.

The Iroquois sometimes acted in concert, sometimes in small groups. The Mohawks observed a separate peace with the Hurons for a time, and only the Mohawks fought with the Mahicans of the Hudson Valley. The defeat of their relatives in southern Ontario forced refugees and French traders to gather around Green Bay on Lake Michigan. However, the Iroquois could now attack unimpeded across the vacated landscape of southern Ontario. Iroquois raiders extended their attacks to the upper Great Lakes and as far as the Mississippi River. Their first big expedition failed, and many were killed by Illinois and Ojibwa counterattacks in 1655. Two years later, however, an army of 1,200 Iroquois moved against Hurons and Ottawas at Green Bay again. The Hurons and Ottawas retreated to the Mississippi around 1658 and eventually moved to Chequamegon Bay on Lake Superior.

In 1657 Mohawk and Onondaga warriors went to Quebec to persuade Huron refugees to come home with them. A village of perhaps 570 Hurons was built near the three Mohawk villages that existed at the time. The refugees, who were staunch Catholics, were welcomed by the Jesuit missionaries, who were having mixed results in their efforts to convert the Iroquois. A decade later Jesuit missionaries would note that two-thirds of the Mohawk village of Caughnawaga was made up of Huron and Algonquian captives and adoptees.[12]

The Fourth Mohawk–Mahican War began in 1658. The Mohawks and Onondagas expelled the Jesuits in the same year, as sentiment against the French and their Algonquian allies grew. Mohawk ties with the Dutch continued to develop, and in 1661 the Mohawks deeded Schenectady to van Curler. In 1662 Sokokis from the upper Connecticut River attacked a Mohawk village, bringing quick retaliation. Like many other Algonquian allies of the French, the Sokokis retreated, many of them moving to New France. It seemed that the Iroquois were becoming increasingly isolated, their only allies being the Dutch. But this too ended abruptly. Iroquois culture had been in the throes of rapid and profound change for decades, and it was about to face yet another completely new set of circumstances. In 1660 Charles II had acceded to the restored throne of England, and English policies began to change.

### The Rise of English Power

The English seized New Netherland in 1664, precipitating the Second Anglo-Dutch War, which lasted until 1667. Beverwyck became Albany and the province of New Netherland became New York. The Mohawks quickly signed a treaty with the English at Fort Orange, even as they were still fighting with Indians allied with the English in New England and Pennsylvania. The other Iroquois nations drew closer to the French in the face of these events, but the Mohawks were now close neighbors of the English and they saw the future more clearly than the others.

The western Iroquois nations signed a peace treaty with the French in 1665. Mohawk intransigence led de Tracy to lead a French attack that destroyed the Mohawk villages in the following year. Fortunately for the Mohawks, the Fourth Mohawk–Mahican War ended in the same year in a peace that was brokered by the English. However, the English were unable to bring other Algonquian nations into the accord and the Mohawks recognized that there were limits to English protection. They finally joined the other Iroquois nations in a treaty with the French, and once again accepted Jesuit missionaries to live with them.

The defeat of the Hurons and Neutrals inspired the Senecas, Cayugas, and Oneidas to establish permanent villages on the north side of Lake Ontario. Beginning around 1665, a string of seven such villages were founded from the vicinity of modern Hamilton to the Bay of Quinte. They lasted for over twenty years. However, by 1687 a coalition of Ottawas, Mississaugas (southeastern Ojibwas), Ottawas, and refugee Hurons began attacking the Iroquois villages, forcing them back to the New York side of the lake with severe losses. By the end of this fighting, the Mississaugas were defeating the Iroquois on the same land where the Iroquois had destroyed the Hurons 40 years earlier. By 1696 the Mississaugas were in possession of the village sites on the north shore of Lake Ontario.

### The Middle Ground

The Iroquois were finally all at peace with the French in 1667. French farmers, no longer afraid of attacks by the Iroquois, began settling at La Prairie, across the St Lawrence from Montreal. Some Oneidas were even persuaded to move there. The unique cultural arrangement that had been forming between the French and various Indian nations for decades was coming to full flower. They came together on what Richard White has figuratively called the Middle Ground. French men often roamed westward, dressing and traveling like Indians. English colonists more often moved as complete families, establishing European-style settlements along a moving frontier. French traders

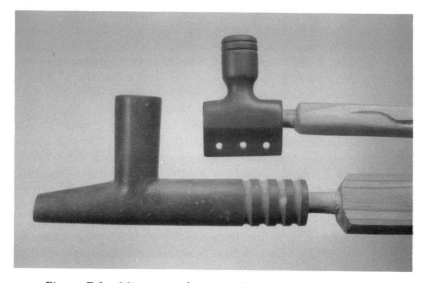

*Figure 7.3    Micmac style pipe (above) and calumet with
wooden stems*

often took Indian wives, an arrangement that served both partners
well in seventeenth-century North America. The Indian women often
enjoyed prestige and wealth that they could not have acquired had
they kept to more traditional arrangements, while the French men
also made the best of their two worlds. The world that they shared,
the Middle Ground, was one in which they both thrived, playing the
roles of cultural brokers and creating a new culture as they went
along. Their descendants are still known as Métis.[13]

The early Métis of the Middle Ground were responsible for many
of the innovations that have sometimes been attributed to Indian
cultures alone. Distinctive "Micmac" smoking pipes were made by
French craftsmen and traded to Indians throughout the Great Lakes
system. Later the French and Métis traders would spread the calumet
pipe and its associated ceremonies throughout much of eastern North
America (Figure 7.3). Although the calumet (or peace pipe) is popu-
larly assumed to have been thoroughly Indian, it is an artifact that
is steeped in the culture of the Middle Ground. It was the product
of interaction between cultures, not the product of one of them alone.

Many of the Indian inhabitants of the Middle Ground were Northern Algonquians. Women were less central to traditional politics in
these cultures than was the case in Iroquois culture. Thus the Iroquois
played roles on the Middle Ground that were different from those of

the Algonquians. Iroquois men more often traveled in all-male parties, bound by invisible ties to their mothers, sisters, and wives, who remained at home in their bark castles. Iroquois women were less often available (or less inclined) to become wives to French *coureurs de bois*. French traders did not penetrate Iroquois society so easily as they did Algonquian society. For their part, the Iroquois preferred formal diplomacy to informal mediations, a preference that drew them closer to the English than to the French.

Euro-American women who were captured by the Iroquois often stayed with their adoptive families even after opportunities to return home became available. There were three reasons for this. First, Euro-Americans regarded most such women as ruined, making it difficult or impossible for them to truly re-enter Euro-American society. Second, the status of women in Iroquois society was high enough to make life there attractive to captives. Third, people captured as young children and socialized in Iroquois society usually thought of themselves as Iroquois. Thus in later years, Mary Jemison, often referred to as the "White woman of the Genesee," remained a Seneca all her life, and was influential well into the nineteenth century.[14]

### The Covenant Chain

Most of the southern New England Algonquians were by now hostile to the Mohawks and other Iroquois. This was largely because the Mohawks continued to trade with the Mohegans, and the Mohegans were pariahs among the other New England Indians. Armed with English guns but not much military sense, a poorly equipped party of Massachusett men, women, and children laid siege to the Mohawk village of Caughnawaga in August 1669. The attackers fell back exhausted after a few days, but were overtaken by the Mohawks, who killed or captured most of them.[15]

The Iroquois were busy fighting the Susquehannocks, the New England Algonquians, and the Shawnee in the 1670s, leaving the Ottawas and their allies with time to recuperate. The Shawnee left the Ohio Valley during this time in order to escape the Iroquois, who seemed relentless despite occasional defeats.

The center of English power in America was shifting to Albany, and the Mohawks enjoyed their proximity to it. By 1672 they and the other Iroquois had effectively destroyed the Susquehannocks. The Third Anglo-Dutch War (1672–8) came and went as part of the more general Dutch War in Europe. In 1673 the Dutch temporarily recaptured New York, but the English were soon back in control.

They returned in 1674 and Edmund Andros was appointed Governor of New York and New Jersey by the Duke of York, later King James II. Andros was committed to consolidating English control over both the English and Indian inhabitants of the northern colonies.

Southern New England Indians recognized the shift in the center of power and Algonquian emigrants from that region founded a new community at Schaghticoke on the Hoosic River, a tributary of the Hudson north of Albany. Still others moved directly to the Mohawk Valley and took up residence with the Mohawks, undertaking a cultural conversion that had been made by many others in earlier years.[16]

Many Iroquois had by now converted to Catholicism under the influence of French Jesuit missionaries. Mohawk converts broke with tradition and found themselves in the shadow of rising English influence and scorned in turn by traditionalists. Catholic Mohawks moved to Canada, joining Oneidas already settled at La Prairie. By 1673 there were more Mohawk warriors at La Prairie than in the Mohawk Valley. Onondagas, Hurons, and others came as well, but the Mohawks dominated culturally, and the settlement came to be known as Caughnawaga after the old Mohawk village in New York. On the other hand, the Mahicans were by now virtually powerless, and it was clear to all that the Iroquois (especially the Mohawks) were pre-eminent in New York.[17]

Among the Mohawks at Caughnawaga was a young woman named Kateri Tekakwitha, who had moved there from the Mohawk Valley in 1677 (Figure 7.4). Her mother had been an adopted Christian Algonquian who had married a Mohawk chief. Kateri's parents and siblings had all died in a smallpox epidemic when she was a small child. She grew up in her uncle's household, and came under the influence of Jesuit missionaries, who returned to the Mohawk Valley in 1667. She was baptized in 1676, and became a particularly devout Catholic. Kateri and other Christian Mohawks were harassed by traditional Mohawks, and many were persuaded to move to the village of Caughnawaga on the St Lawrence. She moved there in 1677, but died only three years later in 1680. She was beatified by the Catholic Church on the 300th anniversary of her death, and may yet be the first American Indian to become a saint.[18]

### King Philip's War

The Mahicans were neutralized, but the southern New England Algonquians remained a threat to the English. King Philip's War

*Figure 7.4   Kateri Tekakwitha*
*Source: image courtesy of the Friars Minor Conventual.*

broke out between them in June 1675. The Iroquois stayed out of the conflict, even though the Mohawks had every reason to side with the English. Early in 1676 Metacom (King Philip) came to the upper Hudson in an attempt to recruit the aid of the Indians north of Albany at Schaghticoke and the neutral Mahicans. An epidemic swept through his party, and he was set upon by a force of Mohawks that had been goaded into action by Governor Andros. The survivors returned home dispirited to face certain defeat at the hands of revitalized English colonists. From this point on New England was English and its Indian inhabitants were refugees in their own land.[19]

Many more southern New England Algonquians fled to Schaghticoke, north of Albany, where some feared they might form a new center to threaten English interests. The Mohawks, however, continued to attack the Mohegans and exert their dominance over all non-Iroquois Indian communities. Andros saw an opportunity to consolidate his power over both New York and New England while at the same time enlisting the Iroquois to do the same with the Indians of the region. Andros sent Wentworth Greenhalgh to visit all the villages of the Iroquois in 1677, as a means to assess the strength of the confederacy. The Jesuits saw the inevitability of English control of Iroquois affairs and began to pull out of their Iroquois missions, taking the remaining converts with them to Canada.

Greenhalgh observed the social consequences that absorption of refugees and captives was having for the Senecas, although he probably did not fully comprehend what he was seeing. The Senecas maintained their population at around 4,000 throughout the latter part of the seventeenth century, but so much of it was made up of immigrants that even the standardized longhouse had been abandoned for small extended-family cabins. For the Senecas the longhouse was already just a metaphor.[20]

Governor Andros called a meeting in Albany in April 1677, the purpose of which was to get the Mohawks and Mahicans to pledge not to raid Indian allies of the English in New England. In return, the New England colonies agreed not to treat separately with the Iroquois. New York became supreme, with New England and the Iroquois receiving secondary but equal importance. All other Indian nations were deemed children of the Iroquois. This agreement was the founding of the Covenant Chain, which bound the English and the Iroquois from this point forward, and provided the English with their claim of hegemony over all of the Indian nations construed as subordinate to the Iroquois.[21]

---

### The Green Bean Ceremony

The seventh moon of the annual cycle brings the Green Bean Ceremony. Our Life Supporters dances form the major rites of the Green Bean Ceremony, just as they do the Planting Ceremony. As is customary in all Iroquois ceremonies, this one begins and ends with the Thanksgiving Speech. Tobacco would be burned in an invocation near the beginning were the life supporters not so close by, but their proximity makes this unnecessary. Our Life Supporters dances include the Women's Dance, the Corn Dance, the Stomp Dance, the Hand-in-hand Dance, the Striking-the-Pole Dance, and the War Dance.

---

The arrangement did not work immediately. The Mohawks continued to attack New England Indians. But by 1679 the last Jesuits and Catholic Mohawks left for Canada. In 1681, Andros was recalled to England at the insistence of the New England colonies, but the Covenant Chain remained unbroken. By 1684 the Mohawks agreed to treat the Massachusetts and Mohegans as clients of the English colonies, a renewal of the Covenant Chain that ended the political significance of the southern New England Indians.

Iroquois diplomacy put great value in the linking of arms, and the Covenant Chain was an extension of that metaphor. Alliances were forged by leaders who attracted followers by their personal traits and reputations. Kin ties were important. Clan brothers were easily linked, but links with one's father's clan could be important too, even in this strongly matrilineal society. Men traveled in parties often composed of clan brothers. In the larger engagements of the colonial wars, such units sometimes included men from two or more Iroquois nations that happened to share common clan names. In one later case a fighting unit of Mohawk clan brothers joined a particular English army unit because one of its recruiters was adopted into their clan.[22]

Thus, while the Covenant Chain was to the English a hierarchical structure, to the Iroquois it was a nearly flat network of linked arms. The links all strengthened each other, but they needed constant nurturing. Gift exchange, most importantly the transfer of wampum in the seventeenth century, maintained the network and prevented it from dissolving into the normal human condition of constant warfare.

Subtle differences in relative standing were signaled by terms of address. Equals called each other "brother," but the Mohawks, Onondagas, and Senecas were "elder brothers" to their Oneida, Cayuga, and (later) Tuscarora "younger brothers." Dependent tribes were more often called "nephews," and they reciprocated by calling the Iroquois "uncles." No one spoke from authority, for all speakers merely spoke for their constituents. Reciprocity was a matter of constant attention, as it had been in the League of the Iroquois for many years. Thus decisions came slowly, only through the gradual development of consensus, always with an air of ritual, and preferably in private.

The English later noticed that the Iroquois were most comfortable when the Condolence Ceremony of the League preceded treaty negotiations. But while the English were usually interested in the details of an agreement, and often wanted to settle matters once and for all, the Iroquois usually focused on the need for clear and open communication, and the renewal of the alliance itself. Treaty conferences went on for days, as spokesmen rested, conferred, deliberated, and considered all things at length, even then sometimes avoiding any clear conclusion.

The Iroquois expeditions reached as far west as the Illinois Valley in 1680. The Iroquois maintained their Covenant Chain with the

English, but were increasingly disturbed by the growth of French trade to the west. The Senecas attacked the Illinois in 1680 in order to forestall French expansion. The French planned an expedition against the Senecas in 1684, but it faltered after sickness struck the French troops. However, the French strengthened their forts in the west and Iroquois attacks on Fort St Louis and Chicago later in the decade were their last probes westward.

Charles II died in 1685 and was replaced as King of England by James II, a Roman Catholic with little political support. Edmund Andros returned to head the new Dominion of New England the next year. This included all of New England, New York, and New Jersey. The Iroquois now began attacking French outposts regularly. They attacked both Fort Chambly and Fort Frontenac in 1687. The French finally were able to launch an attack against the Senecas with the Denonville expedition of the same year. The Senecas fell back before the attack, and the French destroyed their villages and fields before moving on to build a fort at Niagara. But the attack only tormented the Senecas into stepping up their raiding.

By 1687 there were Mohawks living at the Sulpician mission at the Lake of Two Mountains, along with Nipissings and Algonquians. Like the Mohawks at the new Caughnawaga near Montreal, these people were all firmly in the French camp.

### King William's War

James II was deposed in 1688. Governor Andros was seized and sent home when word of the coup reached New England. William and Mary then assumed the English throne as joint sovereigns, and declared war on France. The new conflict was called King William's War in North America. William and Mary restored some but not all autonomy to the colonies, and both sides began to contend for Indian allies.

The French abandoned their forts at Niagara and Frontenac, and in 1689 the New York Iroquois attacked and razed the French settlement at Lachine Rapids. The massacre at Lachine led the Caughnawaga Indians, now largely regarded as Catholic Mohawks, to flee to Montreal. They returned to the south bank a year later, but built a new village a few miles upstream. The French and their Indian allies retaliated by attacking and burning Schenectady, New York, in 1690.

The French attacked Mohawk villages in 1693, aided by Caughnawaga Mohawks. In 1696 Frontenac attacked the Onondagas and the Oneidas as well. Amid all this the Caughnawaga Mohawks moved their village farther upstream once again. King William's War ended in 1697 with the Peace of Ryswick, but the Iroquois and the French kept on fighting. Thus in effect the English and French continued the war through the end of the century by proxy.

### The Grounds for Torture

These were times of widespread and pervasive violence. Warriors killed one another for revenge, prestige, and power, not for nationalistic or economic reasons. Iroquois warriors apparently never committed rape, and European commentators attributed this to weak sex drives, making even this virtue seem a weakness. The real reason was that Iroquois men believed that sex could sap them of fighting strength, a belief that clearly separated sex from violence in their minds.

Iroquois warfare throughout the seventeenth century was fueled by desires for revenge and for captives to replace lost relatives. Many captives were adopted and became full members of their adoptive nations. Others were allowed to live, but only as slaves. Those that were not incorporated in these ways were often subjected to protracted torture and painful death. In these cases cannibalism was sometimes practiced, at least in ritual form, as the torturers attempted to invest themselves with the bravery and prestige of their victims.[23]

Torture took many forms, beginning with the removal of fingernails so that the captive could not easily untie his bindings. Prisoners who survived the journey back to an Iroquois village were forced to run a gauntlet in which everyone, even small children, was allowed to strike or stab at the prisoner. If the prisoner was marked for death, (s)he would often be placed on a scaffold and tortured by a variety of means. Red-hot iron axes were hung as a necklace on the prisoner; fingers were burned or cut off. A prisoner might be forced to eat his own flesh. Resolute prisoners clung to their dignity, singing their death songs in the face of excruciating pain until they lost consciousness. Occasionally they would be revived so that the torture could continue, but once their condition became grave they were killed. Children were anointed with the blood of brave victims, and warriors consumed their hearts, all so that they might acquire a portion of the victims' courage. More extensive cannibalism sometimes followed.

The three-year captivity of Pierre Radisson provides us with a detailed description of these practices. Radisson was marked for adoption soon after he was captured by Mohawks in 1651 on the St

Lawrence. His captors painted his face red and took delight in dressing his hair and teaching him the rudiments of their language. When they reached their home village, his trip down the receiving line was cut short, and he was almost immediately taken in by a family that had recently lost a son. After a failed escape attempt, Radisson was brought back to the same village, this time to face the full torture treatment. His adoptive parents bought his freedom with wampum and saved him from certain death after he had endured many hours of torture. He stayed with them voluntarily for many months, but eventually escaped by way of Fort Orange in 1654.[24]

Had Radisson's face been painted black by his captors, he would certainly have been killed, and we would know nothing of his story. The opposite of black or dark purple in traditional Iroquois color symbolism was white, clear, or sky blue-green. Red was both vivid and ambivalent. Red, like blood, connoted life as opposed to death in positive contexts, but it also connoted violence and hostility. The wampum that was draped around Radisson's neck was balanced with patterns of white and dark purple beads. Yet with a fresh coat of red paint a wampum belt could be converted instantly into a symbol of war.[25]

Torture and cannibalism are at once repugnant and fascinating to many modern readers. These practices were, of course, not unique to the Iroquois; there have been many parallels from cases far removed in time and space. Thus it is possible to compare historically unrelated cases in order to say something about the cultural conditions that cause these practices to arise. As it happens, there are a half dozen conditions that are always present. First, militarism and intergroup conflict are always prominent. Second, the taking of prisoners is always an important objective of conflict. Third, there is invariably a great social emphasis on conformity, compliance, and generosity, which displaces aggression on to outsiders. Fourth, the world view must be personalistic, where all everyday occurrences, both good and bad, are regarded as the doings of supernatural forces or other human beings. Fifth, sacrifice to supernaturals must be part of regular religious observance. Finally, there must be intensive intergroup competition for scarce resources, with great uncertainty about outcomes. These may not be sufficient conditions, but they are necessary ones. All of these conditions were met in seventeenth-century Iroquoia, and the Iroquois behaved as people sometimes do under those circumstances. The Iroquois were not monsters to any greater or lesser degree than any other human beings; they were only acting as many humans have done when faced with a particular set of predilections and stressful conditions.[26]

## *Iroquois Society around 1700*

Evidence from oral tradition, the work of nineteenth-century anthropologists, and historical documents allows the reconstruction of Iroquois life around 1700. The senior women in a household approved and arranged the marriages of their daughters and sons. The marriage was confirmed by an exchange of gifts. The most important traditional principle was that one married outside one's household, and preferably outside one's clan. This rule was extended even to adopted captives, showing just how strongly adoptees were integrated into the community as substitutes for lost relatives. Marriages repeatedly tied matrilineal households together, constantly recreating the links of community in the village, and providing new relatives with whom to share communal tasks.

Residence after marriage was in the woman's household, where her husband was always a guest when not away from the village. Should a woman die, her husband was encouraged to marry one of her sisters (the sororate), so that remarriage would not threaten the stability of the lineage. At the same time, divorce was an easy remedy for brittle marriages. Estranged spouses could come back together again after a period of separation. At other times the breakups were permanent and led to bitter jealousies. The most extreme cases could lead to revenge-motivated violence or suicide.[27]

The status of women was derived from their economic importance and from the extension of the kinship system into Iroquois political life. The village and its surrounding fields was the traditional domain of women. The world of Iroquois men was the forest, where war, trade, and hunting went on.

Adults cooperated in longhouse construction, clearing, planting, hoeing, and harvesting. Major events requiring mutual aid were often regular occurrences in the seasonal round, and thus marked by a formal ceremony.

Men who distinguished themselves might become War Chiefs or Pine Tree Chiefs. Those with the proper disposition were candidates for hereditary sachemships, so long as they belonged to one of the lineages holding these titles. Upon being selected for a sachemship, a man became that chief, and he gave up the identity implied by his old name.

The chiefs and clan matrons, and the lineages from which they came, formed a class apart. The chiefs were known by their hereditary names, but they were also referred to in other deferential ways that made their status clear. War Chiefs and Pine Tree Chiefs earned their way into this social class, making it larger than it might have been. Their traditional status and power reflected well upon the matrons and the other members of their lineages, and it set them all apart. War Chiefs can also be thought of as first among equals within a separate warrior class.

The general public was the second great social class. These were people who were said to be "like women." Much was later made of this identification by people who assumed that the term was one of denigration or supposed to be taken in some literal way. The absorption of the Delaware Indians into the League of the Iroquois as a subject nation of "women" has been particularly misunderstood. However, the Iroquois emphasis was on the role of women as providers and peacemakers, a domestic definition that clearly defined this middle class.

The third class was that of captives who were either temporarily or permanently not incorporated by adoption. Such people could be called slaves, for they were used as drudges and did not have places in the Iroquois kinship system.[28]

# 8

# Iroquoia in the Balance, 1700–1750: The Green Corn Moon

By 1700 two-thirds of all Mohawks were living in Canada. Most were located in a village on the south bank of the St Lawrence at Sault St Louis (Lachine Rapids), which had been founded in 1676. They gave the village the name Caughnawaga, an old village name from the Mohawk Valley. The village was rebuilt farther upstream after the massacre at Lachine in 1690; it was moved again in 1696, and yet again, farther upstream, in 1714. Two years later, a final move brought the village to its present site in the Canadian Mohawk reserve, where it is known by the phonetically more appropriate spelling "Kahnawake."

The Senecas maintained their population at around 4,000 by continuing to absorb adoptees in large numbers, but at considerable cost to their social fabric. The longhouse had long since become standardized into three- or four-hearth structures throughout Iroquoia, and in some villages these were giving way to even smaller cabins. The social stresses of the seventeenth century had already led to individual or two-family Seneca houses (Figure 8.1). These initially had central fireplaces on dirt floors and end doors. The eastern Seneca village had moved to the site of Ganondagan, now a state park, by 1677. At that time Wentworth Greenhalgh saw the same number of Seneca cabins as had been reported for its predecessor village eight years earlier: about 150 of them. In the 1670s about 40 per cent of the Seneca population of 4,000, or 1,600 people, must have lived in the 150 cabins of the eastern village. Cabins holding an average of only ten or twelve people must have been designed to accommodate extended families, but not the much larger lineages of earlier times. It seems likely that these new family units were often made up of three generations. Even the old rule of matrilocal residence may have been honored in the breach as often as not by this time.[1]

An able man could arrange a suitable adoption for himself, thus

*Figure 8.1   Cabins at Onondaga*
Source: *photograph courtesy of Ste Marie among the Iroquois,*
*Onondaga County Parks.*

gaining access to a traditional sachemship. Alternatively he could
work to gain power and prestige outside the traditional system, eventually earning the special status of Pine Tree Chief. Either way, such
a man had little need to subordinate himself to an elderly longhouse
matron, and he would have been motivated to live apart in his own
cabin, surrounded by his wife, children, and grandchildren.

### A Move to Neutrality

The turn of the century brought a new realization to the Iroquois.
They were badly divided within, and demands for alliance from both
the French and the English were threatening to tear the League and
even its constituent nations apart. The Iroquois form of government
allowed no faction to gain authority, and it became clear that the
only solution for the League was to seek a state of deliberate indecision. In practical terms this meant seeking alliance with both the
French and English so that the Iroquois could survive by remaining
neutral in colonial conflicts.

At the national or village level, disputes could still be resolved by fissioning. Angry factions could still pack up and move out. Traditional slash and burn horticulture allowed and even encouraged this form of dispute resolution. The fragmentation of Iroquois longhouse villages into dispersed clusters of cabins made it even more unlikely that matrons would be able to hold communities together in the face of political disagreements. Households of disgruntled Iroquois from all five nations began appearing in Ohio and other areas far from Iroquoia.

So long as fissioning remained available as a solution to the stresses of political factionalism, a more coercive form of Iroquois government was unlikely to evolve. Furthermore, expanding Euro-American settlement had an adaptive advantage that guaranteed its ultimate dominance. English farmsteads were built to be permanent. Even English fields were enclosed and designed to be permanently maintained by crop rotation and pasturing. The Iroquois practice of abandoning exhausted fields and moving villages condemned them to constantly fall back before encroaching Euro-Americans.

For the time being the Iroquois still held their pivotal military power as a bargaining chip. Even with this leverage, however, they increasingly found themselves with only land to trade for the manufactured goods they wanted. By the end of the century they would lose all of their military leverage and be left with only their land as capital.

While the European powers each sought a bilateral alliance at the beginning of the century, the Iroquois would give them only promises of nonaggression. This was consistent with Iroquois tradition, for even the League of the Iroquois itself was little more than a mutual nonaggression pact. Political and military action remained in the hands of *ad hoc* leaders, who occasionally had the charisma to seize the moment and take concerted action. The power of such leaders always passed with the moment as well.

The Iroquois leaders traveled to Montreal to negotiate the Grand Settlement with the French in 1701. The agreement to neutrality enabled the pro-French Senecas, Cayugas, and Onondagas to travel freely to Montreal and Quebec. Meanwhile the pro-English Oneidas and Mohawks were not impeded in their relations with Albany. The new arrangement changed the Covenant Chain only a little from the point of view of the Iroquois, although the English took a more alarmed view of the new development and countered by getting a "deed" to the American interior (centered on Detroit) from the Iroquois. The sale came about as a result of the efforts of Robert Livingston, then secretary for Indian affairs in Albany. Livingston

argued that the Crown should acquire Iroquois lands and then rein-
state the Indians as tenants, one of several ploys he used to try to
wrest land holdings from the Iroquois. King William's War had officially ended in 1697, but it was extended by proxy in Iroquoia until
settled by these uneasy agreements.[2]

The emergence of Iroquois neutrality in the coming conflicts between the French and English allowed the Iroquois to turn their
attentions to the western nations. New chains of friendship, and the
menacing implications of their absence, extended westward into
the Ohio Valley and the upper Great Lakes. But the position of the
Iroquois gradually weakened as the century grew older and both
the French and the English established forts in and west of Iroquoia.
The Iroquois could not control their own hunters, much less the
western nations, and the network of the Covenant Chain became
frayed as links broke more rapidly than new ones could be forged or
old ones repaired.

---

### The Green Corn Ceremony

The Green Corn Ceremony stands opposite the Midwinter Ceremony
in the seasonal round, and rivals it in importance among the calendrical
ceremonies. Like midwinter, this is an appropriate time for naming.
Children born since midwinter receive their first names, while a few
others take new ones. It may be that a child is adopting an adult name,
or an adult is assuming a faithkeeper name. The ceremony marks the
time when sweet corn can be harvested and eaten, a time when a good
harvest seems assured.

Our Life Supporters dances form the major rites of the Planting,
Green Bean, and Harvest ceremonies. These include the Women's Dance,
the Corn Dance, the Stomp Dance, the Hand-in-Hand Dance, the
Striking-the-Pole Dance, and the War Dance. The Green Corn Ceremony has these as well, but to them were added the Four Sacred
Rituals in the early nineteenth century. These are the Feather Dance,
Thanksgiving Dance, Rite of Personal Chant, and Bowl Game, which
added days to the ceremony. As is customary in all Iroquois ceremonies, this one begins and ends with the Thanksgiving Speech.

---

Into the chaotic uncertainty of neutrality stepped a new Iroquois
personality. Theyanoguin was a Mohawk whose charisma and diplomatic skills made him into a new leader among equals. His emergence from obscurity in 1710 shifted the center of Iroquois power from
the Onondagas to the Mohawks.[3] Theyanoguin was probably born

*Figure 8.2 Theyanoguin, also known as Hendrick*
*Source: New-York Historical Society.*

between 1675 and 1680, near Westfield, Massachusetts. His father was Mohegan and his mother Mohawk, a circumstance that made him Mohegan to the English but entirely Mohawk in the eyes of the Iroquois. His adult Mohawk name was Theyanoguin, which means "the western door is open." He was later also known as Sharenhowaneh, the traditional title name of the fourth League sachem of the Mohawks. He became known to the English as Hendrick, and was later called King Hendrick by them.

Theyanoguin moved to the Mohawk Valley at a young age and took his place with the Wolf clan. Around 1690 he was persuaded to convert to Protestant Christianity and he later became a preacher.

### Queen Anne's War

Queen Anne's War (called the War of the Spanish Succession in Europe) broke out in 1702, and the Iroquois found themselves under heavy pressure to support the English. Theyanoguin was persuaded to recruit warriors to join Francis Nicholson's planned attack on Canada in 1709. The expedition was aborted, but Theyanoguin's participation put him solidly on the side of the English interest. Peter Schuyler and Francis Nicholson took Theyanoguin, his brother Cenelitonoro (John), Sagayonguaroughton (Brant, the grandfather of Joseph Brant), and a Mahican man to London to meet Queen Anne in 1710. All of them were treated to expensive dinners and entertainment. All four sat for portraits by a leading artist of the day. Theyanoguin and the others addressed the Queen at length, stressing their loyalty to England and their rejection of French influence. The Queen responded by passing their request for religious assistance on to the Society for the Propagation of the Gospel.

Theyanoguin might have already been a League sachem in 1710, although while in London he did not go by the sachem name he would sometimes later use. If not, he became one soon after his return from London. His request for missionaries was successful. The Queen funded missionaries and established a chapel at Fort Hunter in 1711. The fort, located at the confluence of Schoharie Creek and the Mohawk River, quickly attracted Mohawk residents, and the new village came to be known as the Lower Mohawk Castle. Queen Anne also ordered the construction of a chapel and a house for two missionaries, and she arranged for the Mohawks to receive a six-piece silver communion set. The communion set was later divided between Mohawks who fled to Niagara and the Bay of Quinte

*Figure 8.3  Brant, also known as Sagayonguaroughton*
*Source: John Verelst, 1710, oil on canvas, 91.5 × 64.5 cms,*
*Documentary Art and Photography Division, National Archives of*
*Canada, Ottawa (Accession No. 1977–35–2).*

respectively during the American Revolution. A matching set that was originally intended for the Onondagas remains in Albany.

By 1709 the Palatine Germans living along the upper reaches of the Rhine could no longer bear the constant war and religious persecution that raged there. Many sought refuge in England, which could not absorb them all. Queen Anne decided to resettle most of them elsewhere, and many were sent to New York, where homes were found for them around Livingston Manor in the Hudson Valley. They were there for two years, during which time they were supposed to repay the Queen's kindness by producing pine tar for her navy. This arrangement did not work well, and by 1710 the Palatines were agitating for farmland in the Schoharie Valley. Theyanoguin offered them land through Governor Hunter upon his return from London, and they moved to the Schoharie in the fall of 1712.

### The Coming of the Tuscaroras

The Tuscaroras also began moving north around this time. Intrusive European settlers had made their lives intolerable in North Carolina and their defeat in the resulting Tuscarora Wars (1711–13) prompted the survivors to flee north in search of refuge among the Iroquois. Tuscarora is a Northern Iroquoian language, but along with Nottaway and Meherrin it was separated from the others several centuries earlier. It may be that when most ancestral Northern Iroquoians expanded into the lower Great Lakes region, the ancestors of these three moved to the coastal plain of Virginia and North Carolina, where they were found by European settlers. In any case, the Iroquois were ready to take in the displaced Tuscarora by 1712. About 500 Tuscarora families arrived in New York in 1713. Some settled along the Susquehanna or its tributaries, while many others settled in a village located somewhere between the Oneidas and the Onondagas.[4]

Theyanoguin was deposed ("dehorned") in the winter of 1712–13, apparently because he objected to tithing 10 per cent of his income to the new chapel. He was in a minority and the matrons turned him out. The incident is often cited as evidence of the power of women in Iroquois society. Tempers cooled, and he was restored to his position as League sachem by 1720.[5] Queen Anne's War ended in 1713 with the Treaties of Utrecht. The settlement gave England Newfoundland and Hudson's Bay, but this had little effect on the Iroquois.

Some time late in 1722 or early in 1723 the Tuscaroras were formally adopted into the League of the Iroquois as a sixth nation of the confederacy. Their chiefs were raised up like other Iroquois chiefs. Yet while they sat as younger brothers with the Cayugas and the Oneidas, the Tuscaroras were not invited to send sachems to sit as part of the Grand Council. The roll call of 50 was not expanded to include them, and none of the established nations offered positions to the Tuscaroras. For their part, the Tuscaroras seemed to accept the political processes of the League without adopting all of its ritual. Despite this, the Tuscaroras were considered to be members of the League, and they participated in conferences and treaty signings from this time on.

In 1727 Cadwallader Colden published the first part of a history of the Iroquois that would not be finished until 20 years later. In it he attributed empire to the League, a claim that he fabricated in order that the colonial government might use the Covenant Chain to assert sovereignty over much of interior North America. Empire is a term that usually applies to nation states that are based on intensive agriculture. Conquest implies standing armies and permanent garrisons to hold imperial acquisitions. The Iroquois engaged in neither empire building nor conquest, yet Colden attributed both to them. "Lacking a reasonable alternative until the French could be forced off the continent, the British donated an empire to the Iroquois in order to claim it for themselves."[6]

### King George's War

King George's War, which was called the War of the Austrian Succession in Europe, broke out between the French and English in 1744. The Iroquois remained nominally neutral. The Indian commissioners of Albany resigned in 1746, and Governor Clinton appointed William Johnson as colonel of the Six Nations, later commissary of New York Indian Affairs. Johnson was still in his early thirties at the time, having arrived in America in 1738 at the age of 22 or 23. He was supposed to be in service to his uncle, but by 1739 he had bought his own land on the north side of the Mohawk River. William Johnson built his first home by 1743, the same year that a Mohawk child, who would later be called Joseph Brant (Thayendanegea), was born in Ohio. Theyanoguin became a close friend and confidant of Johnson. The two visited each other frequently, for Theyanoguin was Johnson's principal link to the Mohawk leadership in the years before the emergence of Joseph Brant as a Pine Tree Chief.

The Iroquois put great stock in dreams, which are considered to be expressions of suppressed desire. There is a famous story that Johnson appeared one day in a new scarlet uniform. A while later Theyanoguin told Johnson that he had dreamed that Johnson had given him the uniform. Johnson knew Iroquois culture, and he knew that he had little choice but to hand it over as a gift. But with the gift Johnson revealed that he had dreamed that his friend Theyanoguin had given him 500 acres of good Mohawk land. Theyanoguin had no choice but to comply, but he added: "I will never dream with you again."[7]

Akwesasne, sometimes called St Regis, was founded on the south side of the upper St Lawrence by disaffected people from Caughnawaga in 1747. They remained pro-French and strengthened French control of the river. King George's War ended in 1748 with the Peace of Aix-la-Chapelle. William Johnson subsequently finished building a new home along the Mohawk River, a place now called Fort Johnson. Another Iroquois village called Oswegatchie was founded on the south bank of the St Lawrence that same year, this time at the site of modern Ogdensburg. This new village was comprised mainly of pro-French Onondagas who had moved north for political reasons, and further strengthened the French interest on the St Lawrence.

Around this time the French induced Indians at various missions to come together in a partly religious, partly political confederation known as the Seven Indian Nations of Canada. Its membership included the Mohawks, Algonquians, and Nipissings then living at the Lake of the Two Mountains (later known as Oka or Kanesatake), the Caughnawaga (later Kahnawake) Mohawks, the Onondagas and Cayugas at Oswegatchie, the St Francis Abenakis, and the Hurons at Lorette. After Oswegatchie broke up it was agreed that the Mohawks at Akwesasne would take their place in the confederation. These communities were united mainly by their Catholicism, but they remained united in their loyalty to French interests through the coming conflict with the English.

# 9

# The Loss of Independence, 1750–1800: The Fresh Moon

### The Iroquois in the Balance

In 1750 the English were at peace with the French again, but the French busied themselves with trying to convert the Ohio River Iroquois (Mingos) to their interest. Johnson perceived that if that happened the Six Nations would have to go over to the French cause as well. Johnson consequently begged Clinton to come to Albany to brighten the Covenant Chain with the Iroquois. Yet meetings between the English and the Iroquois were increasingly strained.

Attention was diverted in 1752 when the ginseng fad created an economic boom along the Mohawk. Ginseng is a small plant with five leaflets on the end of each of three stalks. It has a root like a parsnip, and its leaves can be used for tea. The root was exported to China, where it was believed to be an aphrodisiac. The demand for the American species of ginseng was so strong that Mohawk incomes soared while the fad lasted. It was a welcome alternative to the declining fur trade.

By now most Iroquois were living in cabins, and the traditional longhouse was maintained only as a public structure for meetings and for housing visitors. As the male heads of these smaller family units found new ways to earn money, and as female heads found themselves increasingly independent in food production, the old social system faded. Talented men became chiefs, sometimes called "Pine Tree Chiefs," irrespective of their access to traditional positions. Traditional sachems no longer commanded as much respect, for they were no longer the sole legitimate conduits for goods coming into the community. Similarly, clan matrons no longer commanded large cooperative groups of women in the fields.

Johnson arranged for the construction of a fort to protect the Upper Castle Mohawks in 1753. These were Mohawks who lived in a village 50 kilometers upstream from the Lower Castle at Fort Hunter. The new fort was built across from the mouth of East Canada Creek, west of modern Fort Plain, and it was initially called Fort Canajoharie.

### The Albany Plan

The aging Theyanoguin, often called King Hendrick by the English, still hung on to both his sachemship and to the prestige it carried, but mainly because he had developed a strong personal relationship with Johnson. Theyanoguin was present at the 1754 conference in Albany in which Benjamin Franklin proposed his famous Albany Plan of Union. Much of the conference was given over to mollifying the Iroquois. Land sharks were pestering the Mohawks and Clinton's arrogance was not helpful.[1] Conrad Weiser saved the day by advising both sides, smoothing ruffled feathers, and rebutting Theyanoguin's attacks on Virginia and Pennsylvania. The incident reveals the ways in which the politically weakened Iroquois played the English and French off against each other. It also reveals once again a fundamental premise of Iroquois diplomacy: no treaty settled anything once and for all. The Iroquois regarded friendship as a condition that needed constant nurturing and renewal, not to mention a steady flow of essential goods. In the absence of new treaties the Iroquois believed that things would soon devolve into their natural state of war.

Much has since been made of the Albany Congress and the Plan of Union Franklin proposed. Franklin had previously witnessed Iroquois diplomacy at a conference in Pennsylvania, and he was impressed by what he knew of their system of government. However, he was also aware of the weakness of the League of the Iroquois, and his plan assumed principles very different from those of the League. The League emphasized consensus rather than executive authority, unanimity rather than majority rule, and equality rather than hierarchy. Franklin knew that these principles would not work in a federal union, so he concentrated on the form rather than the substance of the Iroquois model. The plan called for 48 representatives to be chosen unequally by eleven colonies (Georgia and Delaware were not included). The colonial assemblies were to select the members of this Grand Council, but there the parallels end. Franklin's plan went nowhere, but had it come to anything, it would surely not have replicated the League of the Iroquois in its operation. European principles of hierarchy, authority, proportional representation, and majority rule were too strong to have allowed that to happen.[2]

As the conference broke up, John Lydius got Theyanoguin and 15 other chiefs drunk at his house and tricked some of them into signing the infamous Wyoming Deed. In fact, Theyanoguin and other leading men refused to sign. Lydius later rode to the Mohawk castles in an attempt to get more signatures. He made the fraudulent deal on behalf of Connecticut, which was looking for western lands. In the end it caused serious fighting between the colonies and helped precipitate the Wyoming Massacre of 1778.[3]

### The Final Colonial War

By 1755 the French and the British were once again moving towards open warfare. A 'General Map of the Middle British Colonies in America' made by the English at this time shows the boundary of the Six Nations running along the St Lawrence and Ottawa rivers and including all of Lake Huron, Michigan, and Illinois southeast of the Illinois River. This was the empire that Colden had given the Iroquois, and which the British were now claiming as their own.

Meanwhile the French built forts at Presque Isle, on the southern shore of Lake Erie in what is now Pennsylvania, at Lake Le Boeuf at the head of French Creek, at Venango where French Creek enters the Allegheny, and at Fort Duquesne at Pittsburgh. Braddock tried to dislodge the French at Fort Duquesne, but was defeated. Thus effective control of the imaginary Iroquois empire fell to the French.

Governor Shirley appointed William Johnson to the rank of general in 1755. Fort Lyman (later Fort Edward) was built at one end of the portage from the upper Hudson to what was by now called Lake George. Johnson then built Fort William Henry at the other end of the portage, the southernmost tip of Lake George. He also reinforced Fort Canajoharie, which was by this time beginning to be called Fort Hendrick in honor of Theyanoguin, and Fort Herkimer farther up the Mohawk. For their part the French built Fort Carillon (later Ticonderoga) at the other end of Lake George where it flows into Lake Champlain. With that, most of the pieces were in place for renewed conflict. Once again the Iroquois were in a position to tip the balance one way or the other.

The French appeared to be ready to advance on Albany by August 1755. Theyanoguin led over 200 Mohawks up the Hudson to Fort Edward to assist the English. Unfortunately, the French had many Caughnawaga Mohawks on their side, and the New York Mohawks thus faced the unpleasant possibility of fighting kin. They arranged to meet with them in no-man's-land, providing their own men as pickets for the English so that they would not be mistaken for the enemy when they returned.[4]

Theyanoguin expressed alarm at the negligence of English sentries. He went on to urge Johnson to take the advice of the Iroquois when fighting in the wilderness. Johnson nevertheless made the error of sending out three detachments of 500 men to take the French at their rear. Theyanoguin was alone in disagreeing with the plan.[5] They marched into a French trap south of Lake George (Figure 9.1). One of the French Mohawks was later said to have deliberately fired his musket early in order to warn the English Mohawks of the trap. Nevertheless Theyanoguin and Tarageorus (both Mohawk League sachems) and many others were killed in the fighting.

The defeat left Johnson weakened and without his principal friend and ally among the Iroquois. Nevertheless, in 1756, Shirley was removed as commander in chief and governor of Massachusetts, and Johnson was made baronet and superintendent of Indian affairs, a post he held until his death. England and France formally declared war. This war, which was called the Seven Years' War in Europe, was the last of the French and Indian wars in North America.

Many Mahicans moved to the Mohawk Valley, and many Canadian Mohawks came home to the valley as well. The French took Fort Oswego, having already taken Fort Frontenac and Fort Niagara. In 1757 General Montcalm took Fort William Henry at the south end of Lake George, but later fell back. During this time William Johnson became increasingly a man of two cultures. He has been said to have married Molly Brant, a prominent Mohawk woman, in this year or the next, although there is little proof. She was certainly his common-law wife, even though there was also a woman of German extraction living with him who could have claimed the same status. Just as important as Molly was her equally intelligent younger brother, Joseph Brant (Thayendanegea), who was still in his teens. These two would come to replace Theyanoguin as Johnson's links to the Mohawks and the Iroquois generally.

The fighting went better for the English in 1758. Johnson and Abercrombie assaulted Fort Carillon and fell back, but Johnson was confident enough to found Johnstown in the Mohawk Valley and Fort Stanwix at the portage near the source of the river. The English captured Louisburg, Oswego, Fort Frontenac, and Fort Duquesne. The following year they captured Fort Carillon and renamed it Fort Ticonderoga. Johnson also captured Fort Niagara.

Rogers' Rangers attacked the Abenaki settlement at St Francis, Quebec, in September 1759, dispersing them to find refuge with one or another of the other members of the Seven Indian Nations of

Canada. Many went to Akwesasne (St Regis), where they eventually came into conflict over land with the largely Mohawk population there. They eventually returned to St Francis in 1771. Montreal fell to the British in 1760, effectively ending the war in America, but the peace treaty was not signed for three more years.[6]

### The Rise of Joseph Brant

Through all of this the New York Mohawks had been pro-English, but the Senecas had been mainly pro-French. Resolution of the fighting in favor of the English left the Mohawks in an especially strong position. In 1761 Johnson sent Joseph Brant and two other Mohawks to Wheelock's Indian School in Connecticut. There Brant learned English, and later returned to serve as an interpreter and begin his long path to power as a Mohawk Pine Tree Chief.

Livingston's efforts to acquire Mohawk land in 1754 came back to haunt the Indians after the war. In 1761, George Klock settled in the valley, taking land in the supposed Livingston patent that he claimed was now his. The Livingston family had long since given up the claim, and tenants on the patent were paying rent to the Mohawks. Klock was having none of that, however. He intimidated the tenants and plied young Mohawks with liquor. Johnson detested Klock and made every effort to remove him. Even the discredited Lydius purchase of 1754 resurfaced again in 1762 when the claim was pressed in London.[7]

### An Unbalanced Peace

The Treaty of Paris ended the Seven Years' War in 1763. However, Pontiac's War soon broke out as an Indian attempt to hold their land now that they could no longer play the French and English off against each other. King George III signed the Proclamation of 1763 in which the crest of the Appalachians was made the boundary of Indian country. This was an attempt to forestall conflict between English settlers and the Indians, but it left the Iroquois still in an ambiguous state, with the Mohawks and the Oneidas not clearly protected from encroachment.

The Iroquois realized that without the threat of the French and their Indian allies, the English colonies really did not need them. Furthermore, peace allowed the English to travel to the west and buy furs directly, bypassing the Iroquois, making them economically

The place where the Brave Coll: Williams was
ambush'd & Killed, his Men Fighting on a Retreat
the Main Body of our Army. Also where
Cap: McGennes of York & Cap: Fulsom of New
Hampshire Bravely Attack: d y Enemy Killing many
Rest Fled leaving their packs & Provisions and
also shews y Place where the Valiant Col: Titcomb was Killed
being the westerly Corner of the Land defended in y general
Engagment which is Circumscribed with a double line, westerly
Southerly, within the P.d double line is y Form
our Armys Entrenchment which shews the Gen.ls
& Each Col: Apartment.

N.o 4

The Waggon Road 1 Inch to 120 Rods

Inch to a Mile.

4 A Hill from which the
Enemy did us much harm, and
during the Engagement, the
Enemy had great advantage they
laying behind Trees we had fell
within Gun Shot of our front.

VI, the place where the Wagoners
were Kill'd.

Col. Cockn

Col. Harris

Col.

Col.
Dyer.

Gen.t man

Col. Cha

56.

RIVER

ll Water 8 Miles.   Saratoga   Falls   A Quick Currant   Fort Edward

The Waggon Road to Lake Geo

Fort William H

Figure 9.1   Battle of Lake George
Source: Sir William Johnson Papers.

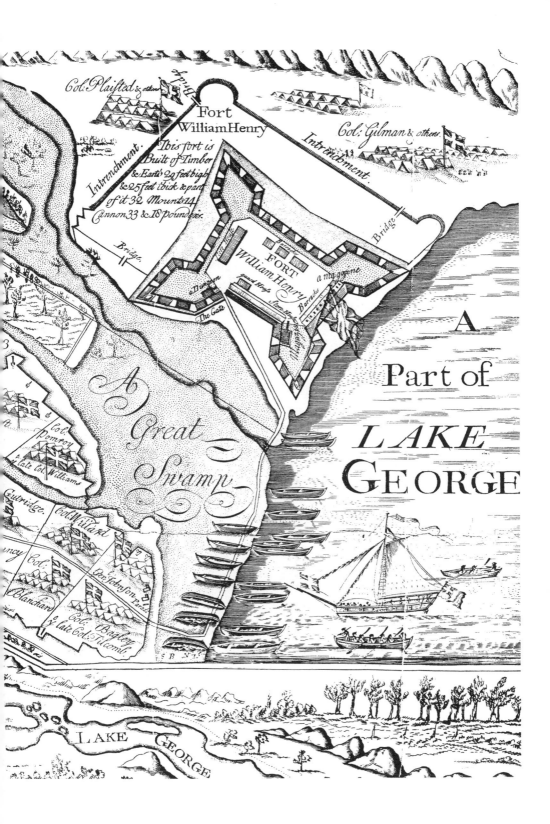

*Figure 9.2   Joseph Brant, also known as Thayendanegea*
*Source: William Berczy, c.1807, oil on canvas, 61.8 × 46.1 cms,*
*National Gallery of Canada, Ottawa.*

superfluous as well. Nevertheless, in 1764 the Lords of Trade instructed Lieutenant Governor Cadwallader Colden to recommend to the New York Assembly that the patents of Kayaderosseras and the Corporation of Albany be vacated, a move that was designed to protect Mohawk lands.

The Treaty of Oswego was signed in 1766 with William Johnson and Pontiac both present. This ended Pontiac's War. Two years later the Kayaderosseras patentees gave up part of their patent and paid the Mohawks for the rest. A council at Fort Stanwix then established a new boundary along tributaries of the Susquehanna and down the Ohio, once again to protect the Indians from further English encroachment. Without the French, the Iroquois had little political or economic leverage to exercise against the English. The 1768 agreement at Fort Stanwix left them without influence over the Shawnees, Delawares, and Wyandots living in the Ohio Valley. The English no longer felt the need to extend easy credit and gifts to the Iroquois. The new boundary also left the Oneidas and Mohawks exposed to further encroachment, but this was balanced to some extent by better local property boundary definitions around their settlements and their proximity to Johnson's protection.

Samuel Kirkland came to establish a mission among the Oneidas and Tuscaroras in 1767. Kirkland was a New England Puritan, not an Anglican, and his powers of persuasion were strong. He converted many Oneidas, mostly from the ranks of the warriors. Like other missionaries, he unwittingly served as provider of an alternative belief system for members of a faction that already had other reasons to split from others in the community.[8] William Johnson, who had the ear of the hereditary chiefs, did not like Kirkland very much, for he had given the Oneida warriors a way to challenge the traditional political structure. As conflict between the Americans and the English approached, the Oneidas found themselves pulled in opposite directions. Calvinist revolutionaries at Oneida eventually came to dominate Anglican loyalists in the struggle.[9]

In 1768 Joseph and Molly Brant contributed land at the Upper Mohawk village for the construction of the Indian Castle church, an Anglican mission. The church still stands, albeit in modified form (Figure 9.3). Joseph may have regretted making the gift in 1772, when an Anglican clergyman refused to marry him to his recently deceased wife's half-sister. The clergyman was ignorant of the custom of the sororate, which preserved Iroquois matrilineages by finding men new wives within the same families whenever possible.[10]

Johnson bought 123,000 acres from Oneidas west of German Flats in that same year, and later acquired the Kingsland Royal Grant of

*Figure 9.3   Indian Castle church, Mohawk Upper Castle*

99,000 more acres. Johnson continued to acquire more patent shares in the years leading up to the American Revolution. In 1774 he collapsed and died during an Indian conference at his mansion in Johnstown.

### The American Revolution

William's son John Johnson inherited the title of baronet and moved into Johnson Hall on his father's death, and William's nephew Guy Johnson became superintendent of Indian affairs. The new arrangement did not last long, for revolutionary rumblings soon forced the younger Johnsons to flee to Canada.

Their departure left the Mohawks in limbo. Most of them were in favor of continued British rule, for their association with English interests had served them well for over a century. Yet the revolutionary sentiments of many of their Euro-American neighbors isolated them politically. The nominally Mohawk Indians at Akwesasne signed a treaty with the Americans at Albany in 1775, a move that secured them in the long term, but within two years the Mohawks remaining in their native valley would choose to become refugees.[11]

The great invisible longhouse of the Iroquois League came apart in 1776. While many New York Mohawks were pro-English, many Oneidas and Tuscaroras were pro-American, a measure of Kirkland's influence. The Onondagas, Cayugas, and Senecas were generally pro-English. The League Chiefs met in council, trying to find consensus, but the search was futile. An epidemic struck the assembly at Onondaga, killing three League Chiefs and many others. Finally, in 1777, as war raged between the English and the Americans, the League of the Iroquois covered the council fire at Onondaga. This action symbolically suspended the work of the League, with no promise that it would ever be resumed. No united Iroquois course of action was possible.[12]

The Mohawks were attacked by the Americans and had no choice but to flee. The Upper Castle Mohawks living near Fort Hendrick fled mainly to Fort Niagara. The Lower Castle Mohawks who had lived around Fort Hunter mostly went to Montreal. Some from both settlements went to Oquaga, a refugee village containing mostly Oneidas and Tuscaroras that was located in the town of Windsor, along the Susquehanna River near the Pennsylvania line. The Oquaga community later joined the Upper Castle Mohawks at Fort Niagara. Pro-American Oneidas seized Mohawk property in the Mohawk Valley or camped outside Schenectady.

After a dozen years of peace, the American Revolution offered the Iroquois a chance to once again influence the balance of history by the application of their relatively small weight to one side or the other. Many traditional chiefs, particularly those in the western nations, saw the wisdom of Iroquois neutrality. But outrages precipitated by American revolutionaries soon pushed most Iroquois over to the British side.

The western Iroquois nations had stayed in place, but in 1779 the Americans decided to expel or destroy them. Generals John Sullivan and James Clinton launched a three-pronged expedition against the Onondagas, Cayugas, and Senecas. The first line of attack was from the Mohawk Valley westward into Onondaga country. Clinton moved down the Susquehanna from Schenectady, then waited at Tioga for Sullivan to join him from Pennsylvania. A third force moved up the Allegheny River from Fort Pitt. Joseph Brant led raids as far as southeastern New York in an attempt to divert the campaign, but with little success. The combined armies of Clinton and Sullivan marched through Cayuga and Seneca country, facing serious fighting only at Elmira. Virtually all of the Iroquois crops and villages in western New York were destroyed. Brant's raiders burned Oneida and Tuscarora villages in retaliation for their support of the Americans. Iroquois refugees fled to Fort Niagara, where they camped without adequate clothing or shelter for the duration of the war. By the end of the war their population was halved.

Iroquois warriors raided the American frontier and defended the British cause. Joseph Brant led raids in the valleys of the Mohawk and its Schoharie tributary. The purpose was to terrorize American settlers and prompt them to abandon their farms, thus denying the revolutionary army an important source of provisions.

As early as 1783 New Yorkers were worried that the success of the Clinton and Sullivan campaign would lead to a federal claim of conquest over all of Iroquoia. They consequently moved quickly to declare state jurisdiction over what is now western New York. Then they took it a step further, asserting that only New York had sovereignty over Indians within its borders. The matter remained unclear during the years that the nation was organized under the Articles of Confederation.

### The Longhouse in Ruins

The 1783 Treaty of Paris made no provisions for the Iroquois. Individual Iroquois nations had made their own deals as best they could. The Lower Mohawks moved to Tyendinaga (also called Deseronto) on the Bay of Quinte in Ontario, under the leadership of John Deserontyon. The Upper Mohawks moved to Grand River, Ontario, under the leadership of Joseph Brant, after General Haldimand was allowed to buy land for them there from the Mississauga Indians. Most Oneidas remained in place, temporarily protected by their support of the revolution. Some Onondagas remained in place at Onondaga Creek, some moved to Grand River with the Mohawks, and some moved to Buffalo Creek with the Senecas. The Onondagas at Oswegatchie dispersed to other reservations. Some Cayugas remained in place at Cayuga Lake, some moved to Grand River with the Mohawks, and some moved to Buffalo Creek with the Senecas. Many Senecas remained in western New York at Buffalo Creek, Cattaraugus, Allegany, and Tonawanda. Some Senecas moved to Grand River with the Mohawks. The Tuscaroras initially split themselves between Grand River and the Big Tree village on the Genesee, but the latter group moved to the Niagara River after 1790.

Two new Iroquois leagues formed as fires were rekindled at two

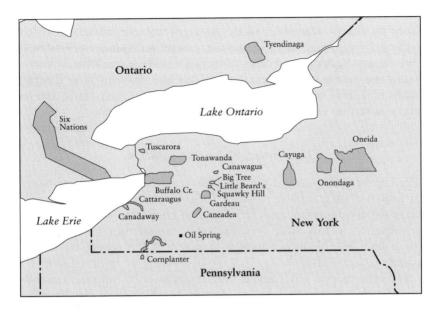

*Figure 9.4   Iroquois reservations of western New York and the nearby reserves in Ontario as they appeared around 1800*

places, one at Grand River (the modern Six Nations Reserve) and the other at Buffalo Creek. Two sets of League Chiefs emerged, each with a portion of the wampum that had been at Onondaga before the Revolution. The great longhouse of the Iroquois was now permanently broken apart.

The New York Iroquois who had opposed the American Revolution were nearly helpless at the 1784 Treaty of Fort Stanwix. They had no choice but to give up claims in Pennsylvania and Ohio. Earlier claims of Iroquois empire, which the English had appropriated, were now irrelevant. Not even Iroquois leaders (namely Cornplanter) could now accept the idea that the Iroquois spoke for all the Indians.

The Cayugas sold all but a 100 square mile reservation around the north end of Cayuga Lake at a 1789 treaty in Albany. They sold most of even this in 1795, retaining only two small tracts totaling just three square miles. In addition, a single square mile was given to Fish Carrier, a prominent Cayuga War Chief. It would later be found significant that these sales took place after the adoption of the United States Constitution, a circumstance that threw their validity into question.

The Oneidas and Tuscaroras fared a bit better, but even they were uncertain about the future. Governor Clinton spoke warmly to the Iroquois at Fort Stanwix, and the state government moved swiftly to outlaw land purchases from the Indians by individual non-Indians. But the state also passed laws to facilitate state acquisition, subdivision, and resale of Iroquois land. Thus the reason for outlawing individual sales was not to secure the Indians on their lands, but to make sure that the profits from sales came to the state.[13]

### The United States Constitution

The United States Constitution of 1790 reasserted federal sovereignty in Indian affairs, a blow to New York. Governor Clinton was particularly disappointed, and he refused to cooperate with the federal government in this area, even though it would turn out that New York had little financial interest in much of the remaining Indian country.

Had the federal government been more assertive on this constitutional point during the coming decade, the history of the Iroquois might have been very different. However, it has been quite another issue regarding the relationship of the Iroquois to the United States Constitution that has attracted most attention in recent years. Franklin's aborted Albany Plan of Union probably drew some inspiration from the League of the Iroquois. A few writers have recently proposed that the substance of the plan and even the substance of the later United States Constitution also drew upon ideas embedded in the League. This idea is very popular with the general public and with politicians; New York's Governor Cuomo and the United States Congress have even given it credence. There is, however, little or no evidence that the framers of the Constitution sitting in Philadelphia drew much inspiration from the League. It can even be argued that such claims muddle and denigrate the subtle and remarkable features of Iroquois government. The two forms of government are distinctive and individually remarkable in conception. It serves no legitimate long-term purpose to confuse the two, or to attempt to make either a derivative from the other. Yet the temptation to demonstrate that the United States Constitution was derived from a Native American form of government remains, for ephemeral political purposes, too strong for some to resist.[14]

### The Struggle for Land

The Treaty of Paris had stipulated that what is now western New York was part of the United States, but it did not specify to which state the area belonged. Both New York and Massachusetts claimed it. A Solomonic agreement made in Hartford in 1786 gave sovereignty over the Seneca land to New York, but gave to Massachusetts the sole right to purchase the land from the Iroquois. Two years later Massachusetts sold this pre-emption right to Oliver Phelps and Nathaniel Gorham. They promptly purchased all of the Seneca lands east of the Genesee River as well as a tract west of it. For this they paid the Senecas at Buffalo Creek $5,000 and an annual annuity of $500.

But Phelps and Gorham were unable to make their payments to Massachusetts, and all but the tracts that they had purchased from the Senecas were conveyed back to Massachusetts in what amounted to a foreclosure. Massachusetts then resold the pre-emption rights to Robert Morris of Philadelphia. During 1792 and 1793 Morris in turn resold much of this to various individuals, who subsequently joined together as the Holland Land Company in 1796. The catch in all of this was that Morris was attempting to sell land itself, not the right to acquire it, although he did not yet own the land.

The Americans forced separate treaties on the Shawnees, Delawares, and Mingos in the Ohio Valley. These were dubious transactions, and the Indians later repudiated them, taking up arms against the settlers who were pushing their way into the territory. The Iroquois stayed out of the fight, gaining friends on neither side, until the Ohio Indians were defeated at the Battle of Fallen Timbers in 1794.

Not everything was disastrous for the Iroquois in the years after the American Revolution. Certainly they fared better than their Mingo kin in the Ohio Valley. The 1794 Canandaigua Treaty with the federal government recognized the land in western New York as belonging to the Senecas, while the Senecas agreed to quit claim to Ohio. In 1796 Pennsylvania gave Cornplanter land next to the Allegany Reservation in recognition of his service. The Senecas had good title to their land, and they would have been secure for the future had they been able to provide for themselves through some means other than selling their land. For his part, Robert Morris had to find a way to extinguish their title before the Holland Land Company would pay for it. At the 1797 Treaty of Big Tree near Geneseo, the Senecas sold most of their New York land to the Holland Land Company for $100,000. They reserved 310 square miles in eleven tracts, seven of them very small areas scattered mostly along the Genesee River. The four big reservations were Tonawanda, Cattaraugus, Buffalo Creek, and Allegany. It was the beginning of the reservation system.

In eastern New York the Mohawks claimed ownership of land in the Adirondacks as far south as the Mohawk River. The pro-English

Mohawks were gone, but the claim was kept alive by the Mohawks at Akwesasne (St Regis), who had sided with the Americans in 1775. In 1796 New York made an agreement with all the Seven Indian Nations of Canada (including Akwesasne), in which the Indians surrendered their claims beyond Akwesasne itself and a few other small parcels for an annual payment. Other possible Mohawk claims in the state were extinguished by another treaty in the following year.[15]

The new landscape wrecked Iroquois morale. Many believed that their traditional leaders had sold them out for personal advantage. The traditional chiefs still maintained their positions by redistributing bribes and annuities, and in this sense the old system remained intact. However, most Iroquois had seen enough of Euro-American culture to know that the system facilitated the concentration of wealth, something that many Iroquois still regard as offensive. Worse, the new arrangements made them all wards of either the new United States government or the British government. Without either corporate or individual independence, and without their traditional means to gain power and prestige, many succumbed to alcoholism. There they languished, without faith in their traditional national leaders, and without a single coherent League of the Iroquois.

Most Iroquois were living in small cabins on reservations ("reserves" in Canada) by the end of the eighteenth century. Quakers visiting the traditionalist Seneca village of Burnt House on the Allegheny in 1798 found people living in what were said to be longhouses. However, there were 30 houses for 400 people, and an average of only 13 people per house was a far cry from the great longhouses of the past. They were still constructed of poles and bark, but they were small and not very Iroquois in form. Most houses would have had only two fires, and illustrations from the nineteenth century indicate that they had gabled roofs in the European style rather than the arched roofs of traditional longhouses.[16]

When disputes arose, no faction had the option of removing to a new location. Reservation boundaries inhibited both this traditional form of dispute resolution and the traditional form of slash and burn agriculture, with the frequent village relocation it entailed. Many Iroquois correctly saw the new reservations as securing them in their homes and agricultural lands, but they also believed incorrectly that they could continue to hunt on the vacant land they had given up. That vacant land soon began to fill up with settlers, and the Indians found themselves shut out of their traditional hunting grounds.

With the beaver largely gone, with little land left to sell, and without access to other resources, some Iroquois turned to the manufacture of ash splint baskets. These they could sell to non-Indians for cash. While the use of ash and other splints had been long known to the Iroquois, the new basket forms were derived largely from Euro-American traditions. Swedes had introduced the use of ash splints for large baskets to the Delawares early in the eighteenth century, and Shaker craftspeople were selling their own splint baskets by the end of the century. The Oneidas and Mohawks were the first of the Iroquois to pick up the craft after the American Revolution. It spread quickly to most Iroquois reserves and reservations, and thousands of baskets were made by Iroquois men and women in the nineteenth century. The craft persists today, particularly on Mohawk reserves.[17]

The departure of the French had nearly ended the traditional diplomatic activities of Iroquois men, and the Treaty of Paris effectively finished them. Without diplomacy and hunting, Iroquois men were condemned to remain on their reservations. Most had no choice but to help with the farming, which in Iroquois culture had traditionally been women's work. While women continued to be economically important in the evolving society, men were stripped of their traditional roles and often derided for their impotence. At the end of the eighteenth century, the once proud Iroquois were reduced to a squalid alcoholic existence on small fragments of their former domain. If they were to survive another seven generations, something verging on the miraculous would have to occur. The revival they needed so desperately came with the turn of the century.

# 10

## Revival and Subjection, 1800–1850: The Harvest Moon

### Handsome Lake

We come now to the third great piece of Iroquois cosmology. The departure of the French, and then the American Revolution against English rule, were disastrous for the Iroquois. These events were a disaster in political terms, but their significance went much deeper than that. The Senecas retained fractured holdings of eleven reservations after 1797, only four of them sizeable. The Allegany band retained a reservation 42 square miles in size along both sides of the Allegheny River in southwestern New York. Part of the band lived on the adjacent Cornplanter grant just to the south in Pennsylvania, under the leadership of Cornplanter himself.

The new reservation system might have worked well. The Iroquois regarded the reservations as secure home bases from which they could hunt, travel, or gather food over unoccupied lands they had ceded. The Indians sold splint baskets and beadwork to non-Indians, or even secured employment among them. Cornplanter hired non-Indians to operate smithies and mills on his grant. Quakers moved into this optimistic setting, intent to show the Senecas the way to civilization. They did not necessarily seek to convert the Indians to their faith, but rather to teach them literacy, mathematics, modern farming, and various arts and crafts. Despite these good intentions, the reservations slid into deplorable wilderness slums. Iroquois men no longer ruled the world beyond the edge of the woods, abroad for months on end to deal with hunting, diplomacy, and warfare. Rather, they found themselves confined to a woman's world of farming and village affairs. Hunting was restricted and villages could not relocate easily when soil declined, so the Iroquois had to adopt plow agriculture and domesticated animals that provided fertilizer. At a time when the Plains Indians were approaching the apogee of their new equestrian adaptation, oxen become more important than horses to the Iroquois.

Fueled by alcoholism, families fragmented, the mechanism of reciprocal condolence came apart, and Indian society fell into a darkness of mutual suspicion and rumors of witchcraft. The cycle of endless offense and revenge, which the Peacemaker had ended within Iroquoia centuries earlier, began anew. Families that had previously been parts of extended matrilineal households had to survive on their own at the very moment at which stress on the traditionally weak marriage link reached its maximum. The traditional ceremonies, with their emphasis on thanksgiving, solidarity, and catharsis, did little to relieve the general hostility. By the end of the century, Iroquois culture was near death.

Cornplanter had a half-brother, a man named Handsome Lake (Skanyadariyoh) who had been raised up to the office of the Turtle clan League sachem in about 1795. Handsome Lake was living with Cornplanter in 1799, bedridden by prolonged alcoholism. In June of that year Handsome Lake collapsed and appeared to die, at the end of a stressful spring during which a suspected witch had been executed. Blacksnake, his nephew, discovered that he was still alive, but in a coma. It was while he was in his coma that Handsome Lake had the first of a series of visions in which the Creator spoke to him. Three people in traditional Iroquois dress appeared to him and instructed him to give up alcohol or die. They also warned that witches must repent and confess their sins. Handsome Lake was commanded to spread these words and to ensure that the Strawberry Ceremony was held that year and each year from then on.

On his recovery, Handsome Lake conveyed these messages in council and to the local Quaker schoolmaster. In a vision a few weeks later, Handsome Lake was taken on a tour of heaven and hell. He met George Washington and Jesus, neither of whom appeared to be in ideal circumstances. These features surely reflect the long contact the Iroquois had experienced with Christians. He was also shown vignettes having to do with drunkenness, witchcraft, promiscuity, wife abuse, quarreling, and gambling. All of these led to the definition of an explicit moral code, which Handsome Lake was compelled to take to his people. The code was called the *Gai'wiio*, "The Good Message."[1]

The Iroquois put much stock in dreams, and have traditionally maintained a relatively modern view of their significance. While the Algonquian shamans of New England saw dreams as out-of-body experiences, the Iroquois thought them to be the expressions of suppressed desires. Dreams not acted upon would cause the dreamer to

fer a disruptive imbalance that could lead to personal illness or
th, or even misfortune for the entire community. The higher the
rank of the dreamer, the more likely it was that a dream had far-
reaching significance. So it was that the visions of Handsome Lake
came to have wider significance.

During the following winter, Handsome Lake had a third vision.
In it he was instructed to ensure that the traditional ceremonies were
continued, especially the Midwinter Ceremony. The consequence of
not doing so, he believed, would be the destruction of the world by
fire. He revived the Midwinter Ceremony by adding four sacred
rituals as a second segment. These were the Feather Dance, Thanksgiving Dance, Rite of Personal Chant, and Bowl Game, which added
as many as four days to the ceremony.

Most games are just that. However, the Bowl Game was elevated
to sacred status by its inclusion in the Midwinter Ceremony as one
of the four sacred rituals. The Bowl Game (called the Peach Stone
Game after the introduction of that fruit) is played with flat fruit pits.
The pits, which are colored black on one side, are tossed six at a time
in a shallow bowl by thumping the bowl against the ground. Players
collect counters by turning up five or six pits of the same color. The
length of the game depends upon the number of counters used.

The central themes of revived Iroquois ceremony remained the
traditional ones. They were and are thanksgiving and appreciation
for the goodwill of the supernatural, and attention to the meaning
of dreams. Iroquois dances are regarded as either sacred or social.
Sacred dances are usually performed in the longhouse as part of a
ceremony. Social dances are for fun and relaxation. These are also
the dances that are performed outside the longhouse, at powwows,
and at festivals attended by non-Iroquois. The most sacred of dances
are the Feather Dance and the Thanksgiving Dance (sometimes called
the Drum or Skin Dance), which Handsome Lake added to the
Midwinter Ceremony. Other less sacred dances include the Women's
Dance, Corn Dance, Stomp Dance (also called Trotting or Standing
Quiver), Bean Dance (also called Hand-in-Hand or Linking Arms),
Striking-the-Pole Dance, and War Dance.

Social dances, which are most likely to be performed in more
public settings today, are numerous. They have names like Fish,
Raccoon, Chicken, Sharpening a Stick, Choose a Partner, Shake the
Pumpkin, Garter, Pigeon, Duck, Robin, Skin Beating, Cherokee,
Grinding the Arrow, Knee Rattle, Alligator, and Rabbit. There is also
a new Women's Dance, which is in addition to the sacred dance of
the same name and can be performed socially. As may be clear from
their names, several of these were borrowed from other Indian nations.

The Eagle Dance[2] began as a war dance derived from the Calumet Dance of western Indians. Over the last two centuries it has evolved into a curing society dance. Most dances are round dances, with people alone or paired according to the requirements of each dance. Except for certain dances for the dead, movement is almost always counterclockwise. Every dance has its own specific steps, and everyone participates regardless of proficiency.

Handsome Lake's health improved. He began spreading the word as a new Iroquois prophet. He even went to Washington to solicit the support of President Jefferson. Visions and periods of meditation led to more revelations, and over the course of the next 15 years, Handsome Lake gradually compiled a complex code of behavior. He did not argue that witchcraft did not exist, but rather that it should be given up. While Handsome Lake lived, the *Gai'wiio* was called the New Religion by some Iroquois in order to distinguish the movement from the Old Religion of the Iroquois. This distinction was not very important to many traditional Iroquois at the time or for many decades later, but it would be revived by some late in the twentieth century.

For a while Handsome Lake was obsessed with witch hunting. He came to believe that the traditional medicine societies were covens of witches, and he demanded that they be disbanded. Some members pretended to comply, but continued to practice their rituals in private. It was for this reason that a century later Parker would refer to them as secret medicine societies.[3] Handsome Lake ordered people to confess to witchcraft, and those that refused were sometimes killed. Inevitably, he eventually began throwing such accusations at the famous Seneca Pine Tree Chief known as Red Jacket and other political rivals, nearly precipitating a war in one instance. But overall, his code began to have some positive effects. Handsome Lake realized that the Quakers had some things right. Iroquois men could no longer afford to insist that farming was women's work. Nor could the tradition of easy divorce continue to work in the absence of extended matrilineal households. He realized that the strong matrilocal extended family was a thing of the past, and argued that gossip and family meddling (especially by women's mothers) had to end. These points became first principles in Handsome Lake's evolving code, which he preached as an extended oral tradition in a classically Iroquois manner.

Handsome Lake opposed any further land sales. He also opposed the participation of Iroquois men in the United States military, particularly in the case of the War of 1812. In these and other things, his code was conservative. He was calling the Iroquois to revive and adapt the best of traditional Iroquois belief. His teaching sought to

reinforce the old myths and ceremonies, not replace them. But he
also sought to replace the catharsis of acting out dreams with thera-
peutic confession and the repression of illicit desires. Whether he
realized it himself or not, Handsome Lake was helping traditional
Iroquois belief to adapt to the realities of reservation life.

Handsome Lake deliberately struck at the central link in Iroquois
society as a means of reinforcing the new nuclear family unit. He
realized that the bond between husband and wife was more important than that between mother and daughter now that the longhouse
residence was gone. He did not threaten the clan system or the rights
of clan matrons to appoint chiefs, but he did everything he could to
subvert the authority of matriliny at its root. It may well be that the
Iroquois survived the nineteenth century because Handsome Lake
made it acceptable for men to work the fields, and made it difficult
for women to accuse their sons-in-law of adultery.

---

### The Harvest Ceremony

Our Life Supporters dances formed the major rites of the Harvest
Ceremony, just as in the cases of the Planting and Green Corn ceremonies. As is customary in all Iroquois ceremonies, this one begins and
ends with the Thanksgiving Speech. Tobacco would be burned in an
invocation near the beginning were the life supporters not so close by,
but their proximity makes this unnecessary. Our Life Supporters dances
included the Women's Dance, the Corn Dance, the Stomp Dance, the
Hand-in-Hand Dance, the Striking-the-Pole Dance, and the War Dance.

---

Quaker-inspired technology and Handsome Lake's religious revival
gave new spirit to the Iroquois. Like all nativistic movements, this
one claimed to revive traditional religious values while it was in
reality carefully selective of those values and inventive in finding
innovative solutions to new problems.

### Giving up the Land

While all this was going on, the Iroquois continued to lose their land
base. The Cayugas remaining in New York lived mainly with refugee
Tutelos among the Senecas at Buffalo Creek. Many others had gone
to Six Nations Reserve after the American Revolution. A few Cayugas
had remained in their homeland around Cayuga Lake, but most of

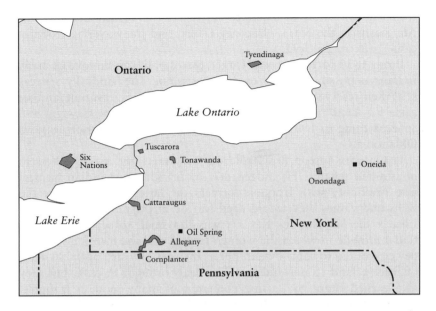

*Figure 10.1  Modern Iroquois reservations of western New York and the nearby reserves in Ontario as they appeared by the middle of the nineteenth century*

this had been given up in the 1795 Treaty of Cayuga Ferry. The small tracts that they retained were eventually sold in 1807 and 1841, although none of the Cayuga League Chiefs still resident on parcels totaling only three square miles agreed to the 1807 sale. Fish Carrier, who lived in Canada by now, was responsible for these sales, and he also sold his own grant in 1841.

Some Cayugas moved with other Iroquois to the lower Sandusky River in Ohio, where they all came to be known as the Sandusky Senecas. These Iroquois kept the old cultural pattern going as best they could, the men fighting with the Americans in the War of 1812. Their reservation was enlarged in 1818 partly because of this.

At the Six Nations Reserve the Iroquois contemplated going over to the Americans during the War of 1812. Many thought that Upper Canada would fall to the Americans anyway. Considerable numbers of the Iroquois declared their neutrality, and only a few volunteered to fight with the British. The chiefs made a display of moving to protect the mouth of the Grand River, which did not need protection, in order to move away from the anticipated American invasion from the direction of Detroit. However, the British defeated the Americans in the Battle of Stoney Creek, and the wavering Iroquois came back to the fold.

From 1830 to 1846 it was United States policy to remove as many Indians as possible to west of the Mississippi. The Sandusky Senecas sold their reservation in 1831 and moved to new reservation land set aside for them in Indian Territory. So it was that some Cayugas and Senecas came to live on a reservation in what is now northeastern Oklahoma.

In Ontario, Joseph Brant sold off vast tracts and leased others to non-Indian tenants. He judged that by bringing non-Indian farmers into proximity with Iroquois farmers the latter would acquire the skills and values they would need for life in the nineteenth century. Clearly the Six Nations Reserve was too small to support a traditional lifestyle in which the women farmed and the men hunted. The device worked to some extent, but at the cost of losing 350,000 acres of reserve land to non-Indians. The deals brought in cash, but they also earned Brant the lasting contempt of many modern Iroquois. Hated by Americans for his raids during the American Revolution and hated by many Iroquois for his wealth and political machinations, Brant nonetheless died with broad if sometimes grudging respect in 1807.[4]

In New York, David Ogden bought the right to acquire remaining Seneca land from the Holland Land Company in 1810. Handsome Lake's witch hunting caused many other Senecas at Cold Spring to turn against him. The prophet was forced to leave Cold Spring on the Allegany Reservation, and he moved to Tonawanda where his mother was buried. He continued his preaching, traveling from one Iroquois reservation to another. In 1815 Handsome Lake died at Onondaga and was buried under the floor of the frame structure that was usually referred to as the longhouse. Gable-roofed frame or log longhouses had been serving as meeting houses on most reservations for years, and where Handsome Lake's teachings took hold these were taking on renewed ceremonial significance. Later the longhouse at Onondaga would be moved, and a stone monument erected over Handsome Lake's grave.

From this time on the state of New York continued to reduce Indian sovereignty by enacting statutes that violated the United States Constitution. The Iroquois were not always informed of these acts, and were even less often aware of their significance. They came back to haunt the government of New York State in the twentieth century, and various law suits, some of them land claims, are still pending. However, not all of the state's moves were malevolent. New York took over responsibility for educating Indian children in 1855 with at least some good intentions.

A council was held at Buffalo Creek in 1818 to discuss religion, and this was followed by a 12-day council at Tonawanda for the same purpose. Iroquois leaders debated Christianity and the teachings of Handsome Lake. This led to renewed polarization of Christian and pagan parties. Although the division had been present since the seventeenth century, it now became the major division in Iroquois society, even though the Christians were not particularly devout. Both sides agreed that they should not allot reservation land to individuals or move to new reservations in the west, as they were being pressured to do.

In the early decades of the century, pressure increased on the Senecas to sell their remaining lands. The Senecas sold much of their territory to Ogden in the 1826 Buffalo Creek Treaty, but still retained four large tracts in New York at Buffalo Creek, Tonawanda, Cattaraugus, and Allegany. They also continued to hold the tiny reservation at Oil Spring, which remains Seneca today. The lands sold included the portion of the Gardeau Reservation on the Genesee that Mary Jemison had not sold in 1823. Annuities were paid for manufactured goods and the labor of white gunsmiths and blacksmiths, and this eased the continuing economic transition.

The Handsome Lake religion was becoming codified by this time and was being recited at annual events. The women Faithkeepers at Tonawanda asked Jemmy Johnson (Shosheowa'), Handsome Lake's grandson, to recount the teachings of Handsome Lake. He politely declined and was just as politely asked again, a formality often followed in Iroquois tradition. He did the job well and it was so successful that they decided to do it every year at Tonawanda. So it was that Tonawanda became the center of The Good Message, the longhouse religion as conceived by Handsome Lake. The teachings of Handsome Lake as recounted by Jemmy Johnson were first recorded in 1845 by Eli Parker, a Seneca sachem who would later achieve fame as a Civil War general. Still later, in 1848, the teachings of Handsome Lake as recounted by Jemmy Johnson were recorded by Lewis Henry Morgan, Parker's friend and arguably the founder of American anthropology.[5] Later anthropologists erroneously concluded that there had been a lapse in the teaching of the Code of Handsome Lake between the time of his death and these events of the 1840s. This has even been followed by the further fiction that the oral tradition has changed little since 1850. But the truth is that the code has been recited more or less continuously, and with the steady modifications inherent in all oral tradition, ever since 1815.[6]

### The Buffalo Creek Disaster

The New York State Legislature permitted and ratified leases of Allegany Reservation land to non-Indians in 1835. Three years later the traditional Seneca sachems sold out completely to the Ogden Land Company. In the 1838 Buffalo Creek Treaty the Iroquois gave up not just the four remaining Seneca reservations but also their allocation in Wisconsin. The deal was that the Senecas would give up everything and move to Kansas. Ogden paid only $202,000 for this fraudulent purchase of land worth over $2 million. Moreover, only 43 of the 81–91 chiefs signed the treaty: of these, sixteen had been bribed and still others were coerced. Some of the signatures were simple forgeries.

Most Senecas were outraged by the fraud and opposed to any removal to Kansas. They had the help of the Quakers and other non-Indians in western New York, and in 1842 they were able to negotiate a compromise agreement. Unfortunately, even the compromise was a defeat, for it required the Senecas to give up both the Buffalo Creek and the Tonawanda reservations, leaving them with only Allegany and Cattaraugus. The Buffalo Creek council fire was moved back to Onondaga. The New York League wampum was also returned to Onondaga after Captain Cold, the firekeeper at Buffalo Creek, died at Tonawanda in 1847.

By 1840, the state was trying to tax Indian lands that it claimed had been sold in 1838. The United States Supreme Court struck down the offending statute. New York was clearly trying to turn the Iroquois into just another set of citizens, and the state continued to try to ignore the federal Constitution on this point. On the other hand, the state also began providing education and health care on reservations.[7]

### The Mohawks and Oneidas

Eleazar Williams was a Caughnawaga Mohawk who had also lived at Akwesasne before settling among the Oneidas to preach the Episcopal faith. He managed to convert most traditional Oneidas to Christianity by 1816, finishing the work begun by his missionary predecessor, Samuel Kirkland. Williams proposed that the Oneidas sell their land in New York and move to a new location near Green Bay, Wisconsin. New York politicians and the Ogden Land Company were eager to see this happen, and Williams somehow persuaded most of the Oneidas to negotiate for land with the Menominees and Winnebagos of Wisconsin. They started moving in 1823 and by 1838 there were 654 Oneidas in Wisconsin.

The disastrous 1838 Buffalo Creek Treaty split the remaining New York Oneidas into three factions. Some left to settle on land they purchased near London, Ontario. There were few League Chiefs in this group. However, Six Nations chiefs came by and helped them set up a council of eighteen hereditary chiefs, nine of them League Chiefs. This arrangement was very much like that found earlier at Buffalo Creek and later at Tonawanda. The other two Oneida factions comprised those who wanted to stay and those who wished to move somewhere other than Wisconsin or Ontario. By 1848 there were only 200 Oneidas left in their traditional homeland. Three years earlier New York had passed legislation to permit allotment of Oneida land to individuals. The gradual alienation of most of their land followed over the next 100 years. Meanwhile, some additional Senecas and Cayugas from Buffalo Creek joined their relatives in Oklahoma in 1846. New York was gradually losing even the last remnants of the Iroquois nations.

### Cultural Retrenchment

Abraham Hogeboom recruited Iroquois to move to Kansas. He needed some minimal number, and eventually had to recruit even some Canadian Iroquois to make his quota. Sixty-six Senecas migrated west to Kansas in 1848. What they found was treeless prairie rather than paradise. Twenty-six of the Kansas Senecas soon died. All but two of those that did not die came back. Euro-American settlers flooded Kansas after this and simply squatted on the land that had been reserved for the Iroquois. The Seneca then moved to recover compensation for the lost land.[8]

In 1841 the chiefs at Six Nations Reserve realized that the continuation of Joseph Brant's policies was leading to the gradual alienation of virtually all of their land. In response to government concerns, they agreed to surrender most of their remaining land to the Crown to be held for them in trust. The Canadian government then evicted all non-Indians from the reserve, and secured its boundaries for the future.

In 1848 the Allegany and Cattaraugus Senecas adopted elected governments out of fear that the traditional chiefs would sell them out again. Many people wanted annuities to be distributed directly to heads of households rather than through the traditional chiefs. Cattaraugus and Allegany thus formed the Seneca Nation of Indians, ruled by a council of sixteen elected chiefs. The Tonawanda Senecas did not participate in this because they were still holding out on their land. They had not agreed with the fraudulent land sale of 1838 and none of their chiefs had signed the compromise agreement in 1842. They consequently felt that none of the sales was binding on them. They held out for a just settlement, and believed that any tampering with the traditional system of government would weaken their case. Time would prove them right. The Onondagas too continued to be governed by a traditional council of the 14 League Chiefs plus 13 assistant chiefs (Thadodaho does not have one). Some parts of this system of government and the council fire of the New York League of the Iroquois still survive at Onondaga.

At the beginning of the century the Mohawks at Akwesasne were governed by hereditary chiefs appointed by clan mothers in traditional fashion. There were 12 of these, three from each of four clans. In addition to the Turtle, Bear, and Wolf clans, the Mohawks had acquired the Snipe clan, probably by absorbing Cayuga people of the Snipe clan who had lived for a time at Oswegatchie. In 1802 the New York State Legislature passed a statute that led to the election of three Akwesasne Indians as trustees for the tribe. The state subsequently conducted its business with these chiefs. The hereditary chiefs continued as well, being responsible for internal affairs. In 1818 the Mohawks on the United States side of the boundary at Akwesasne were allowed to form a local government. The three trustees continue today as the three elected chiefs of the tribal council.[9]

### Morgan and the Iroquois

Most people think of Indian agents as government bureaucrats, but the nineteenth-century Iroquois had an agent in the twentieth-century sense. An upstate New York lawyer made both himself and the Iroquois famous by inventing anthropology and promoting the Iroquois as his primary subject.

Lewis H. Morgan was born in 1818 in Aurora on Cayuga Lake. He was a natural organizer, starting a boys' club to read the classics before going on to Union College in Schenectady. Later he founded a club named The Gordian Knot, made up mostly of former Cayuga Academy students. After a time he converted it to The Grand Order of the Iroquois, which he conceived as a new Iroquois confederacy that would replace the dying old one. He sought to organize additional chapters in other towns. When one eventually formed at

*Figure 10.2  Lewis H. Morgan as a young man*
*Source: University of Rochester*

Waterloo, it became the Seneca chapter. The Aurora chapter thus became known as the Cayuga chapter.

Morgan and his friends initiated Abram La Fort, a well-known Onondaga, into the Cayuga chapter in 1844, probably so that they could have him as a source of information on how an Indian society should be organized. Morgan's reading of Stone's biography of Joseph Brant and other books did not give him the information he wanted.

Morgan then happened to encounter Eli Parker in an Albany bookstore. Morgan was in town on business, and Parker was there to interpret for three Tonawanda chiefs who were visiting the capital. Parker was eager to learn about United States law and Morgan was eager to learn about the Iroquois, and they immediately became friends.

Morgan met the chiefs that evening. They included Jemmy Johnson, Handsome Lake's principal disciple, and a nephew of Red Jacket. Morgan quizzed them about names for Iroquois chiefs and other officers. He found out that the Senecas had eight League Chiefs and two War Chiefs. He also found out that they had eight clans. From this he jumped to a series of false conclusions. He surmised:

*Figure 10.3    Eli Parker*
*Source: photograph courtesy of the New York State Museum.*

1 that each clan had a League Chief,
2 that each of the six nations had eight clans,
3 that each of the six nations had eight League chiefs, one from each clan,
4 that there were therefore 48 League chiefs for the six nations, and
5 that each nation had two War Chiefs.

Morgan thus served as a model for all anthropologists who jump to premature conclusions in the early stages of their work. The chiefs had said that there were about 50 League Chiefs in all, and Morgan took that to mean 48. In fact they gave an approximate number because there was disagreement about whether the unfilled Mohawk position originally held by Hiawatha should be counted. But Morgan did not yet have any notion of the (to him) unfamiliar principles underlying the structure of the League, and he incorrectly attempted to solve the puzzle using a Eurocentric algebra.

Morgan later presided over the annual council of what he called the "New Confederacy," at which time the club made changes in the constitution based on what Morgan thought Parker and Johnson had told him in Albany. They decided that the New Confederacy would have six nations and that each would be comprised of eight "tribes" corresponding to the eight clans of the Senecas. That would allow for 48 chapters. Morgan also came up with Seneca words for the offices of sachem, head warrior, prophet, treasurer, and librarian. The prophet was in charge of initiations ("indianations"), which were everyone's favorite activity. Morgan decided that only the Wolf and Snipe tribes could have head warriors, because that was all the old League allowed. Morgan delivered speeches about the inevitable replacement of the old League by the new league. At this stage of his life he was clearly still acting out juvenile fantasies.

Eli Parker came to Aurora to become an honorary member of The Grand Order of the Iroquois and to tell the boys some of the realities of Iroquois life. Parker also enrolled in the Cayuga Academy, but went to Washington the next year at the time the Smithsonian was founded. Joseph Henry, the first secretary of the Smithsonian Institution, also moved to Washington from Albany when the institution was founded.

Morgan moved to Rochester later in 1844. There he began to have some financial success, making a fortune as a corporation lawyer; he also went to Albany to serve in the legislature for a while, and began to organize a Turtle tribe of the Seneca nation. The new chapter had eight charter members, including Morgan.

In Rochester Morgan was still the "grand tekarihogea" of the new league, so he was responsible for the annual meeting in Aurora in 1845. He got Henry Schoolcraft to come to Aurora from Albany in August of that year to speak. Schoolcraft was writing a report on the Six Nations for the legislature. The meeting involved yet another modification of the constitution. This one involved the addition of offices for the leader of the war songs and the keeper of the wardrobe. Morgan was by this time styled "supreme chieftain of the Iroquois." The thrust of Schoolcraft's speech was that The Grand Order of the Iroquois should give up its adolescent games and turn to a serious study of the Iroquois.

In September 1845 there was a notice in the *Rochester Daily American* that there would be a meeting of the Grand Council of the Six Nations at Tonawanda. This was to be a condolence council in which new chiefs would be raised up. Morgan and some of his "sachems" attended in order to find out how it was done. It was his first field trip.

Morgan spent some time talking to Abram La Fort, who had also arrived early, finally getting a proper list of the 50 League Chiefs. The condolence council began a day late, but Morgan observed that the Mohawks, Onondagas, and Senecas were on one side and the Oneidas, Cayugas, and Tuscaroras were on the other. Several chiefs had been lost from both sides, and they would raise up replacements at this ceremony. In this case a Seneca chief was the most important of those who had recently died, and the Mohawks, Onondagas, and Senecas were given the role of the bereaved. No one on the clear-minded side knew the ritual, so an Onondaga man named Captain Frost was borrowed from the bereaved side for the purpose of conducting the ceremony.

On the next morning everyone gathered to hear Jemmy Johnson deliver his annual speech, a recounting of the message of Handsome Lake. He spoke for nearly three hours, and Morgan was delighted by the experience despite his inability to understand even a single word. Later Morgan got more information on the structure and procedures of the League through Parker. He learned that there were subchiefs that were raised up at the same times as sachems (League Chiefs), and he also learned that men like Joseph Brant and Red Jacket had been Pine Tree Chiefs, a class different from League Chiefs. These were self-made men possessed of high intelligence and oratorical skills. Even if they came from families that held sachemships, they were considered too charismatic to be appointed to such positions. At about the same time, the teachings of Handsome Lake as recounted by Jemmy Johnson were recorded by Eli Parker.

Morgan wrote to Schoolcraft after this trip, addressing Schoolcraft as "Alhalla" and signing the letter "Schenandoah." Both of these were names that the men had assumed without any apparent prompting from the Iroquois. Morgan promised to write a paper on Iroquois government, and he did so in less than a month. He delivered the paper in Rochester, then did so again in New York as he made his way to Washington to help defend the Tonawanda Senecas in their effort to hold on to their reservation. Morgan had traveled to both Buffalo Creek and Tonawanda in 1845 and 1846 in order to gather information for this purpose.

Yet another new constitution was adopted by the New Confederacy in 1846. Morgan was still the grand tekarihogea and supreme chieftain of the Iroquois. This time they dropped the Tuscarora from the list of League Chiefs and made a few other changes. In the following two years, Morgan published a series of letters in the *American Review*. These later became the core of his book on the League.

In 1847 Governor John Young asked Morgan to acquire Iroquois artifacts for the Cabinet of Natural History in Albany. Morgan made three trips in 1849–50 to Tonawanda and Grand River. He eventually acquired 478 specimens, which were cataloged as 269 entries. In 1911 a fire in the New York State capital building burned all but 71 of the specimens Morgan had acquired.

Morgan also recorded the teachings of Handsome Lake and other information from Jemmy Johnson in 1848 and 1849. Curiously, he took little notice of the medicine societies. This was perhaps because they had been driven underground by the Handsome Lake movement, but it is just as possible that Morgan was simply not interested in them. Later in 1850 Morgan made a trip to Grand River to acquire more specimens. This latter set is preserved along with his papers in Rochester.

Morgan assembled most of this when he published his *League of the Ho-dé-no-sau-nee* in 1851. John Wesley Powell regarded this as the Bureau of American Ethnology's first scientific account of an Indian tribe. Morgan married his cousin, Mary Elizabeth Steele, that same year, and this turned out to be a watershed in his life. He gradually put his New Confederacy notions behind him and turned to more serious scholarship. The organization subsequently died.

In that same year, Francis Parkman published the first of his historical volumes on the conflict between France and England in America. Parkman visited the Onondaga in 1845, but he was no ethnographer, and he had little success eliciting information from the Indians. Morgan used Cadwallader Colden, Charlevoix, and Baron de Lahontan, and he corresponded with Parkman. But he was as uncomfortable with history as Parkman was with ethnography. Nonetheless, because of the influence of both men, the myth of Iroquois empire began to revive. The emerging importance of anthropology and his own role as a founder of the discipline were recognized when Morgan joined the American Association for the Advancement of Science at its meeting in Albany in 1856.[10]

# 11

# The Worst of Times, 1850–1900: The Hunting Moon

The myth of Iroquois empire began to revive after 1850 because of Lewis Henry Morgan's work. With the help of Eli Parker, Morgan gained an increasingly detailed grasp of Iroquois social and political structures. After the 1851 publication of the *League of the Ho-dé-no-sau-nee*, he moved steadily away from playing at being an Indian and toward the serious scholarship that Schoolcraft had urged upon him. This first scientific account of an Indian tribe focused attention on the Iroquois generally and on their system of government in particular. There would soon be attempts to codify that system, to make its oral tradition look more like a modern constitution. The effort paralleled attempts to make Handsome Lake's message look like a Euro-American religious document.

In fact the nineteenth century was a time of widespread religious and social experimentation in New York. Joseph Smith invented Mormonism in Palmyra, New York, in the 1820s, William Miller sowed the seeds of Seventh-day Adventism in 1844, and John Noyes led his followers to establish their utopian community at Oneida in 1847. It was also the heyday of the Shaker movement, which had started out near Albany around the end of the previous century. Neither the Iroquois nor those who could only wish that they were Iroquois were unaware of these and other social/religious movements of the day. Thus much of what was said and written about the Iroquois in the second half of the nineteenth century was reinvention along lines paralleling those movements. Yet through it all, Morgan's work became increasingly objective and careful. Though it may have inspired others to write nonsense, Morgan's own work remains valuable to researchers today.

Morgan was elected to the National Academy of Sciences in 1875. He published *Systems of Consanguinity and Affinity of the Human Family* in 1871, *Ancient Society* in 1877, and *Houses and House-life of the American Aborigines* in 1881. He was a peer of Charles Darwin, Herbert Spencer, and Edward Tyler. Friedrich Engels, who worked with Karl Marx on the *Communist Manifesto* and carried on after Marx's death in 1883, was very taken with Morgan's work. Engels emphasized Morgan's place in history but played down the latter's associations with Francis Parkman, Henry Adams, the Pundits of Rochester, and other capitalists. Morgan died in 1881 at the age of 63, having made a secure place for both himself and the Iroquois in the history of anthropology.

### Holding on to the Land

As the second half of the century began, the Senecas at Allegany and Cattaraugus were still trying to recover payment for the lands they had occupied and then abandoned in Kansas. While many Senecas continued to press for compensation, others feared that they would be forced to abandon their lands in New York if they pursued the matter. A majority even voted against pursuing the claims in 1857. The Senecas had also to contend with state officials who still believed that the language of the United States Constitution regarding Indians did not apply to states that had once been among the thirteen original colonies. In 1856 the state comptroller first argued that the Senecas at Cattaraugus owed the state back taxes, then announced that the state would sell off reservation lands to cover the alleged debt. Of course, both taxing the Indians and selling their land would have been a violation of federal law, so the attempt failed.[1]

The Tonawanda Senecas were finally able to buy back part of their reservation in 1857, but had to give up their share of the Kansas claims in order to do so. Later they adopted a modified form of government with some traditional chiefs and some elected chiefs. This eventually came to be a council of eight League Chiefs and eight subchiefs. Jemmy Johnson died at about this time, but Tonawanda still remained the center of the Handsome Lake religion. A committee at Tonawanda was formed to approve men to preach the *Gai'wiio* at other reservations. In more recent times the Six Nations Meeting has still been called there every fall to recount the teachings of Handsome Lake. In the weeks that follow that meeting, the teachings have been repeated at other longhouses on Iroquois reservations and reserves. Akwesasne and Kahnawake were not included in this circuit. The cycle has been such that it has been heard in every longhouse at least once every two years. The oral tradition has varied in the telling, as it has since 1815.

By 1860 the Senecas were secure at Allegany, Cattaraugus, and Tonawanda, although still under two tribal governments. The Onondagas persisted with a traditional form of government. The Cayugas had all but disappeared in New York, and the Oneidas dwindled on their ever-shrinking allotments. The Grand Council of the New York version of the League of the Iroquois has survived, but has had no formal recognition from the United States government. Treaties were and continued to be negotiated with the individual nations.

### The Canadian Iroquois

In Canada the Senecas and Oneidas were weak at the Six Nations Reserve, but the Confederacy Council there managed to find men to fill all 49 League Chief positions by assigning some names to lineages that had not traditionally held them. The Oneidas that had moved to the Thames in the 1840s were outside this organization and did not send League Chiefs to meetings at Six Nations.

The Canadian government recognized the Six Nations Confederacy Council as the appropriate group to speak for all the Iroquois. Curiously, the same did not happen in New York. Neither the state nor the federal government recognized the Grand Council for formal purposes. Some treaties were supposedly conducted with the New York Grand Council, but this was largely fiction. Few if any League Chiefs had been present at the 1784 Fort Stanwix Treaty. Similarly, the Fort Harmar (1789), Canandaigua (1794), and Buffalo Creek (1838) treaties had all been conducted largely without them.

### The Kansas Claim

The Seneca Nation of Indians, now led by elected chiefs, eventually decided to pursue the Kansas claim and hired agents to do this on a contingency basis. While the Tonawanda band had given up their share of the claim, the other Senecas had not. Some Seneca factions still thought that this was a bad idea and wanted to go back to a government of traditional chiefs. Serious factionalism ensued at Allegany and Cattaraugus. The Kansas claim was debated endlessly, but without any representation from Tonawanda, from 1857 to 1898.

The Kansas claim became a rallying issue for all of the Iroquois of New York, and it breathed new life into the League Council at Onondaga, by this time often called the New York Confederacy

Council. The League Chiefs were unable to reach consensus in the 1888 New York council. They adopted a traditional Iroquois technique to resolve the impasse, dividing up into groups to discuss the matter. The six groups were the Seneca nation, the Oneidas living with the Onondagas, the Onondagas, the St Regis Mohawks, the Tuscaroras, and the Cayugas. Up to this time the St Regis (Akwesasne) Mohawks had not been included in the New York League, and their inclusion marked their formal adoption into the League. The six discussion groups, using a technique as old as Iroquoia but as modern as corporate America, eventually achieved consensus by appointing two agents from every group to act together in pursuing the claim.

The Iroquois were granted federal permission to sue in 1893. They were awarded almost $2 million in 1898. With the settlement, the New York League became much less visible to the non-Indian world and appeared to some outside observers to have ceased functioning. The Kansas claim had kept the profile of the New York League high until the end of the nineteenth century, but as the new century approached, some Iroquois and many of the Euro-Americans around them thought that it was an obsolete institution, and acted accordingly.

### The Civil War

The Iroquois had participated in Euro-American conflicts since early in the seventeenth century. Prior to the War of 1812 their roles had been largely those of scouts and guerillas. By the time of the American Civil War, they were serving in ordinary cavalry and infantry units, fully integrated with Euro-Americans and receiving the same pay. Most served in New York units, although there were some Iroquois in units from Wisconsin, Pennsylvania, and other northern states. Three even served in what were then called Negro regiments.[2]

Army service provided the outlet that combat had always given the Iroquois. It was time away from claustrophobic reservation life and the tensions of ever-present factional disputes. It was also a source of cash for young men having little other access to it.

The Iroquois were at first not allowed to join the army because no law could be found permitting it. Despite his education and experience as a civil engineer, Eli Parker (Donehogawa) was initially rebuffed when he sought an officer's commission. The United States Secretary of State bluntly told him that this was a war between white men, and that Indians should stay out of it. At the time, Indians were not considered citizens, and could not successfully apply for citizenship. In 1862 the government finally decided to allow Indians to enlist, although they were not covered by the draft. Various Iroquois fought in nearly every battle after March 1862. Enlistment of Wisconsin Oneidas was delayed for several more months because the Sioux uprising in Minnesota had made Wisconsin officials generally fearful of Indians. The Oklahoma Iroquois remained officially neutral throughout the war, although a few joined the home guard in Kansas. The few Iroquois still living in Kansas became refugees in the face of raids by Quantrill and his raiders.

When the war was over Washington forced the Iroquois in Indian Territory to apologize for having agreed with the Confederate states to remain neutral. Thus even though no Iroquois had fought for the south and many had fought for the north, the Oklahoma Iroquois were regarded as traitors. The condemnation led to forced land sales.

Eli Parker eventually gained a commission with the help of an old friend from his days in Illinois, Ulysses Grant. Parker became an aide to Grant, valuable because he was more literate than most soldiers, and was present at the surrender at Appomattox. He eventually rose to the rank of brigadier general. Still later, when Grant became president, he appointed Parker commissioner of Indian affairs.[3]

The Civil War moved the Iroquois who stayed home away from subsistence farming and towards market-oriented production, just as it did other farmers. The aftermath brought a new wave of non-Indian population increase, and with it new pressures on Indian land. The war had done nothing to halt the decline in their fortunes, but it set a pattern of voluntary service by Iroquois in the United States military that persists today.

### The Dawes Act

The Dawes General Allotment Act of 1887 clearly defined the direction of United States federal Indian policy. Indians were to be integrated into Euro-American society. Policy-makers thought that the way to achieve this was to encourage the speaking of English, conversion to Christianity, and the pursuit of Euro-American livelihoods wherever possible. Allotment of reservation lands to individuals was designed to break up traditional political institutions and to encourage the growth of family farms in the Euro-American tradition.

The formal and informal pressures on the Iroquois nearly succeeded. By 1900 American Indian populations, as measured by tribal enrollments, bottomed out. Many elders were convinced that the old ways were irrelevant, and even those who disagreed acknowledged that they were dying. The Bureau of American Ethnology had been established to salvage and describe whatever it could of American Indian cultures before they disappeared. As well intended as these early anthropological efforts were, they contributed to the fatalistic view of Indian cultures as inflexible, eroding anachronisms. While Euro-American culture was allowed to be dynamic and adaptive, Indian cultures were conceived as static institutions for which change could only mean loss. Indians and non-Indians alike accepted this ruinous concept of Indian cultures, leaving them nowhere to go but down an inward spiral to oblivion.

### Giving up Tradition

By 1878 only twelve wampum belts remained at Onondaga. Four of the belts were sold to Thomas Webster in 1891. In 1898 the Iroquois nations of New York elected the University of the State of New York as official custodian of the five wampum belts still remaining at Onondaga. The belts were turned over to the New York State Museum. In 1908 the director of the State Museum was proclaimed keeper of the wampum by the president of the Six Nations in New York. The four belts sold at Onondaga to Thomas Webster in 1891 were bequeathed to the New York State Museum in 1927, where they remained until 1989.

The Canadian government took steps similar to the Dawes Act in 1888. Until then they had left the Mohawks at Akwesasne alone, for the most part. However, in that year they passed an Order in Council that replaced the twelve hereditary chiefs at Akwesasne with an equal number of elected councillors, later to become a band council. The pretext was that the hereditary chiefs had been guilty of malfeasance. From this time on Canada dealt with Akwesasne through the band council while the United States dealt with the international community through the tribal council. The hereditary chiefs continued, but were ignored by both federal governments.

Mohawks also continued to live at Caughnawaga (Kahnawake) and Kanesatake (Oka). In the 1880s a group of Mohawks left Kanesatake and established a small community near the modern town of Parry Sound, Ontario. This location near Lake Huron's Georgian Bay is just north of ancient Huron territory. The community called itself Wahta, but would later be more commonly known as the Gibson Reserve.

Traditional Iroquois beliefs persisted with only some modification through the second half of the nineteenth century in many places. Horatio Hale published a description of the burning of a white dog

*Figure 11.1   The Washington Covenant wampum belt*
*Source: photograph courtesy of the New York State Museum and*
*the Iroquois Grand Council.*

in 1885, when the sacrifice was still being practiced. Hale observed this at a Midwinter Ceremony held at a Six Nations Reserve longhouse. The dog was supposed to be pure white, but this one had spotted ears, perfect specimens being hard to find. The animal was strangled, then laid out in the longhouse. It was decorated with red spots, a string of wampum, feathers, and colored ribbons, perhaps a vestige of treatment once accorded human prisoners.[4]

This was a genuinely heartfelt sacrifice. The Iroquois prized their dogs, and each one sacrificed was almost certainly someone's pet. Yet there was no better way to genuinely cast off one's sins than to give up something one truly valued. Tobacco was burned, the smoke rising and carrying a message of thanks to the sky. Near the end of the Midwinter Ceremony the dog was burned as well, the smoke carrying the accumulated sins of the community skyward.

Political deliberations at Six Nations also preserved traditional forms. They were conducted in Mohawk, and the Mohawk–Seneca side always spoke first. The matter then passed across to the side of the Cayugas, Oneidas, and the dependent nations (Tuscarora, Delaware, Nanticoke, and Tutelo). After discussion the matter was returned to the Mohawk speaker, who announced the decision to the Onondagas. The Onondagas had veto power as executives, deciding

*Figure 11.2   The League Chiefs at Six Nations Reserve around
1910*
Source: Rochester Museum and Science Center, Rochester,
New York.

upon whether the decision was in the best interests of the League as
a whole. The speaker and interpreter were generally Mohawks, and
they had considerable power to control outcomes. Thus the Mohawks
dominated, even though they were a minority on the reserve.

The Mohawks also took greater advantage of missionaries and
education. They were more thoroughly Christianized and were more
committed to agriculture early in the century. The Onondagas tended
to be conservative and adherents of the traditional longhouse religion.

The first movement to switch to an elected form of government
occurred in 1861–2. Most Mohawks and Onondagas were initially
opposed to the idea, although for very different reasons. The Onondagas
were conservative and withdrawn, and they distrusted any change
in the traditional government. The Mohawks were innovative and
confrontational, but they had been successful in manipulating the
traditional government. Both sides thus had reason to fear the institution of a new elected form of government. The 1869 Indian Act in
Canada split the two sides. The lower chiefs (mostly Onondaga)
wanted to reassert the traditional League structure in the face of
Canadian domination. The upper chiefs (mostly Mohawks) wanted to
go along with the Canadian government for at least some purposes.

The 1869 law also mandated a patrilineal basis for the determination of Indian band membership, and put an emphasis on legitimate birth. Both principles were completely contrary to Iroquois traditions. The uncertainties caused by this ignorant act led to political and social conflicts on Canadian reserves that are still surfacing today.[5]

## Reviving Tradition

A new figure rose to prominence amid the debate over government at Six Nations. Seth Newhouse sided with the Onondagas (his mother's people) even though he spoke Mohawk (his father's language) more fluently. He also sided with the warriors, a faction that favored using nativistic arguments to promote innovative policies. Newhouse acted as a Pine Tree Chief and drafted a version of the League constitution in order to validate and codify the position of the conservative chiefs, for he was on their side in opposing interference by the Canadian government.

Newhouse's manuscript was not accepted by the Six Nations chiefs in the 1890s. J. N. B. Hewitt, a Tuscarora scholar, said that this was because Newhouse did not understand the structure of the League. William Fenton has said that it was because the document was too heavily biased toward the Mohawks. The Newhouse version would have also silenced the assistant chiefs and dependent nations' chiefs, who by 1884 made up about half of the council.[6]

The Newhouse version tells us as much, if not more, about political conditions on the Grand River at the end of the nineteenth century than it does about the origins of the League. Problems centered on the dominance of the Mohawks, efforts to replace traditional chiefs with elected chiefs, and customary indecision in the traditional council. Newhouse was deposed in 1884 on grounds that he had traveled too much to New York, among other things. That travel had been prompted mainly by his desire to gather information on traditional League structure. In any case, the chiefs reaffirmed the traditional form of government even while rejecting Newhouse's codification of it.

Newhouse retired from political life, but resurfaced in the 1890s when there was another movement to adopt a system of elected chiefs. But by this time it was too late. Even the traditional chiefs had adopted a system of standing committees that made things operate fairly smoothly, and reversion to the old League format seemed unnecessary even to the conservatives. In 1899, the chiefs set about creating their own written version of the League's constitution under the leadership of Seneca chief John Gibson. Gibson was assisted by chiefs Jacob Johnson and John Elliott. The official copy was made by Hilton Hill, another Seneca, and this one too was reviewed by Albert Cusick. This version, written in perfect English, was approved by the chiefs in 1900. No mention was made in this text of the longhouse of the Six Nations. This might have been because the longhouse image was too closely associated with the Handsome Lake movement at the time. However, the Canadian Iroquois also wanted to avoid reference to the metaphorical longhouse, which was previously located entirely in New York.[7]

## Old Age

The Iroquois chiefs were old, and they felt the weight of their years. The years were counted as winters, the hardest of the seasons. An old person was one who had survived many winters. White hair is the sign of an elder, a mark of wisdom, and one who possesses it is due respect. Iroquois oral traditions required the lifelong dedication of people with exceptional memories and oratorical skills. As their abilities to remember recent events inevitably faded, the clarity of old memories served the elders well, and they became encyclopedic bearers of tradition.

The death of anyone left a void, but the death of an elder left an especially deep one in the corporate memory. His or her name returned to the pool owned by the clan, perhaps to be used again when a suitable child reached adolescence. The death of a sachem was particularly traumatic, for a giant pine had fallen, and it was necessary to raise it up again by appointing a new man to the title. But as the century ended, many thought that there would be no real continuation of this great tradition, a view that was encouraged by United States and Canadian government policies.

The elders of this era appeared to think of their society as old too, and the giving up of the wampum belts was a sign that at least some of them thought that Iroquois culture was near the end of its time. As their numbers dwindled, and as Euro-American culture engulfed them, the Iroquois clung mainly to the less vital trappings of their culture.

## Lacrosse

One such trapping is the game of lacrosse (Figure 11.3). Like the longhouse, wampum belts, and medicine masks, lacrosse is quin-

*Figure 11.3  Modern lacrosse game*
*Source: courtesy of the Iroquois Indian Museum, Howes Cave,*
*New York.*

tessentially Iroquois. The game has been a part of Iroquois culture for centuries, perhaps for as long as the Iroquois have lived in the region. It was and is a sport that could be played at any time during the warm months of the year. In recorded history, lacrosse was played on a field between goals 200 to 400 meters apart, depending upon the number and skill of the players. The goals themselves were pairs of upright posts, 3–5 meters long and set 3–9 meters apart, with a cord strung between them to define the goal mouth. The egg-shaped wooden ball was carried in the netting of lacrosse sticks, which might have originally been modeled after traditional Iroquois hoes.

The teams decided how many points would constitute a win at the beginning of the game. After that, almost anything was allowed. To score, the players had to throw or carry the ball through the goal defended by their opponents. Tripping, throwing, holding, and charging were all allowed, so the games quickly became very rough. Many players were severely injured, and a few were known to have been killed while playing.

Players fasted, bathed, and purged themselves before games. Shamans were hired to help one side or the other. Players were chosen at the beginning of the game in pairs. Individuals were matched as closely as possible in terms of their sizes and skills, then the pairs were split into two teams. Goalkeepers, called "door guards," were positioned in front of the goals. The game began much like the modern game does, with the two team captains holding the ball between their sticks. Truly great players were those who could elude an entire opposing team, carrying the ball the length of the field and into the goal for a score. Spectators bet heavily on the outcome, sometimes losing everything, and the game was usually followed at night by a feast and social dancing.[8]

# 12

# The Rise of Modern Iroquois, 1900–1950: The Cold Moon

## The Great Law at Six Nations

John Gibson continued to be an important chief at Six Nations into the twentieth century. The official chiefs' version of the Iroquois constitution, as Gibson and the other chiefs had edited it, was accepted in 1900. Although called a constitution in order to make it look like a political document, it was really much more than that. The actual narrative has three parts. First is the story of Deganawida and the conversion of Thadodaho. (A summary of this story appears in Chapter 4.) The second part is the story of the conversion of the nations, and their coming together as the League of the Iroquois. The third part is a recitation of the principles or laws of the League.

J. N. B. Hewitt worked with Gibson, recording the chiefs' version in Onondaga. But Gibson was not happy with this version, and thought about writing his own. Hewitt was a Tuscarora Iroquois who lived from 1859 to 1937. The Bureau of American Ethnology was founded when Hewitt was 20 years old, and he later joined it as a rare Indian scholar who was committed to recording as much as he could of his own culture. He and Arthur Parker carried most of the load of Iroquois ethnography during the first quarter of the twentieth century. Hewitt was himself a religious man, and was very interested in what he saw as the traces of "aboriginal thought" in Iroquois mythology.[1]

Hewitt published a version of the legend of the founding of the Iroquois League in 1892, and a discussion of the constitution in 1920. In both of these he sought the essential prototype among many versions. Of course, he never found it, for in an oral tradition there is always variation around a general theme. Hewitt went many times to the Six Nations Reserve, revising his earlier work each time in his search for original versions of various myths and tales.

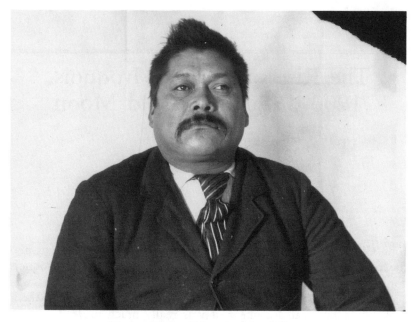

*Figure 12.1   John Arthur Gibson*
*Source: Smithsonian Institution.*

Constitution

Arthur Parker went to Six Nations in 1910 to make casts for the old New York State Museum life groups (Figure 12.2). He met Seth Newhouse and various other chiefs at that time, and discovered that manuscripts codifying the constitution of the League existed. This was news to him, even though scholars like Hale and Hewitt had known about them for years. Parker gave Newhouse's manuscript to Albert Cusick, a New York Onondaga/Tuscarora, for review and criticism, although he later implied that it was Newhouse who had done this. Cusick, who had previously worked with Hale and Beauchamp, worked on the manuscript for a month.[2]

In 1912, John Gibson dictated another longer version of the constitution in Onondaga to Alexander Goldenweiser. Gibson died later in the same year, as did Albert Cusick. Gibson's 1912 version is the most extensive and authoritative of all the written versions of the oral tradition concerning the League, yet it remained unpublished until 1992, when Hanni Woodbury brought out the definitive edition of this classic version.[3]

Before Woodbury took up the task, William Fenton had worked with Simeon Gibson, Hardy Gibson, Howard Sky, and James Skye to produce their own translation of the 1912 Gibson manuscript.

*Figure 12.2  Seneca harvest: museum life group constructed by
Arthur Parker*
*Source: courtesy of the New York State Museum.*

Fenton subsequently analyzed the first and second parts of the legend
of Deganawida and the formation of the League, isolating 179 specific elements. He then compared this list to elements identified in the
chiefs' (1900), Newhouse's (1880), and six other earlier and more
fragmentary versions of the legend. Despite the additions, omissions,
and rearrangements expected of oral tradition, the structure of the
legend is preserved in all of the versions. Indeed, given the variable
nature of oral tradition, it can be argued that one cannot understand
it as anything less than all its versions. Fenton's analysis remains only
partially published.[4]

Parker published heavily edited versions of both the Newhouse
and the chiefs' versions in 1916, failing to mention that the latter had
already been published by Duncan Campbell Scott in 1911. Newhouse
had originally divided his version of the recitation of the principles
of the League into 123 laws grouped in three sections, each associated with a string of wampum. The three sections were called Tree
of the Long Leaves (1–69), Skanawita's Laws of Peace and War
(70–84), and Emblematical Union Compact (85–123). Parker rear-
ranged everything into a sequence of 117 laws grouped into 16 topic
categories, but one can still reconstruct the original order laid out by
Newhouse from parenthetical codes supplied by Parker.[5]

Table 12.1 summarizes Parker's 117 laws and the general categories to which he assigned them. It is important to realize that he
reordered Newhouse's version of the Great Law substantially so that

Table 12.1   Outline of the Great Law as published by
Arthur Parker

| Laws | Sections |
| --- | --- |
| 1–16 | General principles |
| 17–34 | Rights and duties of League Chiefs |
| 35 | Election of Pine Tree Chiefs |
| 36–41 | Rights and duties of War Chiefs |
| 42–54 | Clans and consanguinity |
| 55–65 | Official symbolism |
| 66–70 | Laws of adoption |
| 71–2 | Laws of emigration |
| 73–8 | Rights of foreign nations |
| 79–91 | Rights and powers of war |
| 92 | Treason or secession of a nation |
| 93–8 | Rights of the people of the Six Nations (93–6 borrowed from Lafitau and given to Newhouse by Hewitt) |
| 99–104 | Religious ceremonies protected |
| 105–6 | Installation song |
| 107 | Protection of the longhouse |
| 108–17 | Funeral addresses |

he could group them in sections that made sense to him and brought the Great Law into closer conformity with a Euro-American political constitution. It is also important to remember that all versions of the Great Law vary substantially, as one should expect of a complex covenant sustained in oral tradition. From that perspective, Parker's elaborate editing can be viewed as just another variation on the theme, neither better nor worse than any other.

Goldenweiser was livid. Parker had not mentioned Scott's prior publication, and he had edited the Newhouse version so extensively that it had been converted into an essentially modern document. What had started out as a code had become a political constitution in Parker's hands, and Goldenweiser was not about to let him get away with what he regarded as a fiction.

Hewitt blasted Parker in his own separate review. He accused Parker of failing to explain the differences between the Newhouse and chiefs' versions, for not mentioning that one was intended as a substitute for the other, and for failing to report (or perhaps even to know) that the Newhouse version had been around for 30 years prior to Parker's discovery of it. He even pointed out that some sections that Newhouse had included were based on information that he (Hewitt) had found in Lafitau and had later given to Newhouse.

Hewitt was himself guilty of not fully understanding the nature of oral tradition. Hewitt looked vainly for the one true version of the Great Law, apparently regarding all of the available versions to be flawed derivatives. But there was no King James to command the creation of a single true text from the available alternatives.

Newhouse also worked with Hewitt, rendering his version of the constitution in Mohawk. At the same time, Newhouse was active in trying to get back the Six Nations wampum, which the keeper had sold to a dealer in Wisconsin. Newhouse died in 1921 at the age of 79. The traditional chiefs of the Six Nations Reserve would be displaced by elected chiefs three years later.

### The Decline of Traditional Leadership

In 1915 the Thames Oneidas in Ontario established a second (elected) chiefs' council, like the hereditary one but separate from it. The hereditary chiefs were Christian, not traditional followers of the longhouse religion. Although they did not hold titles in the League of the Iroquois maintained at Six Nations, they had been in the habit of attending its meetings. In 1921 the Thames Oneidas became involved in a land claim case brought by the Onondagas against New York. The hereditary Oneida chiefs, all of them Christians, stopped going to Six Nations and started going to Onondaga for condolence councils and other League matters, a move that drew them out of the Canadian League and into the New York League.

An elected council finally replaced the traditional government at Six Nations in 1924, and the Royal Canadian Mounted Police seized their remaining wampum. The League Chiefs continued to meet and occasionally attempted to reassert themselves, but without much success. Levi General (Deskaheh), a Cayuga League sachem at Six Nations, even tried to carry their case to the Council of the League of Nations in Geneva. This made him unpopular at home, and he eventually died in exile among the New York Iroquois.

The Thames Oneida hereditary chiefs' council continued, but by 1934 it was meeting once again at Six Nations. An elected council had by this time replaced it as the effective government.

Six Nations

## The Iroquois in New York and Quebec

The State of New York believed that it had an Indian problem, and investigations of it had begun as early as 1855. Once the problem was defined, solutions were not slow in coming. Christianization was proposed as necessary to stamp out paganism. Education, preferably at boarding schools, was proposed as a means to break up intransigent social organizations. Allotment of reservation lands to individual Indians was proposed as a means to promote initiative and free enterprise. All of this was to culminate in the gift of American citizenship, which few Indians coveted. Similar events occurred in Canada, where the Indian Act was imposed upon the Mohawks at Kahnawake in 1877. The act instituted an elected band council in place of the traditional council of chiefs on the reserve.

In 1900, Governor Theodore Roosevelt appointed a commission headed by James Whipple, a Salamanca lawyer, to study the perceived problem once again. The aim of Roosevelt and his commissioners was to solve the Indian problem by assimilation. The goals that whites cherished for the Indians were all reiterated in the Whipple Report. Traditional Iroquois values and traditions were disparaged. Christianization, allotment, and citizenship would lift the Iroquois into civilization.

Whipple had another agenda. He was a friend of Congressman Vreeland of Salamanca, and the two of them concocted a plan to get the Senecas themselves to buy off the Ogden claim. The Ogden Land Company still had the exclusive right to buy Seneca land, and men like Vreeland were eager to find a way to force allotment and eventual resale under the terms of the Dawes Act of 1887. But the Ogden claim was too strong to be extinguished, and the city of Salamanca, like the rest of Seneca land, remained in Indian country. Ironically, the Ogden Land Company was thus partly responsible for the survival of the Seneca nation in New York in the first decades of the twentieth century.

Nearly all of the efforts of the New York State legislature to deal with the Iroquois in the twentieth century have focused on efforts to expand jurisdiction over the Indians and draw them under state sovereignty. New York and many other states wanted the power to extinguish Indian land claims, but the federal government reserved that right, if perhaps not for the most noble reasons. The Iroquois were able to survive the nineteenth century in part because the conflicts between the states and the federal government put them once again into a position of being able to play one dominant force off against another.[6]

Another state commission, the Everett Commission, began its work in 1920, just months after the *United States* v. *Boylan* decision had established that the New York Indians were wards of the federal government. Edward Everett issued a report in 1922 in which he stated plainly that the Iroquois had a legitimate claim to six million acres of western New York, having been illegally dispossessed of them since 1784. The other commissioners did not all agree with Everett's report, and anxious state officials made sure that it was buried.

Despite (or perhaps because of) the political currents running against the Iroquois in both New York and Canada, traditional practices revived and spread. The longhouse religion finally came to Kahnawake in the 1920s. It reached Akwesasne in the 1930s. After that, both were included in the biennial circuit of the Code of Handsome Lake. Although the Mohawks of Akwesasne had been admitted to the New York League in 1888, they remained out of the loop of the Handsome Lake revival for another half century. The longhouses at these two reservations also reinstituted hereditary chiefs, who have since come to challenge the authority of the elected chiefs. Kahnawake has even raised up two sets of League Chiefs, sending one set to Onondaga and the other to Six Nations.[7]

Yet the Iroquois balanced traditionalism by embracing the modern world in other parts of their lives. In 1883, St Regis Mohawks found work with the Canadian Bridge Company, which was building a new steel bridge at Cornwall. The Kahnawake Mohawks first learned about high steel work in 1886, when the Victoria Tubular Bridge was built across a lower section of the St Lawrence River. By the turn of the century, many Mohawks were working on a new bridge to span the St Lawrence at Quebec City. On August 29, 1907, the uncompleted southern part of the new span collapsed, killing 33 men.

Despite the catastrophe of 1907, Mohawks continued to be drawn to the new profession. High steel provided Mohawk men with lives not unlike those of their ancestors. They were away from home, working for long periods in a lucrative but high risk profession. The work required physical skill and extraordinary nerve. By comparison the whiskey bottle offered only a fool's courage, for the steel work demanded absolute sobriety. To work high steel put an Iroquois man in touch with his heritage. For the first time in a century, he had access to the kind of prestige and wealth that the ancient chiefs could have understood.

Iron work also inadvertently clarified another issue. In 1925, a Kahnawake Mohawk named Paul Diabo was arrested in Philadelphia as an illegal alien. The arrest was based on the Immigration Act of 1924, which had been passed mainly to keep Asians out of the

*Figure 12.3    Three Mohawk steel workers, left to right:
Angus Mitchell, Joseph J. Jocks and John Alexander Fisher
Source: photograph courtesy of Kanien'kehaka Raotitiohkwa
Cultural Center.*

United States. Diabo argued that he was a Native American, and as such was protected from United States and Canadian immigration regulations by the 1794 Jay Treaty. Clinton Rickard, a Tuscarora, assisted Diabo by establishing the Indian Defense League of America in 1927. Diabo won the case, and as a result the Iroquois still cross the United States–Canada border without impediment. The Indian Defense League still celebrates the victory by staging an annual Border Crossing Ceremony in July.

The Citizenship Act of 1924 made all Indians citizens of the United States, something that many Iroquois did not want. With it came a new threat to sovereignty, an issue that would still be unresolved 60 years later when some Iroquois would travel abroad using passports of their own creation. Beyond these largely symbolic moves, the reality was that the Iroquois were slowly being more fully integrated into Euro-American society. In 1932 the children at Tonawanda became the first of New York's Indians to be integrated into the local public school system.

### The Federal Retreat

The Indian Reorganization Act of 1934 finally defined the word "tribe" for federal purposes. This was a crucial definition because the word was used in connection with a major provision of the United States Constitution. The Act saved some communities from the destruction that was being caused on other reservations by land allotments made to individuals under the terms of the 1887 Dawes Act.

The federal government provided little funding to Iroquois reservations until the programs of the New Deal. Even then it was resisted by activists like Alice Lee Jemison, a Cattaraugus Seneca, who campaigned vigorously for the abolition of the Bureau of Indian Affairs. The state, on the other hand, had several programs for health, education, transportation, and other needs on reservation lands. But there was a cost to the Indians. The Iroquois had to repeatedly fight off attempts to expand state jurisdiction.[8]

The issue came to a head again in 1942 when Senecas brought white leaseholders in Salamanca to court for failure to pay their rent. The entire city of 3,570 acres still sits on leased land on the northern end of the Allegany reservation of the Seneca Nation of Indians. In 1942 leaseholders were paying trivial rents of a few dollars a year, but even these amounts were resisted by people who hoped to wrest the land from Seneca control. The Senecas stood firm, once again looking ahead seven generations while their opponents took a shorter view. The leases would expire in 1991.

In 1948, Congress passed the Criminal Jurisdiction Transfer Act. This Act, passed by large margins in both houses, transferred jurisdiction over criminal matters on Iroquois reservations from the federal government to New York State. Two years later Congress transferred civil jurisdiction as well. This was another move to integrate the Iroquois into Euro-American society. New York would eventually come to wish that it had not been given this gift, for it made the state responsible for the resolution of Iroquois disputes that state officials often could not fully understand, much less resolve.

Congress also defined Indian country in 1948. The definition extended not just to reservations but also to individual allotments made to enrolled members of federally recognized tribes. Thus the definition extended the concept of Indian country beyond the boundaries of reservations, an extension that would become important with the growth of Indian-owned land in the 1980s and later.[9]

### The Approach of Midcentury

The longhouse religion declined generally in the first half of the twentieth century. However, three Seneca longhouses survived. These are the Tonawanda longhouse, the Newtown longhouse at Cattaraugus, and the Coldspring longhouse at Allegany. The last was forced to move from Coldspring to Steamburg in 1965 because of the Kinzua Dam project. Each of these longhouses continues to practice some but not all of the traditional ceremonies. At the same time, longhouse practices spread to Akwesasne and Kahnawake, where Roman Catholicism had been almost universal for over two centuries.

Traditional practices were kept barely alive in many places by people who no longer quite believed in them, and who did not yet embrace them as vital symbols of their cultural heritage. Like many of the Euro-Americans who now surrounded them, many Iroquois paid lip service to traditional beliefs and superficially observed a few annual ceremonies. Anthropologists lamented that the elders who knew the old languages and rituals were dying off without passing the full oral tradition on to younger people. William Fenton describes Seneca men wearing medicine masks roaring along the road at Allegany in an open Model T Ford, their long hair whipping in the wind and their turtle shell rattles beating against the side of the car. It was a modernized observance of an ancient ritual that must have at once gratified, amused, and disappointed an observer.[10]

At mid-century the Iroquois were at risk of succeeding and failing at the same time. Their reservation populations had rebounded from their nadirs of 50 years earlier and many families were individually prosperous. Well-intentioned federal and state Indian policies had failed to convert the Iroquois into just another minority in the larger American society, and the boundaries of most reservations and reserves had stopped shrinking. Yet the Iroquois were still faced with cultural extinction. It was common for non-Indians to ascribe Indianness only to those who sincerely retained all the prescribed attributes: language, dress, beliefs, and subsistence practices. Most Americans were the descendants of immigrants who had gladly abandoned their cultural heritages in order to become "real Americans," and they expected Indians to do the same. Acculturation theory, which dominated anthropological thought at the time and which defined nearly all culture change as loss, seemed to support this view.

Many Iroquois wondered how they were to retain their cultural identity in the face of a larger society that seemed to be telling them that it was all but gone. How could a Mohawk who spoke only a few words of the Mohawk language, dressed in standard middle-class American clothes, drove a late-model Oldsmobile, and made a good living working on high steel ensure the cultural survival of his descendants to the seventh generation? The dilemma was not made easier by well-meaning anthropologists and historians who focused their attentions on elders, and thereby signaled to younger Iroquois that they were beyond rescue. To survive into the next millennium, the Iroquois would have to reinvent themselves once again, and at the same time convince the larger American society that cultural reinvention is itself a legitimate course of action.

# 13

## The Contemporary Scene, 1950–2000: The Very Cold Moon

The Iroquois have undergone endless transformation since their first contact with Europeans.[1] In the second half of the twentieth century outside forces have come in two forms, one of them obvious and often reprehensible, the other more subtle. One of the more obvious forces has been modern industrial development, which has threatened several reservations as explained in more detail below.

Another obvious force has been the United States federal government. After World War II the government adopted a policy of termination. Indians were to be encouraged to leave reservations and join mainstream American society. Eventually their reservations, even the Bureau of Indian Affairs, were to be terminated. The policy, which promised to free the Indians, plunged most of those accepting it into urban poverty. The Iroquois reservations all fought the policy. The Oneidas of Wisconsin and the Seneca–Cayugas of Oklahoma were the most threatened, but even they staved off termination.

At a more subtle level, the Iroquois face the same overwhelming influence of Euro-American culture that confronts cultures everywhere as the century draws to a close. Satellite dishes and cables ensure that television sets are as ubiquitous on reservations as they are elsewhere. Through this and other media the Iroquois are as aware as anyone else of the dominance of Euro-American speech, music, dress, and the rest of popular culture. This too has to be accommodated and resisted at the same time.[2]

### Tuscarora

Tribal government at Tuscarora is still based on hereditary chiefs, as it is at Onondaga and Tonawanda. Clan mothers still nominate chiefs to assume sachemships for life when vacancies arise.[3]

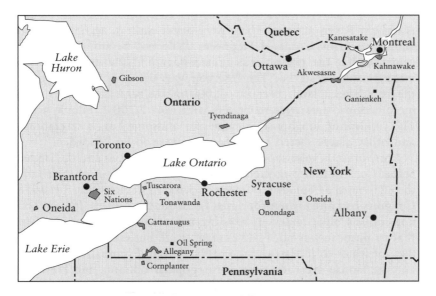

*Figure 13.1   Modern Iroquois reservations and reserves in the northeast*

In the late 1950s, a fifth of the Tuscarora Reservation was taken as a reservoir for the New York Power Authority. The Tuscarora resisted in the courts and behind the barricades, but in 1960 the United States Supreme Court overturned a Federal Power Commission ruling in favor of the Tuscaroras and the project went ahead. Although they lost, the Tuscaroras inspired other Indian nations to stand firm at a time when threats from development were increasing everywhere.

Some Tuscaroras attempted to open a bingo hall there in 1987, but a brief episode of violence put an end to the project.

### The Allegany and Cattaraugus Reservations

Since 1848 the Senecas of the Allegany and Cattaraugus reservations have been governed by an elected government and known as the Seneca Nation of Indians. In the 1960s, a third of the Allegany Reservation was taken for the Kinzua Dam project. This was the heyday of big projects undertaken by the Army Corps of Engineers. Expensive projects having high environmental costs and questionable value were still being funded. The United States government decided that the project was necessary in order to control flooding on the Allegheny River, although there were better ways to accomplish that end.[4] The Army Corps of Engineers could not be stopped, despite evidence that the project was unnecessary and the plan of action incompetently designed. The reservoir was to cover 9,000 acres of the best Seneca land. Because 12,000 of the remaining acres were mountainous, they were to be left with only 2,300 habitable acres. The Coldspring longhouse, the site of Handsome Lake's revelations, and other places sacred to the Senecas were to be flooded.

Army officials were shocked to discover that treaties and the United States Constitution protected the Indians from the loss of their land through normal eminent domain proceedings. However, by 1958 Congress had already appropriated funds for the project. Indians and non-Indians alike joined in resisting the project as it became clear that its purpose was not flood control at all, but rather to ensure the flow of water to industries around Pittsburgh. Eventually the Senate and the House overrode good sense, popular opinion, and President Eisenhower's veto, and authorized the project.

The Senecas sued and collected over $15 million, but their traditional homes were lost under the rising water. About 130 families were forced to relocate to Steamburg and Jimersontown. Burials were dug up and relocated on higher ground. Family homes were vacated and burned. Removal of the Coldspring longhouse fire to a new longhouse in Steamburg in 1965 required a nine-hour ceremony.[5]

A short section of the New York State Thruway was built through the Cattaraugus Reservation in the 1950s. Later the State of New York extended the Southern Tier Expressway through the Allegany Reservation as well. In both cases the Senecas have occasionally demanded the return of land or provision of adequate compensation. The negotiation of and compliance with various agreements between the state and the Senecas regarding that project have often been unusually speedy because unlike non-Indians, the Senecas have been able to use the option of closing the roads when faced with a dilatory bureaucracy.

Cattaraugus was also the site of the Thomas Indian School, which had been established with all good intentions in 1875. Like other Indian schools, it was supposed to serve to integrate Indian children into Euro-American society by forcing them to speak English and to dress and act like non-Indians. Eventually the overcrowded, obsolete, and segregated school was taken over by New York State. It was closed in 1957, the official reason being the need to reintegrate children into mainstream schools. Cost was probably a more important but less presentable reason.

The rise of Salamanca as a major railroad hub in the nineteenth century led the Senecas to lease parcels of land to non-Indians for residential and commercial development. The courts invalidated the leases in 1873 because they had not been approved by Congress, but the federal government then went ahead with a new series of leases. The leases signed in 1892 were to run for 99 years. Thus 1991 was a deadline that was first forgotten, then challenged, and finally dreaded by the residents of Salamanca. Some leases were renegotiated early, but others continued to yield only trivial rents right up to the end. The Senecas, holding the upper hand for the first time in centuries, were magnanimous. Although many of the residents disliked the short term of their new 40-year leases, and others were upset to find that they were never going to gain title, few argued with the fairness of the new rental agreements. The United States Supreme Court rejected an effort to overturn the Senecas' position. In 1991 new leases were signed, and the Senecas entered a new era as powerful landlords. The city of Salamanca found out how powerful only a year later, when they were billed nearly $120,000 for interest and late charges on delinquent rent payments. Some former leaseholders had refused to sign new leases or to pay their rent, but the city found itself responsible for collecting and paying the entire bill owed to the Senecas.[6]

### Akwesasne

Akwesasne persists as a longhouse divided against itself. The community straddles the international boundary, which the 1794 Jay Treaty, by which all Indians may move unimpeded across the United States–Canada border, allows the Iroquois to ignore, at least in their daily routines (Figure 13.2). While the situation at Akwesasne provides some benefits to the Mohawks there, it has also set up conditions that encourage smuggling and unusually complex political factionalism. The United States recognizes only the elected St Regis Mohawk Tribal Council; the Canadian government deals only with the Mohawk Council of Akwesasne, the "band council" mandated by Canadian law. Meanwhile the central fire of the traditional Mohawk Nation Council of Chiefs continues to burn there as well. Quebec and Ontario police have jurisdiction on their respective portions of the Canadian reserve. The New York State Police have jurisdiction on the United States reservation.[7]

Akwesasne lies 80 kilometers upstream from Kahnawake on the St Lawrence River. The St Lawrence Seaway project did less direct and immediate damage to Akwesasne than it did to Kahnawake.

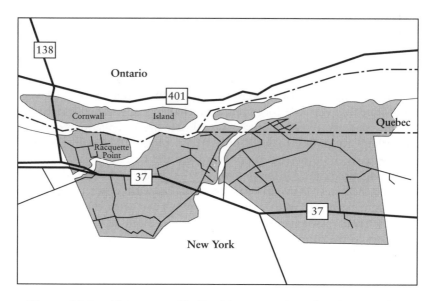

*Figure 13.2    Akwesasne (St Regis) reservation showing portions
lying in Ontario, Quebec, and New York*

Akwesasne straddles the river as well as the boundaries of New
York, Quebec, and Ontario. The seaway thus passes through the
middle of this reservation/reserve. The United States government
expropriated 88 acres of Racquette Point and Barhhardt Island
was taken for dam construction in the 1950s. The Canadian government expropriated land for the construction of a bridge and customs
facilities. Suits calling for just compensation are still in the courts,
although a Mohawk blockade of the bridge in 1969 was necessary
to get the Canadian government to recognize the implications of the
Jay Treaty. A year later, Mohawk occupation of two more islands in
the river prompted the Canadian government to recognize that they
were part of the St Regis Reserve.

Damage in this case has come mainly from heavy industries that
grew up along the seaway just upstream (and upwind) from
Akwesasne. Aluminum and other pollutants have rendered fish in-
edible and gardens hazardous, damaging the quality of life of Mohawks who have lived there for nearly as long as they have been at
Kahnawake.

A strong desire among traditionalists to preserve Mohawk culture
led to the creation of the North American Indian Traveling College
in the 1960s. Traditionalists have also built and operated the

Freedom School for younger children. However, these initiatives have not been universally admired, and both armed confrontations and incidents of arson have marked disputes between the traditionalists and various progressive factions.

Traditional longhouse Mohawks barricaded themselves on Racquette Point on the United States side of the St Regis (Akwesasne) Reservation in May 1979. The dispute flared up over a minor issue, the specifics being now almost irrelevant. The root cause was the fundamental conflict between the longhouse traditionalists who claimed political sovereignty for the Mohawk nation and recognized the League sachems as their only legitimate government, and the elected reservation governments recognized by the United States and Canada. The longhouse Mohawks viewed the tribal council on the United States side as a corrupt puppet of federal and state authorities, a device for maintaining the dependency of reservation Mohawks.

Reservation police had arrested a man who had stopped a tree-cutting project. The traditionalists demanded that the police become right-minded by resigning. This they asked three times in traditional Iroquois fashion. At one point some of them took over tribal police headquarters. The elected government responded by requesting police assistance from the state. And so it was that a little forestry turned into an armed confrontation. Like most human confrontations, this one began with preconditions that took decades to develop, and an immediate cause that seems almost insignificant in retrospect.

A negotiated solution was found in July, but this was scuttled by a county district attorney who refused to drop charges against Loran Thompson, the traditional chief who had stopped the tree cutting in the first place. The stalemate lasted nearly a year. In June 1980 armed supporters of the elected government went to Racquette Point and threatened to attack the barricaded longhouse faction. State troopers arrived, but took no action. The longhouse faction was convinced that the state, which had funded a large increase in the tribal police force, would side with the elected government in the standoff.

The state dithered, caught between an elected government that had federal recognition and a monopoly on legal standing on the one side, and the traditional leadership that enjoyed most of the popular sympathy of non-Indians on the other. Members of the press, unable or unwilling to study the vast Iroquois literature fully enough to understand the complexities of the situation, listened to whoever represented themselves most convincingly as legitimate Mohawks, then rushed off to write unintentionally biased, incomplete, but highly emotional articles for their newspapers.[8]

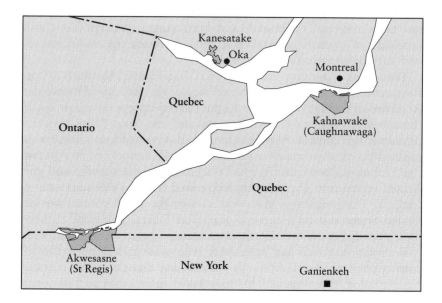

*Figure 13.3　Modern Mohawk reservations in eastern Ontario, southwestern Quebec, and northern New York*

The tribal police force was abolished in 1981, a move that calmed both sides in the standoff. The void in local law enforcement would eventually be filled by self-appointed members of the progambling Mohawk Warrior Society.

Gambling started with a relatively noncontroversial bingo parlor, as it had on many Indian reservations in the United States. By 1984 high stakes bingo was booming, and this soon began to evolve into other forms of gambling. Traditional Mohawks believed that it could turn into a corrupt monster. Progambling Mohawks said that it was the chance they had been waiting for to bring economic self-sufficiency to the reservation. A line was drawn in the sand, and Mohawks began to choose sides.

Gambling was not an issue on the Canadian side, where Indians do not enjoy the gambling option allowed under United States law since 1981. However, even in the United States many reservations, including Akwesasne, are covered by state laws. Las Vegas style casinos operate on federal reservations in places like Minnesota, but transfer of law enforcement from the federal government to New York earlier in the century meant that the Mohawks were constrained by New York's gambling regulations. Nevertheless, high stakes bingo was tolerated by the state, and bigger things were being planned.

In July 1985, Rosemary Tarbell Bonaparte became the first woman to be elected to the tribal council at Akwesasne. By being in favor of gambling on the reservation and indeed by standing for election at all, she aligned herself against some of the longhouse traditionalists. This time most newspaper reports in the non-Indian press appear to have seen it as correct to write articles favorable to a woman chief who was characterized as "standing up to the traditional chiefs of the 'Longhouse'." Once again the non-Indian press resorted to currently popular notions in Euro-American society in its attempt to explain what was going on in an Indian community.[9]

Writing mostly around 1984, Louis Karoniaktajeh Hall produced a manifesto for the Warrior movements at Akwesasne and Kahnawake. In it Hall condemned the Handsome Lake religion and the longhouse beliefs of most of the traditional sachems that are active today. Hall and others in the Warrior movement referenced Iroquois traditions that predated Handsome Lake's revelations of nearly two centuries ago and the religious revival that flowed from them. This revived the distinction between the Old Religion and the New Religion that was commonly made during the years in which Handsome Lake preached his message. Hall was raised a Roman Catholic at Kahnawake, a religious tradition that is older than the Handsome Lake revival among the Iroquois by two centuries. But he rejected this too. He joined the longhouse traditionalists in 1963, taking the name "Karoniaktajeh," but he veered on to a more radical track in a few years. The popular press discovered Hall's writing by 1990. His call for the execution of traditional League Chiefs, his condemnation for cowardice of the great peacemaker Deganawida, and his belief that Euro-Americans should all be sent back where they came from, all make for sensational reading.[10]

By 1987 the situation had changed again. This time the traditional chiefs were asking the state to send in troopers to seize slot machines that were turning up in local stores. The progambling faction had by this time coalesced as the Warrior Society. For their part the Warriors opposed state police intervention, and they threatened armed conflict if the troopers were sent in.[11] In June, New York State Police raided Tony Laughing's casino and seized 192 slot machines. Laughing was charged under state law with promotion of gambling.

On January 9, 1988, arsonists burned the building housing *Akwesasne Notes* and *Indian Time*. The first was a pan-Indian publication that had been publishing for decades, while the second was a younger newspaper that was distributed mainly to Mohawk readers. Douglas George, a traditionalist, was a writer and editor for both. The two newspapers did not cease publication, but the incident forced them to relocate and marked a serious escalation of the conflict.

State and federal officials raided seven casinos at Akwesasne in July 1989, arresting thirteen more Mohawks. State police then sealed off the reservation, setting up road blocks on the state highway running through it. While state officials complained about the high cost of the action, League Chiefs at Onondaga condemned the Warriors and the casinos. In another reversal of positions in a single decade, the Warriors now claimed Mohawk sovereignty while the traditional chiefs sought government intervention. The blockade lasted ten days. Transfer of federal powers on reservations to the state 40 years earlier gave the state power and responsibility that officials by now wished they did not have.

Less than two weeks later the elected chiefs tried to conduct a referendum on the gambling issue. Traditional chiefs anticipated a progambling victory and protested the voting. The antigambling faction was determined not to vote at all, a rejection not just of gambling but of the whole Euro-American notion of voting and majority rule. The elected chiefs then backed down, and sought ways to involve all factions as well as Mohawks on the Canadian side in the decision-making process. Balloting was eventually conducted, with a majority of those voting approving gambling.

The largest casino reopened in August but one was burned down later that month. State police blockaded the reservation once again, and the Warrior faction braced themselves for an anticipated assault by the troopers. But the troopers held back while the traditional chiefs and the two elected councils met to try to find common ground. This "Tri-Council," which had been meeting for years on various issues, labored sporadically to resolve the deep political divisions in later months, but without success.

The casinos reopened with both the traditionalists and the Warriors condemning the tribal council. In January 1990 a man walked into one of the casinos firing a shotgun into the air and sending patrons diving for cover. The incident was said by some to be the result of a personal dispute, but others asserted that it followed months of harassment by the Warriors, who by now had appointed themselves as the Mohawk Sovereignty Security Force in charge of protecting the casinos and maintaining order. Over 100 antigambling Mohawks traveled to Albany to ask Governor Cuomo to intervene, but he declined, reminding all sides of their past claims of sovereignty.

Despite the conviction of one of the casino owners, Tony Laughing, in February, the gambling continued. State troopers kept their distance and the threat of violence actually attracted larger crowds of gamblers. By late April there were armed groups of traditionalists facing equally well-armed Warriors of the Mohawk Sovereignty Security Force, and violence seemed inevitable. Governor Cuomo tried to soothe all sides, but as the weather warmed gunshots were heard in the night-time. Meanwhile there was an armed confrontation between troopers and Mohawks at the new community of Ganienkeh, when the police attempted to arrest a man suspected of having fired on a National Guard helicopter a month earlier.

Antigambling Mohawks blockaded roads leading to the casinos, but progambling Warriors tore the barricades down late in April. Brian Cole, an antigambling leader, was seriously injured in this confrontation. Leaders on the Quebec side of the reservation decided to evacuate about 150 people on the last Friday of April. By 1990 there were perhaps 7,000 people living on the reservation/reserve. Despite the imminence of violence, New York's Governor Cuomo stood firm on his refusal to send in police or guardsmen.

The gunfights in the night-time finally led to the deaths of two men on May 1, 1990. Matthew Pyke, an antigambling activist, was mortally wounded during a battle in the dark. Harold (Junior) Edwards, whose sentiments about gambling seem to have been less clear, was found dead the next morning. New York State Police, the Royal Canadian Mounted Police, and Quebec police sealed the reservation off in a joint operation late the next day. About 500 of them then occupied the portions of the reservation/reserve under their respective jurisdictions, while Ontario police and army troops from both Canada and the United States waited in readiness.

The traditional chiefs were relieved. The Warrior Society and the elected chiefs were defiant. Newspaper reporters seeking to understand the conflict and write engaging stories struggled with shifting definitions of terms like "chief" and "nation," often making sense only to those who already had a better grasp of the situation. Both sides in the conflict argued for Mohawk sovereignty, but both sides had also called for outside intervention when it had been in their interests to do so.

The tribal council and the band council met with federal mediators a few days later. The Justice Department mediators also met with traditional chiefs, but these leaders felt that they were being left out of the loop. Meanwhile Governor Cuomo, eager to get state police off the reservation, called for the creation of a new Indian police force. Negotiations stalled when Harold Tarbell, head chief on the tribal council, refused to participate. Tarbell was opposed to gambling, while the other two tribal chiefs, Lincoln White and David

Jacobs, were both regarded as progambling. Tarbell and some of the traditional chiefs instead went to Albany to meet with Cuomo, whom they regarded as an obstacle to progress. Cuomo's position was that only elected chiefs could participate in formal negotiations. A day later Tarbell agreed to join the other two elected tribal council chiefs in a meeting with Cuomo.

On May 11 a raid by Canadian police revealed that there was more than just gambling at stake at Akwesasne. Cocaine, cannabis, and weapons were seized in the raid on the Ontario portion of the reserve. Akwesasne had long been a conduit for smuggled cigarettes and oil products, all sold tax free to both Indians and non-Indians.

Three days later Quebec police charged Douglas George with the murder of Harold Edwards. Others were also arrested and there was confusion when Canadian authorities realized that because of their Indian status, the defendants could not be forbidden to leave the country, a normal condition of bail. No one was ever charged in the death of Matthew Pyke, and the charges against George were eventually dropped for lack of evidence.[12]

Two of the men arrested with George had been members of the Akwesasne Mohawk Police on the Quebec side, a force that had continued after the disbanding of the tribal police on the United States side. The antigambling faction had found shelter on the Quebec side, and the gunfire that had led to the two deaths had been exchanged largely across the international border between the antigambling faction on the Quebec side and armed members of the Warrior Society on the United States side. The Akwesasne Mohawk Police resigned its commission with the Quebec Provincial Police over the affront.

Meanwhile, Governor Cuomo finally met with traditional Mohawk chiefs in Albany. Cuomo stood firm on his position that formal resolution of the conflict would have to involve only elected leaders. Nevertheless it was expedient for him to meet with the traditional chiefs, a recognition of ancient protocol in Albany.

By the end of June many Mohawks were trying to unite Akwesasne by refocusing anger on a common enemy. Environmentalists were recruited in a campaign against the pollution caused by the nearby Reynolds Metals, ALCOA, and General Motors plants. The move did more to confuse non-Indians, who were still trying to find non-Mohawk bad guys to blame for the mess, than it did to refocus the Mohawks themselves.

Early in July Harold Tarbell was replaced by a progambling cousin, Norman Tarbell, as an elected chief. Both the traditional Mohawks and the Warrior Society boycotted the election on grounds that the elected tribal council violated Mohawk sovereignty. Canadian-side Mohawks might have voted as they had done earlier in the century, but they were forbidden to do so by a New York State Supreme Court ruling. At least one reporter was moved to admit that "sorting out the various groups and their specific interests in such a situation is nearly impossible; Akwesasne can be an enigma to outsiders."[13] Another writer cut through the confusion by simply blaming everything on Mario Cuomo.[14] A state assemblyman, ignoring the United States Constitution, federal and state laws, and recent history, introduced legislation to establish self-government at Akwesasne, as if there were some simple solution that everyone else was avoiding.

As gambling evolved from vice to economic development in the eyes of many Mohawks, so too did it evolve in the thinking of Governor Cuomo. By the end of June, Cuomo was considering compacts with Indian reservations that would allow gambling so long as the state could receive some of the income. The traditional chiefs felt betrayed, but legislators saw a means to help close a budget gap that was widening every year. According to newspaper accounts, the eight casinos and bingo halls at Akwesasne were back in business. By the middle of August, the elected tribal chiefs, now all progambling, were able to consolidate their power. Antigambling tribal staff members were forced out. A year after the murders, at a time when traditional Mohawks believe that the souls of the dead could eventually go to the Other Side, the New York State Police were still maintaining an uneasy peace. The antigambling tribal personnel who had been fired the previous August had been reinstated by a state supreme court judge.

Akwesasne has its own land claims that are now stalled in the legal system. Small parcels that were reserved to the Mohawks in the treaty of 1796 were subsequently given up between 1816 and 1845, but without federal approval. These parcels include a square mile on the Salmon River, and another square mile at modern Messena. Boundary changes after the War of 1812 and subsequent deals also resulted in the loss of land at Akwesasne proper. Negotiation of these complex legal cases is one of the tasks of the Tri-Council at Akwesasne.

Some Akwesasne Mohawks have established themselves in a new home in the Mohawk Valley. They are traditionalists seeking to escape the pollution and political clashes surrounding gambling at home. If they are successful in this new effort, many other traditional Mohawks could also eventually leave Akwesasne, leaving the reservation to the progambling faction. Such a move would perhaps mean the end of the longhouse and the shadow government of League sachems at Akwesasne, leaving local power in the hands of the elected tribal council on the United States side and the band council on the Canadian side of the reservation.[15]

### Ganienkeh

Dissident Mohawks and volunteers from other nations occupied a deserted girls' camp at Moss Lake in the Adirondacks in 1974. Two non-Indians were wounded in the action, in which the Indians asserted that they were taking back ancestral land. The Indians distributed a Ganienkeh Manifesto after the takeover, in which they argued for unification of American Indians from all over the continent, and for formation of an independent North American Indian state.

In the end they settled for substantially less. The Turtle Island Trust was set up in 1977 to act as an intermediary between Ganienkeh and the State of New York. The state gave the community use of 700 acres of state-owned land at Minor Lake in the Town of Altona. Questions then arose as to whether or not the new community was Indian country as defined by the federal government. In some respects it is, but the Ganienkeh community was not federally established and is not federally recognized. Bingo operations continue there amid legal uncertainty but with permission from the state.[16]

The tension at Akwesasne spread to Ganienkeh early in 1990. On March 30 an Army National Guard medivac helicopter was forced to make an emergency landing after being hit by rifle fire while passing over the reservation. A doctor on board was wounded by at least one of three bullets that pierced the helicopter. The Ganienkeh Mohawks then sealed off the reservation and refused to allow the state police to investigate, claiming sovereign status. State police surrounded the reservation and the Mohawks answered with their own barricades.

A month passed before the state police attempted an arrest. Shots were fired and the troopers backed away. Meanwhile gunshots had become a nightly occurrence at Akwesasne, and traditionalists there claimed that Ganienkeh was being used as a refuge by outlaw members of the Akwesasne Warriors Society.

Three months after the incident, a federal grand jury finally indicted 16 Ganienkeh men. In March 1991, one was arrested while off the reservation under a warrant charging him and others with blocking investigation of the helicopter incident. Up to this point only four of the 16 charged had been arrested, for most remained either blockaded at Ganienkeh or in Canada.

## Kanesatake

In April 1990 the little town of Oka, Quebec, made a seemingly innocuous decision to expand its golf course. Residents of the adjacent largely Mohawk reserve of Kanesatake objected, arguing that expansion would carry the golf course on to reservation land. The confrontation led to yet another armed standoff between Mohawks and (this time) Quebec police. Warriors from Akwesasne went to Kanesatake to assist at the barricades, bringing with them weapons and fighting skills. The police moved in on July 11, and there was sustained fighting in which one Quebec police officer was killed. No one knew which side had fired the fatal shot in the course of the fight.

The police continued to blockade the reserve, hoping to starve out the community of 3,000. Mohawks at the nearby Kahnawake Reserve blockaded the Mercier Bridge in solidarity with the people at Kanesatake. Prime Minister Mulroney refused to involve the federal government. Two weeks later the provincial government decided that it might buy the disputed Kanesatake land from the Mohawks, a proposal that completely missed their point. The Mohawks then made their case to a United Nations panel, while Quebec Premier Robert Bourassa continued to treat the matter as if he were dealing with cornered outlaws. While the United Nations Subcommission on Human Rights appealed to Bourassa to rescind his ultimatum to the Mohawks, the Canadian federal government prepared army troops to move in. Meanwhile nearby non-Indian youths in Chateauguay were rioting over the bridge closing and alleged police brutality. Indian groups in Ontario, Manitoba, and British Columbia also began setting up road blocks in sympathy with the Quebec Mohawks. Protesters even appeared outside the Canadian embassy in Washington. The Mohawk Warriors put themselves on "red alert" and broke off talks with the government as the army moved closer at the end of August. Prime Minister Mulroney made it clear that he would never agree to the escalating demands of the Mohawks, and the army tightened its perimeter.

The Quebec government ordered the removal of all the barricades late in August. By now Mulroney was fully involved, and he urged the Mohawks to back down in the face of over 3,000 army troopers. The heavily armed Warriors made no move. By August 29, negotiations had reduced the outstanding issues to only two. John Mohawk, a Seneca mediator from New York, reported that Mohawk demands for immunity from prosecution and government demands for a surrender of weapons remained the only two sticking points.

In September the federal government purchased the disputed 92 acres of land from its non-Indian claimants, a move that cleared the way for them to convey full title to Kanesatake. The arrangement ended the siege, and both sides removed their barricades.[17]

### Kahnawake

From 1955 to 1959, the United States and Canadian governments worked cooperatively on the St Lawrence Seaway project. The authority created for this purpose seized 1,260 acres of the Kahnawake Reserve in order to construct a canal bypass around the Lachine Rapids. A portion of the village that had been there for well over two centuries was sliced away. Chief Matthew Lazare formally complained to the United Nations Human Rights Commission, pointing out that the Mohawks were being offered only monetary compensation, and that it was less than what was being offered to nearby non-Indian landowners. The commission expressed its sympathy, but it took no action.

Kahnawake began maintaining its own police force after a violent dispute with Quebec police in 1979. Members of the Warrior faction at Kahnawake barricaded the Mercier Bridge in support of the Mohawks at Kanesatake in the summer of 1990. This dragged on through the summer, as did the standoff at Kanesatake. Non-Indians, angry over the closing of an important bridge over the St Lawrence, began protests of their own, and this helped finally to draw the federal government into the confrontation. Royal Canadian Mounted Police were brought in to quell a crowd of 3,000 protesters in mid-July.

Mohawks and Canadian troops joined in tearing down the barricades at Kahnawake on August 29. The details of their agreement were not published, but they did not appear to apply to the continuing standoff at Kanesatake. The agreement faltered a day later when the army appeared to be still refusing to allow supplies into the reservation.

The Canadian army finally fired teargas into the barricades on September 19, after the federal government felt that it had taken all necessary steps to resolve the conflict. At last the barricades came down and the army lifted its siege, but at the cost of occupying the reserve.

The army and the Quebec police came back to Kahnawake after an absence of over a decade. Two days of fighting broke out at Kahnawake on January 9, 1991. Twenty-two police officers and eight

Mohawks were injured after the police tried to stop a truck for a traffic violation. The root cause, of course, was anger over the presence of non-Mohawk law enforcement officers on the reserve. The dispute between the Kahnawake Mohawks and the Quebec government continues. Quebec cut off some welfare payments to the Mohawks in 1992, and the Mohawks refused to go along with a native self-government proposal that would have left them under provincial jurisdiction.

Recitation of newsworthy events distorts the pleasant nature of everyday life at Kahnawake, as it does with the other reserves and reservations. In fact, the community prospers in relative peace and quiet most of the time. A cultural center and the work of the Kateri School have helped to refocus the Mohawks there on both traditional values and the special role the Iroquois have in the modern world. Roman Catholic Mohawks continue to hope for the canonization of Kateri Tekakwitha, whose remains still lie preserved in the church at Kahnawake.

### Gibson

The Gibson Reserve is one of the smallest and least familiar of the Iroquois reserves in Canada. It is located near Parry Sound, but like other Iroquois reserves it is invisible on official Ontario road maps. It was established by people from Kanesatake just over a century ago. Today some of the Mohawks there operate cranberry farms, producing up to a quarter of Canada's cranberries.

### Tyendinaga

The Mohawk community at Tyendinaga has been comparatively tranquil since its founding after the American Revolution. Mohawk is no longer spoken in sustained conversations there, and there has never been a longhouse congregation. The clan system has long since ceased to function, and many people are uncertain of their clans. The reserve has been governed by an elected band council since the 1870s. A council of hereditary chiefs persisted until the late 1930s, but has since disappeared.

The reserve covers about 17,000 acres, and there were about 900 Mohawks living there around 1970. Political factions have in recent decades divided along conservative and progressive lines. As sometimes happens in other Iroquois communities, each side occasionally accuses the other of being too much influenced by surrounding Canadian society. While the conservatives are treaty-oriented, the progressives are goal-oriented, both necessarily being outward perspectives. However, neither faction disputes the elected system of government, and the problems that have recently plagued other Iroquois communities are virtually absent here.[18]

## Oneida

In the twentieth century the Oneidas have been reduced to about 32 acres in their traditional homeland. Efforts to recover millions of acres lost before 1790 have not been and are unlikely to be successful. However, a claim for 250,000 acres taken after 1790 is still alive. Oneidas began taking legal action to claim more of their traditional land in 1970. The Supreme Court ruling of 1974 that allowed Indian tribes to bring such claims opened the legal door for the Oneidas.[19] There were, however, complications that arose from problems of federal recognition and the roles of other Oneida communities. The federal government withdrew recognition of the New York Oneida government in 1975 because of factional disputes, and the nature of the Oneida land claim has been such that both the Oneidas of Wisconsin and the Oneidas of Ontario have had an interest. There has even been an effort by the Grand Council chiefs at Onondaga to intervene in this and other matters involving member nations of the League of the Iroquois, although the federal government has never made formal treaties with the League as such.

While all of this has been going on, some Oneidas have taken advantage of the relaxation of government restrictions on bingo operations. This split the Oneida community, as it has on so many other reservations, and there was a violent confrontation between factions when progambling Oneidas began building a bingo hall in 1985. Arsonists eventually burned the bingo hall in 1988, but it was replaced. The New York Oneidas have been led by Ray Halbritter. His progambling faction has gained in power in recent years, purchasing land for a casino close to the New York Thruway and negotiating with the state for permission to operate it in exchange for a sharing of revenues. Meanwhile, new income has allowed the Oneidas to build a new cultural center (Figure 13.4), expand their reservation, and begin planning a new housing development.[20]

The Oneidas of Wisconsin lost large amounts of reservation land as a result of the General Allotment Act of 1887. Once allotted, individual landowners lost their parcels through sales or because they

*Figure 13.4   Oneida cultural center*
*Source: courtesy of the Oneida Indian Nation.*

were unable to pay real estate taxes. The tribal government also fell apart, and the Wisconsin Oneidas nearly lost their identity altogether. The Indian Reorganization Act of 1934 saved them from becoming just another rural minority. They formed a new government, adopted a constitution, and incorporated themselves as a federally recognized tribe. The federal government even assisted by buying back some land for the tribe. Today they prosper, although the language and clan identities are maintained only by conscious effort.

The Wisconsin Oneidas have opposed any casino gambling agreement between the state of New York and the New York Oneidas on grounds that it would scuttle the land claim. Progambling Oneidas claim that the agreement would have no effect on the land claim.

### Cayuga

Cayugas still live in Oklahoma, at Six Nations, and on the Seneca reservation at Cattaraugus in New York. Land claims brought by the New York Cayugas led to a bill that would have given the Cayugas over 5,000 acres of land and an $8 million trust in return for abandonment of the claim. In 1980 the House of Representatives rejected the settlement, and the Cayugas filed a civil suit for a much larger claim. A tentative settlement was still pending in 1985 in which several thousand acres of land in Cayuga and Seneca counties would be granted to them. The settlement was to resolve a dispute stemming from the purported sale of the last small Cayuga reservation in central New York in 1807. The settlement was disputed in court by various non-Indian interests. By 1993 the case was still not settled, although continued court victories by the Cayugas appeared to be driving up the cost of the final settlement.

## Onondaga

Onondaga is one of only three Iroquois reservations in the United States at which the federally recognized government is still that of traditional hereditary chiefs. The other cases are Tuscarora and Tonawanda.

Modern Onondaga is a 6,100 acre reservation south of Syracuse. It was much larger in 1790, but the Onondagas sold the land on which Syracuse is located to New York State in 1793 and 1795. There were smaller sales in 1817 and 1822, all of which might have been illegal. These offer the potential for land claims.[21]

There was an attempt to open a bingo hall at Onondaga in 1985, but the tribal government there remains traditional in form, and the chiefs were able to stop the project. Leon Shenandoah (Thadodaho), Irving Powless, Jr, and Oren Lyons (Faithkeeper) are among the Onondaga leaders who have achieved international reputations as spokesmen for the Onondagas and the Iroquois generally.

When the American Revolution split the Iroquois longhouse, the League sachems covered the fire at Onondaga and divided the wampum belts. One belt relating to the founding of the League was cut in two in order that each group might have half. After the war the belts were kept at Buffalo Creek, the site of the new council fire of the League in New York. They remained there until 1847 when the Buffalo Creek Reservation was given up, whereupon they moved with the fire back to Onondaga once again.

Some of the belts were sold to collectors at the end of the century. Concerned Onondaga chiefs turned five belts over to the New York State Museum through Harriet Maxwell Converse, later making the director their official Keeper of the Wampum. Four more belts were bequeathed to the museum in 1927. Three were obtained by William Beauchamp for the museum and with the consent of the Onondagas in 1898.

All twelve belts were conveyed back to Onondaga chiefs on

October 13, 1989, in a ceremony in Albany. The four major belts are the Washington Covenant belt, the Wing or Dust Fan belt, the Thadodaho belt, and the Hiawatha belt. The remaining belts are known as the First Pale Faces belt, the Champlain belt, the Caughnawaga belt, the Treaty belt, the Alliance belt, the Remembrance belt, the Council Summons belt, and the Beauchamp "Path" belt.[22]

### Tonawanda

The Tonawanda Senecas have never given up their traditional government by hereditary chiefs. They had clung to the traditional system after the sellout of 1838, and steadfastly kept it after they were eventually secured on their reservation in 1857.

In 1992 five Senecas were accused of treason and stripped of their enrollment by the tribal council. The men sued for reinstatement in United States district court. The council cut off services to their homes, but did not attempt to evict them for fear that it would lead to violence.

### Six Nations

The Six Nations Reserve has been effectively governed by an elected council since 1924. As was the case in most communities that adopted elected forms of government, women were not initially allowed to vote. This circumstance seems to repeatedly belie the supposed high status of women in Iroquois society. However, women traditionally operated in the domestic world, and on the boundary between that world and the political world of Iroquois men. Stripped of their right to appoint hereditary chiefs by the imposed elective process, women were left for the time being with only auxiliary roles in politics. Women did not get the right to vote at Six Nations until 1951.

Loyalist sachems took their wampum belts with them to the Grand River in 1784, where they rekindled the fire of the League in Canada. As the League became an anachronism, custodians of the belts came to think of themselves as owners instead. Individual Iroquois at Six Nations sold eleven wampum belts to T. R. Roddy, a dealer, in 1899. George Heye later purchased all of them through another dealer in 1910, bringing them to the Museum of the American Indian in New York City. The trustees of the museum returned the eleven belts to the chiefs at the Onondaga longhouse at Six Nations on May 8,

1988. The Iroquois and various anthropologists had tried to gain the return of the belts since at least 1914.[23] The museum has since been absorbed by the Smithsonian Institution.

At the same time, William Montour, chief councillor of the current government of elected chiefs, graciously returned to the traditional hereditary League sachems a mace of seven strings of wampum that had been held in the council safe since they had given up power in 1924. This signaled the elected chiefs' decision to delegate custody of all belts to the League sachems.

All of the belts probably date to the second half of the eighteenth century. Cayuga Chief Jake Thomas recited the meaning of the Friendship belt and the Two Row belt. The set of eleven belts also included the Brant belt, a Mohawk belt, and a Five Nations War belt. The belts, alienated from Six Nations for almost nine decades, now repose in the place where they came to rest after the American Revolution.

On March 5, 1959, a group of hereditary chiefs tried to reclaim control of the reserve government by taking over the band council offices and proclaiming an end to the elective system. They were evicted by the Royal Canadian Mounted Police a week later, but dissatisfaction continued. Cooperation between the elected chiefs and the hereditary League sachems on the occasion of the return of their wampum belts signaled the beginning of a more cordial coexistence between them.

### The Iroquois at Century's End

Part of the revival of Iroquois culture in the second half of the twentieth century has been the effort by young emerging leaders to resensitize key topics and objects. While members of older generations were not usually opposed to sharing ceremonies with or selling artifacts to sympathetic non-Iroquois, these practices have become taboo in recent years. Thus there was no controversy when Arthur Parker edited and published the myth of the origin of the Little Water Medicine Society along with a description of its ceremonies in Harriet Maxwell Converse's 1908 publication. Nor was there any apparent objection to the efforts of Philip Tarbell (a Mohawk) to reprint the book in 1981. However, there was a storm of indignation, not all of it from the Iroquois, when Edmund Wilson published a description of the ceremony in the *New Yorker* in 1959. The piece was subsequently included in his *Apologies to the Iroquois*. This happened because he (and perhaps some of the Iroquois) apparently misunderstood the terms of his participation. Accounts of both the myth and the ceremony are paraphrased here from versions already published by Iroquois scholars, Parker and Tarbell.

*Origin of the Little Water Medicine Society*

*There was once a young hunter who was loved by the animals for the kindness he showed them. He never took unfair advantage of an animal when hunting, and he always left food for them when he could. One day the young hunter was scalped and left for dead by his enemies. The wolf found him and licked his wounds, howling to attract the other animals. The bear kept him warm in his arms, and the other animals agreed that he should be saved. Together they concocted a powerful medicine from minuscule but potent contributions, which altogether barely filled an acorn cap. To this they needed add only a little water.*

*The animals knew that the hunter needed a scalp, so one of the birds flew off to the village of his enemies to retrieve it. Together they restored the dried scalp, reattached it to the hunter's head, and revived him with the medicine.*

*While lying unconscious the hunter realized that he could now understand the language of the birds and animals. Later he was able to remember every word. It was the song of the medicine animals, and they told the hunter that when the people needed a favor or simply wished to express their gratitude, they should make a ceremony and sing the song. He asked for the secret of the medicine, but they told him that he could not have it for he was married. The formula would be given only to an unmarried man at the proper time.*

*Later the formula was given to another young hunter. The animals taught him the Ganodah, the song that gave the medicine strength, warning him that the medicine had to be strengthened periodically in all-night ceremonies lest it weaken and the neglect anger the animals. The medicine was called Niganigaah, "little water," because the dose was so small.*[24]

The sensitivity of certain objects has also heightened in recent years. While some Iroquois continue to make and sell medicine masks to non-Indians, others object to the practice. Some even insist that medicine masks should not be illustrated photographically on grounds that not just the masks but images of them are all cultural patrimony. Similar contradictions are voiced with regard to turtle shell rattles, husk face masks, wampum, and other objects used in Iroquois ceremonies. Some museums are now returning some sacred or otherwise culturally significant objects to Indian nations, particularly in cases where they were acquired by inappropriate means. Wampum belts that found their way from Six Nations to the Museum of the

### The Little Water Ceremony

In the summer of 1959, Corbett Sundown conducted the Little Water Ceremony at Tonawanda. The medicine is vulnerable, so there must be no smoking, no drinking, and no menstruating by anyone present. Sundown poured fresh strawberries into pails, and pulled two gourd rattles from a large white bag. He laid out three reed flutes and the medicine, all of which was covered by a sheet of white muslin. The muslin was part of the annual payment still made by the federal government under the terms of the 1794 Canandaigua (Pickering) Treaty. Tobacco was laid out in two rows of four, indicating that it was for all eight of the Seneca clans. Sundown later cast the tobacco bit at a time into the stove, invoking the sun, moon, stars, winds, and so on through the Thanksgiving Speech. The ceremony moved on, through the night, through stages of different songs and at different tempos. In the end, just as the sun was rising, the Little Water medicine was renewed, and the morale of the community was lifted.[25]

American Indian, now known as the National Museum of the American Indian, have been returned. Iroquois belts that were legally transferred from Onondaga to the New York State Museum were restored to the Onondaga nation in 1989. These included seven belts that were transferred to state custody in 1898, four that were purchased privately and then bequeathed to the museum in 1927, and one that was acquired in 1949.[26]

The new federal Native American Graves Protection and Repatriation Act is resulting in the return of human remains and associated grave offerings as well. Some people are also arguing for the return of medicine masks and other sacred objects. There is certain to be continuing debate about which objects are sacred and which are not, as well as who has a right to make a claim on them. The Grand Council of the League of the Iroquois in New York often provides a focus for debates over repatriation and other issues of general importance to all Iroquois.

Looted or stolen sacred objects have sometimes ended up in museums, and it seems clear that these should be returned. But museums just as often purchased objects directly from their makers, both parties acting in good faith, and it is difficult to see what claim any third party could have on such an object under the law. Regardless of how these issues are resolved, it is clear that museums have entered a new era with regard to their relations with the Iroquois nations and other Indian groups.

Modern Iroquois are often indistinguishable from non-Indians in their dress. Some might wear clothing that seems vaguely western, a favorite Indian necklace, long hair, or some other symbol of ethnicity. Special occasions usually bring out ribbon shirts, a traditional *gustoweh* headdress, or even more elaborate versions of traditional dress. Modern powwows prompt some to wear Plains Indian war bonnets and other stereotypical paraphernalia that both Indians and non-Indians often expect to see as evidence of ethnicity.

The popular press continues to be sympathetic but often misguided. In an effort to make sure that the voices of the Iroquois are heard, many non-Indians have failed to recognize that the Iroquois do not always speak with one voice. At times uncritical political correctness has been allowed to overtake rational scholarship. Many journalists are still too ready to ignore both the details of history and the subtleties of culture in order to be able to take the simple stance of blaming present difficulties on current government policies and personalities. A June 1993 editorial decrying the ignorance of insensitive white politicians was illustrated by a medicine mask, a gaff that was certain to prompt comments about insensitive white columnists by at least some Iroquois.[27]

Fortunately the lives of modern Iroquois are not defined by the sensational newspaper stories through which most non-Indians have come to know them. In the 1990s, few Iroquois are engaged in agriculture and most Iroquois children speak only English. Many reservations look like special purpose suburbs, with children getting on buses to go to school each day while their parents commute to jobs in nearby towns. Yet essential things have survived the worst that time could visit upon them, and political conflicts have not defeated the Iroquois. The longhouse survives as an institution, just as the clans survive, having persisted through expulsions, epidemics, wars, adoptions, and hostile outside government policies. Their belts, their languages, their games, their cuisine, their dress, their character, their humor, and their fundamental sense of community all survive as well. That these things all persist in evolved rather than pristine forms only proves that the Iroquois are dynamic and human. The Iroquois are in the throes of reinventing themselves yet again, a tradition that is itself seven times seven generations old. For the most part, these are wise and principled people, who understand that nothing is ever settled once and for all, and who have learned to live comfortably with the uncertainty that understanding entails. Despite everything that has occurred through their long past and the uncertainty of the future, the Iroquois prepare the way for the seventh generation still to come.

# Notes

## 1 Origins, AD 900–1150: The Midwinter Moon

1 Bakker (1990) argues convincingly for a Basque origin of the word "Iroquois." Earlier etymologies have proposed several fanciful origins, all of which Day (1967) has discussed and rejected. The only one that Day considered possible in 1967 was that it might have come from Montagnais *irno kuë-deck*, "terrible people." But even this was regarded as very unlikely (Goddard 1978b: 320). Bakker's hypothesis is currently the strongest contender.

2 This story is an abbreviated and paraphrased composite of several versions recorded by Converse (1908: 31–6), Hewitt (1903: 141–339), Smith (1883), and Tehanetorens (1976: 16–22), as well as another summary version by Moulton and Abler (1991: 2). Moulton and Abler drew upon Cornplanter (1938), Barbeau (1915), Hewitt (1903, 1928), Parker (1923), Waugh (1912), and Rustige (1988). The myth, which is common to all Northern Iroquoians, was first noted by Sagard (1939: 169) in 1632. Fenton (1962) provides an excellent analysis.

3 An inconclusive *Time* magazine essay on the existence of evil (Morrow 1991) prompted one reader to write that the debate "sounds like a rhetorical question that one mouse might ask another mouse in the forest after examining an owl pellet composed of bleached rodent bones and matted hair" (Seymour 1991). Traditional Iroquois beliefs do not lead to such absurdities.

4 The idea that "the earth is our mother" might seem a tiresome cliché to non-Iroquois, but it remains widely believed. "Old people believe that since Mother Earth nurtured her children, they should not tear at her breasts with ploughs, but rather tickle them gently with a stick or hoe" (Snyderman 1951: 17).

5 Duality appears also appears in other forms, as on Janus effigy smoking pipes (Mathews 1981).

6 Because the lunar month is 29.5306 days long, a cycle of 13 lunar months is longer than a year and a cycle of 12 lunar months leaves a remainder of 10.8828 days per year. That means that we gain roughly

a full lunar month in three cycles of 12 months, which the Iroquois insert as a lost moon. The cycle is not precise, however, for at the end of the 37th month, the new moon falls about three days earlier than the day of the month on which the cycle began. There is a cycle of 19 years between the appearance of any particular moon and its recurrence on the same day of the year. There are 6939.6018 days in 19 years. There are 6939.691 days in 235 lunar months (19 x 12 + 7). Thus in 19 years the new moon advances a little under two hours against the time of day, meaning that the 19-year cycle advances a day in a little over two centuries. The 19-year cycle includes seven lost moons. Iroquois observers are not likely to have noticed the 19-year cycle, and might not have even noticed the rough three-year cycle of lost moons.

7   The significance of the Pleiades to the Iroquois and other nations of the region was explored by Lynn Ceci (1978) in a paper that later won her a prize from the American Society for Ethnohistory. But for her untimely death, she would have contributed much more to the subject.

8   The definitive work on the Midwinter Ceremony is that of Tooker (1970). It appears to have been the prototype for all other calendrical ceremonies of the Iroquois. In order to keep to a historical narrative and avoid burdening the reader, I have scattered outlines of the calendrical ceremonies through the book, such that there is one each for most chapters and as a set they complete a single annual round through the course of the volume.

9   The last white dog sacrifice at Onondaga occurred in 1885 (Beauchamp 1885, 1888). Hale (1885) observed the end of the same tradition at the Six Nations Reserve.

10  Lounsbury (1978: 334) has suggested that the Cherokee were separated from the Northern Iroquoians for 3,500–4,000 years, and Goddard (1978a: 70) has guessed that the Eastern Algonquians had been separated from the Central Algonquians for about 2,000 years. Lounsbury (1978: 336) further suggests that languages of the Five Nations diverged in the range of 1,000–1,500 years ago.

11  Lafitau (1977: 57) describes the large wooden mortars and pestles.

12  A more complete discussion of key vocabulary items in Iroquoian proto-languages can be found in Mithun (1984: 271–4).

13  Chafe (1964) has pointed out the antiquity of terms related to the Midwinter Ceremony.

14  Morgan (1962: 5) went so far as to claim that the Iroquois had been slaves of the Adirondack "branch of the Algonquin race," from whom they had learned "husbandry" and then escaped. Parker (1916a: 479–80) ignored clear archaeological evidence from the Mohawk Valley so that he could claim that this part of Iroquoia was not occupied until the Mohawks left the St Lawrence Valley late in the sixteenth century. This allowed him a convenient explanation for the disappearance of the St Lawrence Iroquoians after Cartier visited them in 1534–41, but at the expense of denying archaeological evidence for a prehistoric presence of Mohawk culture in the Mohawk Valley. Similarly, while his ideas about

Onondaga origins conveniently explained abandoned Iroquoian sites in Jefferson County, they denied a local development of Onondaga culture around Syracuse. Tuck's (1971) work later showed that the Onondagas were not simply transplanted northerners. That of Ritchie and Funk (1973) clearly showed the same for the Mohawks.

15 James Griffin (1944) was one of the first to caution against the uncritical use of such migration scenarios as explanations of prehistoric change. It was this kind of criticism that led archaeologists to focus the burden of proof on migration hypotheses, leaving presumed immobility (rather than simple uncertainty) as the default hypothesis. Much of the evidence to refute hypothetical Iroquois migrations was accumulated by William Ritchie over a quarter of a century. Nevertheless, Ritchie (1961) credited Richard MacNeish (1952) with propounding the *in situ* hypothesis of Iroquois origins. MacNeish (1976: 80), in turn, now gives much of the credit to Griffin.

16 Ritchie's (1965, 1969) summary work on *The Archaeology of New York State* outlines Iroquois archaeology as he understood it just prior to his retirement in 1972. In this work he defines Owasco culture and Iroquois culture as he understood them (Ritchie 1969: 272–3, 300–1).

17 Ritchie and Funk (1973: 359).

18 My own work in the northeast began in 1966, and I quickly adapted to the *in situ* model of Iroquoian development. I later looked to historical linguistics for additional clues. Floyd Lounsbury had suggested that the Cherokee had been separated from the Northern Iroquoians for 3,500–4,000 years, and Ives Goddard guessed that the Eastern Algonquians had been separated from the Central Algonquians for about 2,000 years. This led me to look for a discontinuity in the archaeological record at sometime in the period 0–2000 BC. It appeared to me that the break between the Late Archaic and the Frost Island phase of central New York around 1600 BC was the most likely candidate. For the Frost Island phase and all subsequent archaeological phases in the area, like most others I looked for continuity and I found it. The result was published as part of a volume in honor of William Fenton (Snow 1984).

19 See Ritchie (1969: 230) and Ritchie and MacNeish (1949: 100) for more complete details on Point Peninsula ceramics.

20 Tuck (1971); Whallon (1968: 236).

21 Sagard (1939: 109).

22 One early English writer even wondered if the Mohawks might be able to manufacture their own gunpowder using saltpeter extracted from vast beds of pigeon dung.

23 Recent cross-cultural research by William Divale (1984) also forced me to consider alternatives to the *in situ* hypothesis. His assertion is that matrilocality develops as a strategy to allow aggressive expanding societies to migrate and displace subordinate societies. This view is consistent with Sahlins's (1961: 323) argument that "a segmentary lineage system is a social means of intrusion and competition in an already occupied ecological niche. More, it is an organization confined to societies of a certain level of development, the *tribal* level, as distinguished

from less-developed *bands* and more advanced *chiefdoms*. Finally, the segmentary lineage is a successful predatory organization in conflicts with other tribes, although perhaps unnecessary against bands and ineffective against chiefdoms and states; it develops specifically in a tribal society which is moving against other tribes, in a *tribal intercultural environment*."

24   Trigger's (1978) essay on Iroquoian matriliny has the *in situ* hypothesis and the gradual development of Iroquoian society as its central theme. However, the underlying hypothesis has not been supported by archaeological evidence. Whallon (1968: 235–6, 240) found evidence of increasing village endogamy and a shift from smaller extended families to larger matrilineages from Owasco times on in New York. But he cites no evidence for in place development of matrilocality from some earlier custom. I have discussed these and other details more fully in various articles (Snow 1992a, 1992c).

25   Mithun (1988) discusses this and other crucial kin terms.

26   Ritchie (1969: 256). The White site radiocarbon date laboratory number is M-170.

27   Owasco types have been described by Ritchie (1969: 290–1), Ritchie and MacNeish (1949: 107–19), and Ritchie et al. (1953: 18–21).

28   Data and interpretations discussed in this section can be found in Ritchie (1965: 253–65, 1969: 229, 254, 258, 261; 1944: 89), Ritchie and Funk (1973: 354–5), Ritchie et al. (1953: 44–7), and Funk (1976: 97). The radiocarbon date from Turnbull is a calibrated average of two dates, 435±50 BP (AA-7413) and 360±40 BP (AA-7691). That from the Willow Tree site is 955+250 BP (M-177). Other dates and a more detailed discussion of the Hunters Home phase can be found in Snow (1993a).

29   Like other American Indians, the Iroquois are understandably sensitive about the treatment of human skeletal remains. The American Indian Religious Freedom Act and the Native American Graves Protection and Repatriation Act both ensure proper treatment of Iroquois skeletal remains. Any research project involving such remains should not be undertaken unless it is deemed appropriate by *both* the Iroquois community *and* the scientific community.

30   See Mithun (1984), Wykoff (1989), and Stewart (1990) for discussions of the geographic homeland of the Iroquois and the role of Clemson's Island culture.

31   Ingram et al. (1981).

32   Wright (1974).

## 2   Owasco, 1150–1350: The Sugar Moon

1   Shelford (1963: 17–55) provides a nice summary of the region.

2   Clermont (1980) has argued that Iroquoian population growth could not have been rapid enough to generate from a small founding population the aggregate size of at least 95,000 that were alive and well in AD 1600. Population decline did not begin in the region until after that date (Snow and Starna 1989). Clermont concluded that the Iroquoians

must have developed *in situ* out of a Point Peninsula base, because that was the only way to postulate a sufficiently large founding population. However, I have been able to show that even if the time for growth is minimized, the ultimate population size is maximized, and Engelbrecht's (1987) findings regarding slow growth are stipulated, there was more than enough time for the Iroquoians to multiply from a small founding population, even if it was as improbably tiny as 500 (Snow 1992a). The Iroquoians did not have to exceed the modest birth rates observed by later Europeans to multiply beyond 100,000 in only 19 generations (less than 500 years). Growth potential was therefore a favorable condition, not an unfavorable one.

3   Tooker (1970: 7–17, 48–50).

4   Ritchie (1969: 272–3) considered traces of Owasco remains in western New York sites to indicate contact with but not permanent residence of Owasco people there. Wright's (1966: 23) discussion of the contemporary Glen Meyer and Pickering branches of Ontario Iroquois indicates that neither of these was present in the western New York/southeastern Ontario area either. During AD 950–1350 the Niagara Frontier and the adjacent portions of both Ontario and New York appear to have been devoid of Iroquoian occupation, although not altogether empty. It is possible that contemporary sites there would be classified as late Middle Woodland in age except for the presence of a little Owasco pottery and pipes. Ritchie noticed the same pattern in the Hudson Valley, where what he assumed were resident Algonquian speakers picked up a few Owasco ceramics, perhaps by means of capturing the women who manufactured them (Ritchie 1969: 274).

5   Ritchie (1969: 274) discusses the place of Pillar Point in the context of a wider discussion of the distribution of Owasco sites. Wright (1966) defined Pickering and Glen Meyer in Ontario.

6   Puniello (1980: 147) has pointed out that "if the historic record was limited to only aboriginal ceramic evidence, the Minisink would undoubtedly be included in the same cultural unit as the Mohawk, Oneida and Onondaga." Yet the historic inhabitants of the upper Delaware and the lower Hudson were indisputably speakers of Eastern Algonquian languages (Goddard 1971; 1978a). Kraft's work at the Harry's Farm site in the upper Delaware Valley illustrates the ease with which Owasco and Iroquois pottery types can be applied in New Jersey. He defines the remains dating to roughly AD 1000–1400 as Pahaquarra culture, noting that the associated pottery types are equivalent or similar to corded Owasco types (Kraft 1975: 124–34). He does not attempt to explain the mechanisms by which these Algonquian speakers came to make pottery that was so thoroughly Iroquoian in appearance, but he does express some skepticism about the utility of types as units of archaeological analysis. The tendency for Delaware and Hudson Valley sites to be occupied for very long periods when compared to frequently relocated Iroquoian villages is discussed by Puniello (1980: 149).

7  Kuhn (1985).

8  Calibrations of published radiocarbon age determinations using the Stuiver and Reimer (1993) program are important because dating methods other than radiocarbon are beginning to have some use in the northeast, and because key global climatological trends are tied to calendrical rather than uncalibrated radiocarbon dates. Most of the radiocarbon dates referred to here can be found in Ritchie and Funk (1973: iv).

9  The Iroquois lived in multifamily houses from Early Owasco times on. Although Divale's theory on the development of matrilocal residence in preliterate societies (Divale 1984) predicts that Iroquois multifamily houses would have been matrilocal from the beginning, there is little independent evidence to support the idea. Coult and Habenstein's (1965: 358) cross-tabulations of Murdock's world ethnographic sample show that of a sample of 52 societies with extended family households, 26 were patrilocal and 20 were matrilocal. Forty-one of 52 having extended family households were horticultural (Coult and Habenstein 1965: 375), so there are necessarily some instances of patrilocal extended family households in horticultural settings. However, of 84 matrilocal societies, only 18 were not horticultural (Coult and Habenstein 1965: 392). This adds weight to the argument that the Northern Iroquoians have been matrilineal since late Middle Woodland or early Late Woodland times.

10  Specific data can be found in Ritchie (1969: 281), Ritchie and Funk (1973: 166, 199, 227), and Snow (1991b). Ritchie and Funk (1973: 215–16) interpret the post mold patterns at the Sackett site to indicate small round houses, but both Trigger (1981: 12) and I (Snow 1980: 313) independently concluded that their data could be better interpreted as partially uncovered longhouses. Thus the Sackett site was probably not out of step with the times after all.

11  See Rippeteau (1978). Turnbaugh (1977: 228) notes that Owasco pottery types are scarce in the valley of the West Branch.

12  Lafitau (1977: 72), Parker (1910), and Waugh (1916) are our primary sources for the Iroquois uses of maize and other plants.

13  Lafitau (1977: 86).

14  Divale (1973) provides a concise set of definitions for primitive warfare. These are based on a world-wide sample, but apply well to the specific Iroquois case. The description provided by Quincy Wright (1968: 456) covers the Iroquois case very well. Otterbein (1968) has distinguished between internal and external warfare.

15  Wright (1968: 456).

16  There has been a tendency to interpret this as a gradual replacement of earlier types by Owasco types. However, both Ritchie (1969: xxv) and Turnbaugh (1977: 227) describe the dissimilar assemblages as being intermixed, sometimes in the same refuse pits.

17  Ritchie and Funk (1973: 167).

### 3   The Development of Northern Iroquoian Culture, AD 1350–1525: The Fishing Moon

1   Lenig (1965) named Oak Hill as the phase following 1350 on the basis of his work in the Mohawk Valley. Lenig was impressed by the brevity of the development and the widespread distribution of common trends in ceramics, houses, subsistence, and burial customs. Because of this he preferred to think of Oak Hill as a horizon, although Ritchie and Funk (1973: 167) considered it to be a rather "arbitrary slice of a developmental continuum." Ritchie (1952) defined the Chance phase.

2   See Niemczycki (1984: 29–30) for a discussion of developments in the areas of later Cayuga and Seneca development. See Tuck (1971: 93–139) and Bradley (1987: 26–34) for the area of later Onondaga development.

3   Indian hemp (*Apocynum cannabinum*). There are over 60 species in the goldenrod genus (*Solidago* sp.) in the northeast.

4   Vanderlaan (1980) has described the Oakfield phase, while Niemczycki (1988) has discussed their possible influence on the later emergence of the Seneca nation, and White (1967) has proposed their ancestry for the Erie nation.

5   Kuhn (1985) discusses the contrasting patterns for pipes and pots. Sagard (1939: 102) provides virtually our only clear evidence that women made pots and men made pipes, but there is nothing to contradict his words. Bradley (1987: 92) discusses the rise in marine shell trade and the revival of long-distance trading networks around AD 1500.

6   Warrick (1988, 1990) has made a convincing case for rapid population growth in Huronia at this time. More fragmentary evidence from Iroquoia is consistent with this, so there is good reason to believe that it occurred here as well. Noble (1975: 37), Pearce (1984: 288) and others have interpreted all of this as evidence of an increasing reliance on maize horticulture.

7   Dodd et al. (1990) have documented the rise of the torture complex as evidenced by human bone in garbage contexts. Warrick (1984: 66) has suggested that the longer and more variable longhouses resulted from amalgamation of some households under strong military leaders. Hayden (1979) has linked it to differential wealth or status accumulation. Either is possible, but neither is necessary to explain the phenomenon.

8   The general association of matrilocality and large floor areas seems well established (Ember 1973). Fenton and Tooker (1978: 467) argue that at least for the large villages of the early seventeenth century village exogamy was very unlikely. It might have been practiced prior to 1450 when villages were small, numerous, and closely spaced within national clusters. Matrilocal societies should be expected to lack men's houses when men are locally endogamous (Divale 1984: 34).

9 Champlain (1907: 313–14) wrote on longhouses in 1616. He used the term *Antouhonorons*, which is often taken to mean the Oneidas (Campisi 1978: 490), but which might refer to the Onondagas or other Iroquois west of the Mohawks.

10 There are several features common to all longhouses which I have extracted and synthesized from descriptions by van den Bogaert (1988), Lafitau (1974, 1977), Bartram (1751), Sagard (1939), various Jesuit Relations (*JR* 1959, 15: 153, 16: 243, 17: 175–7), and my own research and field experience (Snow and Starna 1989).

11 Maps of the villages around Detroit can be found in Clifton (1978: 728), Feest and Feest (1978: 776), and Tooker (1978a: 400). Census data for the same villages can be found in the Collections and Researches of the Michigan Pioneer and Historical Society (Anon. 1916).

12 There is risk in using the Chance phase outside eastern New York, for Ritchie (1952) included a site from the Hudson Valley in the original description. Nevertheless, several investigators have extended its use as far as western New York. I have argued elsewhere that Ritchie should not have included the Kingston site in his definition of the Chance phase. I argue here that it would be better if the phase name were used nowhere outside the Mohawk drainage, for overextension of late prehistoric phase names can mask important variability in the archaeological record.

13 Ritchie and Funk (1973: 168).

14 Ritchie and Funk (1973: 291–312); Snow (1985).

15 Pratt (1976: 107) carried out the work at Nichols Pond, while Lenig (1965: 73) has compared Oneida and Mohawk ceramics. Lounsbury (1978: 336) has noted the special closeness of the Oneida and Mohawk languages, although this could to some extent stem from the close relations and extensive intermarriage between these two nations in the seventeenth century.

16 Tuck (1971: 93–139) summarizes information on the Onondaga, while Niemczycki (1984: 22–3) deals with the Seneca and Cayuga cases.

17 The Susquehannock are discussed most comprehensively by Kent (1984: 295–307). Cayuga historical linguistics have been studied most extensively by Wallace Chafe, who continues to labor on the complexities of the development of this Iroquoian language.

18 Engelbrecht continues to work on the enigmatic Jefferson County sites (Engelbrecht et al. 1990) while Pendergast (1990) does the same for Saint Lawrence Iroquoian sites on the Canadian side of the river.

19 The evidence presented by both Ritchie (1952) and Brumbach (1975) suggests that we must look beyond ceramics to clearly define ethnicity along the eastern boundary of Iroquoia in this and earlier times. Bender and Brumbach (1992) have proposed that the Mohawk ceramics on Fish Kill do not signal ethnicity, but in light of a considerable amount of independent evidence to the contrary, I am compelled to disagree.

4   *The Rise of the League, 1525–1600: The Planting Moon*

1   Archaeological syntheses can be found in Wray et al. (1987) for the Senecas, Niemczycki (1984) for the Senecas and Cayugas, Tuck (1971) and Bradley (1987) for the Onondagas, Pratt (1976) for the Oneidas, and Snow (1993b) for the Mohawks. Village nucleation reduced the total number of settlements even as population continued to grow. Simple counts of villages by period can lead to the false conclusion that population was declining in the sixteenth century.

2   Longhouses were very flammable, and there were many disastrous fires. Le Mercier describes a fire in a Huron village. "On this same 3rd of May [1637], towards eleven o'clock in the evening, a cabin of our village, only about a musket-shot distant from ours, took fire. There were within only four or five poor children, seven or eight of their relatives having died from the contagion during the winter. They ran out entirely naked, and even then had considerable trouble to save themselves. The fire spread so rapidly that in less than no time the cabin was all in flames. We ran to help them, but it was only to look on and show that we had compassion for them. The wind, a Northwester, proved, thanks to God, very favorable both to the rest of the cabins of the Savages, and to ours; otherwise an entire village is soon despatched and reduced to ashes, —the cedar bark, with which the greater number of the cabins are covered, taking fire almost as easily as saltpeter" (*JR* 1959, 14: 43–5).

3   Data on Garoga can be found in Ritchie and Funk (1973: 313–32) and in the files of the New York State Museum.

4   Abler and Logan (1988) discuss Iroquois cannibalism and human sacrifice in the context of similar cases from around the world.

5   Megapolensis (1909: 177); Lafitau (1977: 189–91).

6   Lafitau (1977: 255–64).

7   Life cycle information comes from Lafitau (1977), Beauchamp (1900), and Bonvillain (1980).

8   The *White Roots of Peace* was published by Wallace (1946). Parker (1916b) published the 1880 Newhouse version in heavily edited form, along with the Six Nations chiefs' version, which had previously been published by Scott (1912). The 1912 Gibson version has recently been published by Woodbury (Gibson 1992). These and other versions are discussed in detail by Tooker (1978b) and Fenton (1968).

9   Hiawatha has unfortunately been misrepresented by nineteenth-century literature. Schoolcraft (1847) confused him with Nanabozho, an Ojibwa culture hero. Longfellow later popularized Ojibwa folklore in poetic form, inappropriately following Schoolcraft and using Hiawatha's name. There is a persistent local tradition that Hiawatha was buried on Van Slyke Island at Schenectady, an island that filling has since joined to the south bank of the Mohawk River.

10  Recorded Iroquois traditions assert variously that the League was formed

one to three lifetimes, two to six generations, or 50–400 years before the first Europeans arrived (Tooker 1978b: 418–21). Just which Europeans are implied by each of these remains uncertain, but variation in their identities might partly explain the wide variation in asserted starting dates. European fishermen began to appear off the coast after 1520. Cartier first explored the St Lawrence in 1534. Dutch traders and French missionaries were not in direct contact with the Iroquois until the early 1600s. More recently developed oral tradition often asserts much greater antiquity for the League than did the oral tradition of the nineteenth century, but this may be for for contemporary political purposes. Archaeological evidence does not support the prerequisite of pervasive warfare until after 1450.

11 I have explored the possible significance of an eclipse at greater length elsewhere (Snow 1991a). Crowe (1992) has argued that oral tradition regarding the darkening of the sun refers only metaphorically to the darkness of grief that was dispelled by the Great Peace.

12 Hewitt (1903: 255) says that "an ohwachira in its broadest and original sense denotes the male and female offspring of a woman and their descendants in the female line only."

13 Tooker (1978b) provides the most concise summary of League structure, which was first laid out by Morgan (1962). Fenton (1950) provides many important additional details.

14 Trigger (1978) discusses the origins of Iroquoian matriliny with arguments that differ strikingly from those presented here. Bonvillain (1980) and Tooker (1984) present balanced views of ways in which women in Iroquois society have been represented in support of more modern causes.

15 Parker's (1916b) recasting of the Newhouse version of the Great Law presents it as a "constitution" comprised of 117 detailed sections. John Gibson's 1912 version of the Deganawida legend and the Great Law filled 525 manuscript pages (Fenton 1968: 40). It was recently translated and published by Hanni Woodbury (Gibson 1992). The Gibson version should be regarded as the most complete of those available, and more true to Iroquois tradition than the heavily edited version published by Parker.

16 Hamell (1987) discusses the symbolism of colors in Iroquois thought.

17 The word "wampum" comes from *wampumpeag*, a southern New England Algonquian word. The Dutch called it *sewant*, the Mohawks called it *o'nekórha'*, and the French called it *porcelaine*. Readers interested in the subject should begin with the papers edited by Hayes (1989).

18 Bradley (1987: 67–9) discusses the appearance of marine shell in Iroquoia, and Sempowski (1992) has demonstrated the reorientation of the Seneca in the late sixteenth century.

19 Heidenreich's (1971) treatment of Huron farming is the most detailed analysis available. Waugh (1916) and Parker (1910) provide valuable earlier monographs on Iroquois farming.

20 Contrary to modern popular belief, the Iroquois and other Indians of the Northeast did not fertilize their crops (Ceci 1975).

21  I have explored this matter by simple computer simulation (Snow 1986).
22  See Herrick (1977). Poison ivy could grow anywhere, but was rampant in old fields. If the plant was touched, the victim rushed to a wet shady spot to find the jewelweed antidote. The crushed jewelweed stem exuded sap that might counteract the poison ivy, or more likely salve the blisters that would develop in a day or two. Both pale jewelweed or touch-me-not (*Impatiens pallida*) and spotted jewelweed (*Impatiens capensis*) are found in wet shady places in Iroquoia.
23  Engelbrecht (1987).
24  Megapolensis (1909: 174) provides us with an early description of this and other customs of the Iroquois.
25  Hewitt (1903: 255).
26  This was Isaack de Rasieres writing in 1628 (Jameson 1909: 109).
27  Mithun (1984) describes the shift in kin terms. Van den Bogaert (1988: 54) provides crucial information that the shift had taken place by 1635. Mithun's explanation differs from the one proposed here because the archaeological evidence has grown since her paper was completed.
28  Lenig (1977) speculates on the source of trade goods bound for Mohawk sites in this period while Bradley (1987) discusses the Onondaga case.
29  Robert Kuhn and Robert Funk have analyzed ceramics from the Garoga, Klock, and Smith-Pagerie sites and have found several specimens bearing diagnostic Jefferson County traits. Engelbrecht has compared these and other Iroquoian ceramic assemblages and has confirmed the close relationship between Jefferson County and Mohawk Valley pottery.

5    *The Coming of Europeans, 1600–1634: The Strawberry Moon*

1  Bradley and Childs (1991) and Fitzgerald (1993) provide some of the most recent evidence of this trade.
2  Snow (1976).
3  Hamell (1987, 1992) explicates Iroquois color symbolism better than any other source.
4  The Jesuit Relations and Allied Documents (*JR* 1959) are a priceless source for ethnohistorians interested in the Iroquois. However, they have their own biases and often omit any mention of things of great interest to us now, for the Jesuits were more interested in saving the Indians through conversion than in documenting cultures that they neither understood nor appreciated.
5  De Laet's comment appears in Jameson (1909: 47).
6  Champlain (1907: 313–14).
7  This was the Failing site (Lenig 1965: 84).
8  Demographic data have been drawn from the results of the Mohawk Valley Project, which was designed to measure Mohawk demographic change from the sixteenth century to the time of the American Revolution.
9  One of the wampum belts returned to the Onondagas by the New York

State Museum in 1989 was found to carry traces of cinnabar, the mineral base for a bright red pigment.

10   Spiess and Spiess (1987).

11   Hale (1883: 72) translated *Kanyenke* as "Place of the Flint," but Hewitt (1903: 309) argued that references to flint were really references to ice or crystal. Hamell (1983) has shown that crystals had considerably more symbolic significance than chert.

12   Fenton and Tooker (1978).

13   Campisi (1978).

14   Blau et al. (1978).

15   The early part of this sequence has been described by Tuck (1971), while the latter part of it has been covered by Bradley (1987). Although Tuck is convinced that two clear village sequences can be discerned, Bradley presents data on additional sites that suggest that the Onondaga sequence is more complicated than that.

16   White et al. (1978).

17   Late Cayuga sites were surveyed by Marian White, but she was unable to publish all of the results before her death in 1975. Niemczycki (1984) has published much of this along with other data in her analysis of Seneca and Cayuga development.

18   Abler and Tooker (1978).

19   Wray and Schoff (1953) first defined the Seneca sequence. This has since been expanded and clarified by Niemczycki (1984) and Wray et al. (1987, 1991).

20   The Mohawk population estimate has been derived from the results of the Mohawk Valley Project. Estimates for the other four Iroquois nations are based on the apparent numbers of large villages lived in by each of them in the first quarter of the seventeenth century.

21   Champlain (1907: 154).

22   Le Jeune's remarks appear in the Jesuit Relations (*JR* 1959, 6: 125, 129–33, 177, 211). He got his information from the Montagnais, but the attitude appears to have been widespread in the northeast, and we may cautiously apply it to the Iroquoians as well.

23   Oswald (1975: 3–20).

24   Peña (1990).

25   Lenig (1977: 79–80).

26   Matrons could encourage men to go to war when it suited their purposes. They could also dissuade them if they thought that the village would be left too poorly defended or for some other reason they thought it ill-advised. Women had substantial influence, partly because they so rarely exercised it. The Iroquois were attuned to nuance; they respected their elders, both male and female, and there was seldom need for more than subtle suggestion. For their part, the elders preferred subtle suggestion to constraining others by more overt means, for they knew that the assertion of power would lead to factionalism.

27   These numbers are derived from an article by Starna and Relethford (1985).

28 The best surviving illustrations are to be found in the four Verelst paintings of three Mohawks and a Mahican, which date to 1710. All four are now in the Collections of the Public Archives of Canada.

### 6 The Year of Death, 1634: The Lost Moon

1 Bradford (1908: 302–3).
2 Bradford (1908: 348) described the earthquake. Roger Williams (1863) recounted the apocryphal Narragansett story in a letter to John Winthrop.
3 *JR* (1959, 7: 221; 8: 43, 87–9; 12: 265).
4 Bradford (1908: 312–13).
5 Harmen van den Bogaert (1988) observed the exile of *Adriochten*.
6 These passages appear in van den Bogaert (1988: 10, 17–18).
7 Computer simulation of this epidemic shows that it would have been virtually impossible for anyone present to escape infection and that 50 per cent mortality for those infected was likely (Snow 1992c).
8 This argument is made in Snow and Lanphear 1988. Some authors, such as Ramenofsky (1987: 71–102), have suggested that there might have been severe epidemics in Northern Iroquoia in the sixteenth century, but recent studies do not support that hypothesis.
9 Although claims for much earlier arrivals continue to be debated, most archaeologists now take a conservative view of the peopling of the Americas. Hoffecker et al. (1993) set their entry at no more than 12,000 years ago (10,000 BC). Even many conservative scholars are willing to accept a date a few millennia earlier.
10 The importance of genetic uniformity in the severity of European crowd infections in sixteenth- and seventeenth-century America has been only recently appreciated by epidemiologists (Black 1992).
11 Williams (1643: 148–50).
12 Fenton (1941); Lafitau (1974: 371–82).
13 General information on medicine masks as well as a longer version of the epic myth can be found in Fenton (1987: 95–6).
14 The medicine societies have often been referred to as secret. This is probably the result of the practice of holding their meetings privately in homes rather than in public locations over the last two centuries. This practice, in turn, might date only to the early nineteenth century, when Handsome Lake repressed and attempted to disband the medicine societies.
15 Krusche (1986) has advanced the idea that medicine masks began as carvings on posts. My own excavations on Mohawk sites have frequently revealed single large post holes within houses that were apparently not for structural support. Debris in the post holes indicates that they were removed when the houses were abandoned and not left behind to decay with the abandoned frames. No examples of these posts have survived to the present.
16 Mathews (1980) and Fox (1993) both discuss these small figures.

17   Mohawk moons are from Fenton (1973). Anglo-American moons are derived from annual editions of the *Farmer's Almanac* dating from 1980 to 1993. Although the latter are claimed to have been taken from northeast Indian traditions, they follow a European pattern.

18   This story is paraphrased from a Seneca version of the Iroquois origin myth published by Hewitt (1903: 251–3).

### 7   The Struggle for Hearts and Minds, 1635–1700: The Green Bean Moon

1   See Richter (1987) and Jennings 1976) for fuller discussion of these events.

2   The houses described by van den Bogaert in 1635 were entirely traditional in form, although things such as iron hinges were already being added. By the 1680s, the Mohawk village of Caughnawaga was composed of standardized longhouses laid out in rows like a modern mobile home park. Galinee (1903: 25) says that in 1669 there were 360 cabins in four Seneca villages, of which 150 were in each of two large villages.

3   Visitors to the coinage display at the National Museum of American History in Washington, DC, can see these exchange relationships at first hand. Rates of exchange have been summarized by Ceci (1977).

4   Salisbury (1987: 62–3).

5   Vanishing native forms were often referred to in Mohawk by old words ending in -*onwe*, meaning "real," or "genuine." The unmodified old words were used to refer to the new replacements (Fenton 1973: 35). Kaolin pipes should be more precisely referred to as white ball clay pipes, but custom and convenience persuade me to retain "kaolin."

6   Treaties between the Iroquois nations and various Euro-American and Indian authorities have been compiled and summarized by Jennings (1985). This is the companion volume for microfilm copies of all those treaties that survive.

7   Hunt (1940) was the chief proponent of this view.

8   Richter (1992) has been eloquent in his advocacy of this view.

9   Tooker (1963) has examined the reasons for easy Iroquois victory in this seemingly equal struggle.

10   Salisbury (1987: 64–6).

11   Fenton (1981: 31).

12   *JR* (1959, 51: 187).

13   White (1991).

14   Seaver's (1992) biography of Mary Jemison is back in print and remains a useful source on this extraordinary woman's life. Many living Senecas can claim descent from her.

15   Gookin (1970: 40–2); *JR* (1959, 53: 137–53).

16   Salisbury (1987: 69).

17   *JR* (1959, 63: 179).

18   Koppedrayer (1993) provides an insightful analysis of Kateri and the process by which she became incorporated into the Catholic pantheon.

19  Salisbury (1987: 71).
20  Greenhalgh (1849–51).
21  This is examined by Jennings (1984). To understand the motives of the Iroquois, or for that matter the English and French, one does better to examine the thinking of modern youth gangs, rather than the thinking of military leaders in modern nation states.
22  Druke (1987: 31); Haan (1987).
23  Mark David Chapman explained in a 1992 interview that he killed the singer John Lennon because he thought that he could acquire Lennon's fame by doing it.
24  Radisson (1967).
25  Hamell (1987) has done much to elucidate Iroquois color symbolism in the seventeenth century.
26  Abler and Logan (1988) have done much to clarify the reasons for both the florescence and the demise of Iroquoian cannibalism. I am inclined to add that it is also folly to suggest that human beings are fundamentally nonviolent by nature. Pious pronouncements about the inherent amiability of humans could serve to blind us to the warning signs of extreme behaviors. Abler and Logan make it clear that certain combinations of conditions could occur in the future, and we would be at risk to ignore such advice.
27  Richards (1967) has argued that specific cases of neolocal, virilocal, and avunculocal residence do not support matrilocal residence as a general pattern. She has suggested that matrilocality might have only recently developed as a consequence of the loss of men and other demographic factors of the seventeenth century. However, the few cases she cites were probably reported precisely because they were exceptions to the prevailing rule, which I have already argued has probably been a key element of Iroquois culture for a thousand years.
28  Many modern anthropologists have held that there was no permanent underclass, but Starna and Watkins (1991) have shown that prior to the 1670s the Iroquois kept some captives in a perpetual state of slavery. The institution probably reinforced Iroquois matriliny. The need to incorporate ever larger numbers of captives in order to maintain population levels caused the institution of slavery to break down in the late seventeenth century. Fenton (1973) discusses other social classes.

### 8  *Iroquoia in the Balance, 1700–1750: The Green Corn Moon*

1  Greenhalgh (1849–51); Galinee (1903: 25).
2  Haan (1987: 52–7). The English attempted to counter the French treaty by getting a deed to the American interior from the Iroquois. Despite his young age, Theyanoguin was one of the signatories to a deed of 800 square miles of Iroquois hunting grounds to William III in 1701.
3  I have dealt with Theyanoguin at greater length in a chapter contributed to a volume edited by Robert Grumet (Snow 1993d).
4  Landy (1978) provides a full sketch of these events.

5   Sources for this story include Wallace (1945: 22) and Lydekker (1938: 35). Some sources say that Theyanoguin was removed from office in 1716 by matrons who were unhappy with his performance.

6   Jennings (1984: 11), from whom this quotation is taken, has exposed Colden's (1958) propaganda for what it was.

7   The story is related by Hubbard (1886: 41–2), among others. It is probably apocryphal, for it was told many times about other men. There is a variant of it that attributes the same roles to Conrad Weiser and Shickellamy (Wallace 1945: 151).

### 9   *The Loss of Independence, 1750–1800: The Fresh Moon*

1   The conference occasioned what Schoolcraft (1847: 416) referred to as "Hendrick's greatest speech" on June 19. Theyanoguin was introduced by his brother Abraham, and he held up the chain belt as he spoke. As Theyanoguin spoke he threw a stick over his shoulder and said, "You have thus thrown us behind your backs, and disregarded us, whereas the French are a subtle and vigilant people, ever using their utmost endeavors to seduce and bring our People over to them" (Stone 1901: 29–30).

2   O'Callaghan (*NYCD* 1853–87 6: 853–92) was one of the first to discuss this issue. It has been revived in recent years and a few writers now argue unconvincingly that the Iroquois had an influence on both the Albany Plan of Union and the later United States Constitution.

3   *JP* (1921–57, 3: 715, 9: 142–5); Wallace (1945: 361–3).

4   *JP* (1921–57, 1: 883, 2: 383).

5   Theyanoguin is supposed to have taken three sticks from the ground and said to Johnson "put these together and you cannot break them; take them one by one, and you will do it easily" (Stone 1901: 31). The quote is oddly similar to one attributed to Theyanoguin by Parker. "Five arrows shall be bound together very strongly and each arrow shall represent one nation. As the five arrows are strongly bound, this shall symbolize the union of the nations" (Parker 1916b: 11). It may well be that both are apocryphal.

6   Frisch (1971) discusses the Abenakis at Akwesasne; Day and Trigger (1978: 795) also mention the Seven Nations of Canada.

7   *JP* (1921–57, 10: 336–9, 484).

8   Campisi (1980) has shown that missionaries did not create factionalism, but rather provided rationales and sometimes sources of external power for those Iroquois who for other reasons sought to split from the status quo.

9   Kirkland's papers (Pilkington 1980) have been published and are an invaluable source on the Oneidas.

10  Stone (1838, 1: 27) describes this incident.

11  Graymont (1972) has dealt comprehensively with the role of the Iroquois in the American Revolution.

12  Graymont (1972: 113).

13 Hauptman (1988: 7) provides an excellent discussion of New York State Indian policy beginning with these events.

14 I trust that in the short term, but only in the short term, this paragraph will be the most controversial offered in this book. Readers wishing to explore the issue further should start with Grinde and Johansen (1991), Tooker (1988, 1990), and Johansen (1990). These will lead to most other relevant sources. Strictly speaking, there is no direct evidence for Iroquois influence on the United States Constitution just as there is no direct evidence for the doctrine of the Trinity in the Bible. Yet both are accepted as articles of faith by many people. Both beliefs arose as products of more recent events, and both should be understood today in those terms. Complete exposition of the current controversy, which would require a book of its own, might be worthwhile if popular interest in it does not fade by the end of the century.

15 A modern land claim by the Mohawks rests in part on the assertion that Joseph Brant, who signed for the Seven Indian Nations of Canada, had no authority to do so.

16 Morgan's (1962: 2) 1851 illustration of a bark house is consistent with this late persistence of bark construction. Nabokov and Easton (1989: 86–7) note that attempts by Morgan and Cornplanter to illustrate earlier longhouse styles were impaired by information from the eighteenth century, when forms from the seventeenth century had already been substantially altered.

17 Brasser (1975) has done the most thorough study of ash splint baskets in the aboriginal northeast. Bardwell (1986) has shown that the Indians were preadapted to take on the craft by a prior knowledge of the use of splints.

### 10    Revival and Subjection, 1800–1850: The Harvest Moon

1 The code, with a biography of Handsome Lake, was published by Parker (1913). It is also at the heart of more recent and well-known works by Wallace (1969, 1978). Tooker (1989) corrects some of their errors.

2 Fenton's (1953) classic monograph on this dance has recently been republished.

3 Parker (1909).

4 Isabel Kelsay's (1984) book is a generally excellent source on Brant. Stone's (1838) earlier two-volume biography offers a somewhat less modern perspective.

5 Tooker (1992) has become the foremost authority on Morgan's relationship with the Iroquois and contemporary scholars.

6 Deardorff (1951) initiated this error, which was perpetuated by Wallace (1969) but corrected by Tooker (1989).

7 Hauptman (1988: 9).

8 Abler and Tooker (1978: 511).

9 Fenton and Tooker (1978: 477) discuss the traditional government at Akwesasne. Starna and Campisi (1992) discuss the selection of the three

trustees that later became the elected council. Starna (1993) discusses this further in light of recent attempts to repeal Article 8 of the 1802 statute.

10  Tooker (1992) provides an excellent summary of the life of Lewis H. Morgan.

### 11  The Worst of Times, 1850–1900: The Hunting Moon

1  Hauptman (1988: 4).
2  Hauptman (1993).
3  General Lee's initial shock at seeing Parker, who he mistook as an Afro-American, betrayed the corrupt principles that lay at the core of the southern cause. Hauptman (1993) details this and other roles played by the Iroquois in the Civil War.
4  Beauchamp (1885, 1888) and Hale (1885) provide nice historical accounts. Blau (1964) and Tooker (1965) provide modern analyses.
5  Hayden (1980) discusses the ways in which uncertainties have allowed the manipulation of band membership rolls.
6  Arthur Parker regarded Newhouse as a Mohawk. Newhouse wrote his version of the League legend in what Parker (1916b: 12) referred to as "Indian English."
7  Weaver (1984) has summarized events at Six Nations in the late nineteenth century.
8  Hewitt (1892b).

### 12  The Rise of Modern Iroquois, 1900–1950: The Cold Moon

1  Much of what has been written about Iroquois myths and tales has been published in monograph form. J. N. B. Hewitt's work stands out in this literature (Hewitt 1903, 1928). Hewitt's 1903 publication contains three versions of the origin myth, one Onondaga, one Seneca, and one Mohawk. All three are recounted in their own languages, with literal interlinear translations into English. There is, fortunately, also a free translation of each version.
2  Parker (1916b: 12).
3  Hanni Woodbury has recently published this version in English and Onondaga (Gibson 1992).
4  The versions examined by Fenton were those of Pyrlaeus [1743], Brant [1801], Norton [1816], Newhouse [1880], Hale [1883], Buck [1892], Gibson [1899], Chiefs [1900], and Gibson [1912]. These are reproduced and discussed in Boyce (1973), Fenton (1949, 1975), Gibson (1992), Heckwelder (1819), Hewitt (1892a), Parker (1916b), Scott (1912), and Tooker (1978b: 440–1). Other versions were too fragmentary or too abstracted to warrant inclusion.
5  Errors and omissions by Parker can be corrected with some effort. Parker split Newhouse's law 23 into two separate ones, and in other places he lumped separate laws together as single ones in his revised list.

He made it appear that Newhouse had used number 84 twice. However, Parker also made it appear that Newhouse skipped number 91. If the second use of Newhouse number 84 is changed to 85, and if numbers 86–90 are all raised by one, the inconsistency vanishes. Parker's omissions can also be corrected. His numbers 65 and 108 correspond to Newhouse's numbers 20 and 109 respectively, although he left this information out of his publication (Parker 1916b: 30–60).

6 Hauptman (1988: 4–6) discusses these issues. Graymont (1972) traces the origins of these policies to the American Revolution and the political struggles that followed it.

7 Fenton and Tooker (1978: 478).

8 Hauptman (1980, 1981) has published a history of the impact of New Deal legislation on the Iroquois.

9 I am indebted to Jack Campisi for his lucid explanation of these points.

10 Fenton (1941: 425).

### 13 The Contemporary Scene, 1950–2000: The Very Cold Moon

1 Readers will reasonably expect to see a table showing current reservation and reserve population figures. Unfortunately, accurate figures are often out of date or unavailable. Many unenrolled people, both Indians and non-Indians, live on the reserves. In addition, many enrolled members of the reserves live elsewhere in the United States and Canada. Where appropriate, I have provided a few very general figures to give the reader some idea of community sizes.

2 Hauptman (1985a) has published a history of the Iroquois in the last half of the twentieth century that covers the main points up to 1985.

3 Graymont has edited and published the autobiography of Chief Clinton Rickard who died in 1971 (Rickard 1973).

4 Unfortunately for copy editors and cartographers, official spellings vary. The Allegheny River flows through the Allegany Reservation.

5 Abrams (1967).

6 Hauptman (1985b) has published a comprehensive summary of the Salamanca lease controversy.

7 "Tribe" and "reservation" are legal terms in the United States. Their Canadian equivalents are "band" and "reserve."

8 Fred Padula's well-intentioned but flawed editorial in the October 19, 1980 issue of the *Times Union* is a good example. While one must sympathize with reporters, who are often given short deadlines for writing detailed articles on unfamiliar subjects, it is unfortunately also the case that most people learn what they think they know from uncritical readings of biased or incomplete newspaper accounts.

9 Mel Reisner in the July 16, 1985 issue of the *Schenectady Gazette*.

10 Hall's (n.d.) privately distributed manuscript appears to be prophetic to some, alarming to others, and comical to still others in the Mohawk community.

11 *Schenectady Gazette*, September 16, 1987.

12 The May 28, 1990, issue of *Time* ran a photograph (p. 27) of George in camouflage fatigues and carrying an assault rifle, and quoted him as saying that "unless we have permanent peace here, we're going to resort to terrorist methods." After the dismissal of charges, George left Akwesasne and now lives at Oneida with his wife.

13 Jones (1990: 9) made this admission.

14 Hoskin (1990).

15 The events of the 1980s at Akwesasne are detailed from an antigambling perspective by Bruce Johansen (1993: 23–132). His book takes the position that the problems at Akwesasne can be blamed on the dominant Euro-American culture of the United States and Canada, as well as certain Mohawk factions. Johansen does not fully explore Iroquois cultural traditions that have also contributed to recent events. Hornung (1991) provides a somewhat different perspective on many of the same events.

16 Landsman (1988) has examined these events and some of the ways in which their meaning was manipulated by various parties, particularly the press.

17 Hornung (1991) provides one perspective on recent events in Mohawk communities as of 1991. Johansen (1993: 133–58) also provides an emotional examination of the details of the Kanesatake conflict.

18 Torok (1967) provides a concise description of modern Tyendinaga.

19 Starna and Vecsey (1988) have edited a set of papers that discuss these and other current Iroquois land claims.

20 Campisi and Hauptman (1988) provide a contemporary set of perspectives on Oneida factions. Shattuck (1991) discusses the Oneida land claims.

21 Blau et al. (1978: 491–9).

22 The event was described in print within a month (Anon. 1989).

23 Fenton (1989).

24 This myth was published in complete form by Converse (1908: 150–6) in a volume edited by Parker. It was reprinted by the State Education Department at the instigation of Philip Tarbell in 1981. A shorter version appears in Wilson (1992: 291–3).

25 The ceremony was observed and described in detail in *New Yorker* magazine in 1959 by Edmund Wilson and later included in his *Apologies to the Iroquois* (1992: 290–310). His apologies apparently did not extend to any regret at having published what both Fenton and the Iroquois thought was a confidence.

26 Return of the Six Nations wampum is described by Fenton (1989). Return of the New York wampum is described in an anonymous press release (Anon. 1989).

27 Swiers (1993).

# Suggestions for Further Reading

Bonvillain, N. 1992. *The Mohawk*. Chelsea House, New York.

Bradley, J. W., 1987. *Evolution of the Onondaga Iroquois: Accommodating Change 1500–1655*. Syracuse University Press, Syracuse.

Campisi, J., and L. M. Hauptman (eds) 1988. *Oneida Indian Experience: Two Perspectives*. Syracuse University Press, Syracuse.

Converse, H. M. 1908. *Myths and Legends of the New York State Iroquois*, ed. and ann. by Arthur C. Parker. New York State Museum Bulletin 125, Albany, Repr. 1981.

Fenton, W. N. 1987. *The False Faces of the Iroquois*. University of Oklahoma Press, Norman.

Foster, M. K., J. Campisi, and M. Mithun (eds) 1984. *Extending the Rafters: Interdisciplinary Approaches to Iroquoian Studies*. State University of New York Press, Albany.

Graymont, B. 1972. *Iroquois in the American Revolution*. Syracuse University Press, Syracuse.

—— 1988. *The Iroquois*. Chelsea House, New York.

Hauptman, L. M. 1981. *The Iroquois and the New Deal*. Syracuse University Press, Syracuse.

—— 1985. *Iroquois Struggle for Survival: World War II to Red Power*. Syracuse University Press, Syracuse.

—— 1988. *Formulating American Indian Policy in New York State, 1970–1986*. State University of New York Press, Albany.

—— 1993. *The Iroquois in the Civil War: From Battlefield to Reservation*. Syracuse University Press, Syracuse.

Herrick, J. W. 1995. *Iroquois Medical Botany*. Syracuse University Press, Syracuse.

Hertzberg, H. W. 1966. *The Great Tree and the Longhouse: The Culture of the Iroquois*. Macmillan, New York.

Hornung, R. 1991. *One Nation Under the Gun*. Pantheon Books, New York.

Jennings, F. 1976. *The Invasion of America: Indians, Colonialism, and the Cant of Conquest.* W. W. Norton, New York.

—— 1984. *The Ambiguous Iroquois Empire.* W. W. Norton, New York.

Kelsay, I. T. 1984. *Joseph Brant, 1743–1807, Man of Two Worlds.* Syracuse University Press, Syracuse.

Morgan, L. H. 1962. *League of the Iroquois.* Corinth Books, New York. Originally published 1851 as *League of the Ho–dé–no–sau–nee or Iroquois*, Sage, New York.

Parker, A. C. 1968. *Parker on the Iroquois*, ed. W. N. Fenton. Syracuse University Press, Syracuse.

Richter, D. K. 1992. *The Ordeal of the Longhouse: The Peoples of the Iroquois League in the Era of European Colonization.* University of North Carolina Press, Chapel Hill.

Richter, D. K., and J. H. Merrell (eds) 1987. *Beyond the Covenant Chain: The Iroquois and Their Neighbors in Indian North America, 1600–1800.* Syracuse University Press, Syracuse.

Ritchie, W. A. 1969. *The Archaeology of New York State*, rev. edn. Natural History Press, Garden City, New York.

Starna, W. A., and C. Vecsey (eds) 1988. *Iroquois Land Claims.* Syracuse University Press, Syracuse.

Tooker, E. J. (ed.) 1985a. *An Iroquois Source Book, vol. 1: Political and Social Organization.* Garland Publishing, New York.

—— 1985b. *An Iroquois Source Book, vol. 2: Calendric Rituals.* Garland Publishing, New York.

—— 1986. *An Iroquois Source Book, vol. 3: Medicine Society Rituals.* Garland Publishing, New York.

Trigger, B. G. (ed.) 1978. *Northeast.* (Handbook of North American Indians, gen. ed., W. G. Sturtevant, vol. 15.) Smithsonian Institution, Washington, D. C.

Trigger, B. G. 1985. *Natives and Newcomers: Canada's "Heroic Age" Reconsidered.* McGill–Queen's University Press, Kingston, Ontario.

Van den Bogaert, H. M. 1988. *A Journey into Mohawk and Oneida Country, 1634–1635*, trans., and ed. C. T. Gehring and W. A. Starna. Syracuse University Press, Syracuse.

Wallace, A. F. C. 1969. *The Death and Rebirth of the Seneca.* Alfred A. Knopf, New York.

Wallace, P. A. W. 1946. *The White Roots of Peace.* University of Pennsylvania Press, Philadelphia.

Wilson, E. 1992. *Apologies to the Iroquois.* Syracuse University Press, Syracuse.

# References

Abler, T. S., and Logan, M. H. 1988. The Florescence and Demise of Iroquoian Cannibalism: Human Sacrifice and Malinowski's Hypothesis. *Man in the Northeast* 35: 1–26.

Abler, T. S., and Tooker, E. 1978. Seneca. In *Northeast*, ed. B. G. Trigger (*Handbook of North American Indians*, gen. ed. W. C. Sturtevant, vol. 15), 505–17. Smithsonian Institution, Washington, DC.

Abrams, G. 1967. Moving the Fire: A Case of Iroquois Ritual Innovation. In *Iroquois Culture, History, and Prehistory: Proceedings of the 1965 Conference on Iroquois Research*, ed. E. J. Tooker, 23–4. New York State Museum and Science Service, Albany.

Anon. 1916. State of Canada in 1730. Cadillac Papers. *Michigan Pioneer and Historical Society Collections and Researches* 10: 73–84.

—— 1989. Wampum Belts Returned to the Onondaga Nation. *Man in the Northeast* 38: 109–17.

Bakker, P. 1990. A Basque Etymology for the Word "Iroquois." *Man in the Northeast* 40: 89–93.

Barbeau, C. M. 1915. *Huron and Wyandot Mythology*. Geological Survey of Canada Memoir 80. Government Printing Bureau, Ottawa.

Bardwell, K. 1986. The Case for an Aboriginal Origin of Northeast Indian Woodsplint Basketry. *Man in the Northeast* 31: 49–67.

Bartram, J. 1751. *Observations on the Inhabitants, Climate, Soil, Rivers, Productions, Animals, and Other Matters Worthy of Notice, Made by Mr. John Bartram, in His Travels from Pensilvania to Onondago, Oswego and the Lake Ontario, in Canada*. Printed for J. Whiston and B. White, London.

Beauchamp, W. M. 1885. The Iroquois White Dog Feast. *American Antiquarian* 7: 235–9.

—— 1888. Onondaga Customs. *Journal of American Folk-Lore* 1: 195–203.

—— 1900. *Aboriginal Occupation of New York*. New York State Museum Bulletin 32. University of the State of New York, Albany.

Bender, S. J., and Brumbach, H. J. 1992. Material Manifestations of Algonquian Ethnicity: A Case Study from the Upper Hudson. Paper presented at the meetings of the Society for American Archaeology, Pittsburgh.

Black, F. L. 1992. Why did they die? *Science* 258: 1739–40.

Blau, H. 1964. The Iroquois White Dog Sacrifice: Its Evolution and Symbolism. *Ethnohistory* 11: 97–115.

Blau, H., Campisi, J., and Tooker, E. J. 1978. Onondaga. In *Northeast*, ed. B. G. Trigger (*Handbook of North American Indians*, gen. ed. W. C. Sturtevant, vol. 15), 491–9. Smithsonian Institution, Washington, DC.

Bonvillain, N., 1980. Iroquoian Women. In *Studies on Iroquoian Culture*, ed. N. Bonvillain, 47–58. Occasional Publications in Northeastern Anthropology 6. Rindge, New Hampshire.

Boyce, D. W., 1973. A Glimpse of Iroquois Culture History through the Eyes of Joseph Brant and John Norton. *Proceedings of the American Philosophical Society* 117 (4): 286–94.

Bradford, W. 1908. *Bradford's History of Plymouth Plantation*, ed. W. T. Davis. Barnes and Noble, New York.

Bradley, J. W. 1987. *Evolution of the Onondaga Iroquois: Accommodating Change 1500–1655*. Syracuse University Press, Syracuse.

Bradley, J. W., and Childs, S. T. 1991. Basque Earrings and Panther's Tails: The Form of Cross-Cultural Contact in Sixteenth Century Iroquoia. In *Metals in Society: Theory Beyond Analysis*, ed. R. M. Ehrenreich, 7–17. MASCA, The University Museum, University of Pennsylvania, Philadelphia.

Brasser, T. J. 1975. *A Basketful of Indian Culture Change*. National Museum of Man, Mercury Series. Canadian Ethnology Service Paper 22. National Museums of Canada, Ottawa.

Brumbach, H. J. 1975. "Iroquoian" Ceramics in "Algonkian" Territory. *Man in the Northeast* 10: 17–28.

Campisi, J. 1978. Oneida. In *Northeast*, ed. B. G. Trigger (*Handbook of North American Indians*, gen. ed. W. C. Sturtevant, vol. 15), 481–90. Smithsonian Institution, Washington, DC.

—— 1980. Fur Trade and Factionalism of the Eighteenth Century Oneida Indians. In *Studies on Iroquoian Culture*, ed. N. Bonvillain, 37–46. Occasional Publications in Northeastern Anthropology 6. Rindge, New Hampshire.

Campisi, J., and Hauptman, L. M. (eds) 1988. *Oneida Indian Experience: Two Perspectives*. Syracuse University Press, Syracuse.

Ceci, L. 1975. Fish Fertilizer: A Native North American Practice? *Science* 188: 26–30.

—— 1977. The Effect of European Contact and Trade on the Settlement Pattern of Indians in Coastal New York, 1524–1665: The Archaeological and Documentary Evidence. PhD dissertation, City University of New York.

—— 1978. Watchers of the Pleiades: Ethnoastronomy among the Native Cultivators in Northeastern North America. *Ethnohistory* 25: 301–17.

Chafe, W. L. 1964. Linguistic Evidence for the Relative Age of Iroquois Religious Practices. *Southwestern Journal of Anthropology* 20: 278–85.

Champlain, S. de 1907. *Voyages of Samuel de Champlain, 1604–1618*. Barnes and Noble, New York.

Clermont, N. 1980. L'augmentation de la population chez les Iroquoiens préhistoriques. *Recherches amérindiennes au Québec* 10: 159–63.

Clifton, J. 1978. Potawatomi. In *Northeast*, ed. B. G. Trigger (*Handbook of North American Indians*, gen. ed. W. C. Sturtevant, vol. 15), 725–42. Smithsonian Institution, Washington, DC.

Colden, C. 1958. *The History of the Five Indian Nations Depending on the Province of New-York in America*. Great Seal Books, Ithaca, New York.

Converse, H. M. 1908. *Myths and Legends of the New York State Iroquois*, ed. and ann. Arthur C. Parker. New York State Museum Bulletin 125, Albany. Repr. 1981.

Cornplanter, J. J. 1938. *Legends of the Longhouse*. J. B. Lippincott, Philadelphia.

Coult, A. D., and Habenstein, R. W. 1965. *Cross Tabulations of Murdock's World Ethnographic Sample*. University of Missouri Press, Columbia.

Crowe, P. 1992. The Eclipse that Never Was. Paper presented at the Iroquois Research Conference, Rensselaerville, New York.

Day, G. M. 1967. Iroquois: An Etymology. In *Iroquois Culture, History, and Prehistory: Proceedings of the 1965 Conference on Iroquois Research*, ed. E. J. Tooker, 57–61. New York State Museum and Science Service, Albany. Also in *Ethnohistory* 15 (1968): 389–402.

Day, G. M., and Trigger, B. G. 1978. Algonquin. In *Northeast*, ed. B. G. Trigger (*Handbook of North American Indians*, gen. ed. W. C. Sturtevant, vol. 15), 792–7. Smithsonian Institution, Washington, DC.

Deardorff, M. H. 1951. The Religion of Handsome Lake: Its Origin and Development. *Bureau of American Ethnology Bulletin* 149: 77–107.

Divale, W. 1973. *Warfare in Primitive Societies: A Bibliography.* American Bibliographical Center. Clio Press, Santa Barbara, California.

—— 1984. *Matrilocal Residence in Pre-Literate Society.* UMI Research Press, Ann Arbor.

Dodd, C. F., Poulton, D., Lennox, P. A., Smith, D. G., and Warrick, G. 1990. The Middle Ontario Iroquoian Stage. In *The Archaeology of Southern Ontario to AD 1650*, ed. C. J. Ellis and N. Ferris, 321–59. Occasional Publication of the London Chapter, Ontario Archaeological Society, 5. London, Ontario.

Druke, M. A. 1987. Linking Arms: The Structure of Iroquois Intertribal Diplomacy. In *Beyond the Covenant Chain: The Iroquois and Their Neighbors in Indian North America, 1600–1800*, ed. D. K. Richter and J. H. Merrell, 29–39. Syracuse University Press, Syracuse.

Ember, M. 1973. An Archaeological Indicator of Matrilocal versus Patrilocal Residence. *American Antiquity* 38: 177–82.

Engelbrecht, W. E. 1987. Factors Maintaining Low Population Density among the Prehistoric New York Iroquois. *American Antiquity* 52: 13–27.

Engelbrecht, W. E., Sidler, E., and Walko, M. 1990. The Jefferson County Iroquoians. *Man in the Northeast* 39: 65–77.

Feest, J. E., and Feest, C. F. 1978. Ottawa. In *Northeast*, ed. B. G. Trigger (*Handbook of North American Indians*, gen. ed. W. C. Sturtevant, vol. 15), 772–86. Smithsonian Institution, Washington, DC.

Fenton, W. N. 1941. Masked Medicine Societies of the Iroquois. In *Annual Report of the Smithsonian Institution for 1940*, 397–430. Smithsonian Institution, Washington, DC.

—— 1949. Seth Newhouse's Traditional History and Constitution of the Iroquois Confederacy. *Proceedings of the American Philosophical Society* 93: 141–58.

—— 1950. The Roll Call of the Iroquois Chiefs: A Study of a Mnemonic Cane from the Six Nations Reserve. *Smithsonian Miscellaneous Collections* 111 (15): 1–73.

—— 1953. *The Iroquois Eagle Dance: An Offshoot of the Calumet Dance.* Bureau of American Ethnology Bulletin 156. Washington, DC.

—— 1962. This Island, the World on the Turtle's Back. *Journal of American Folklore* 75: 283–300.

—— 1968. Introduction. In *Parker on the Iroquois*, ed. W. N. Fenton, 1–47. Syracuse University Press, Syracuse.

—— 1973. Mohawk. MS in the author's possession.

—— 1975. Lore of the Longhouse: Myth, Ritual and Red Power. *Anthropological Quarterly* 48 (3): 131–47.

—— 1981. The Iroquois in the Grand Tradition of American Letters: The Works of Walter D. Edmonds, Carl Carmer, and Edmund Wilson. *American Indian Culture and Research Journal* 5: 21–39.

—— 1987. *The False Faces of the Iroquois*. University of Oklahoma Press, Norman.

—— 1989. Return of Eleven Wampum Belts to the Six Nations Iroquois Confederacy on Grand River, Canada. *Ethnohistory* 36: 392–410.

Fenton, W. N., and Tooker, E. J. 1978. Mohawk. In *Northeast*, ed. B. G. Trigger (*Handbook of North American Indians*, gen. ed. W. C. Sturtevant, vol. 15), 466–80. Smithsonian Institution, Washington, DC.

Fitzgerald, W. R. 1993. Late Sixteenth-Century Basque Banded Copper Kettles. *Historical Archaeology* 27: 44–57.

Fox, W. A. 1993. Owls and Orenda. *Arch Notes* 93 (3): 19–25.

Frisch, J. A. 1971. The Abenakis Among the St Regis Mohawks. *The Indian Historian* 4 (1): 27–9.

Funk, R. E. 1976. *Recent Contributions to Hudson Valley Prehistory*. New York State Museum Memoir 22. Albany.

Galinee, R. B. de 1903. Exploration of the Great Lakes, 1669–1670, Dollier de Casson and Brehant de Galinee: Galinee's Narrative and Map, Part 1, ed. James H. Coyne. Papers and Records of the Ontario Historical Society 4. Toronto.

Gibson, J. A. 1992. *Concerning the League: The Iroquois League Tradition as Dictated in Onondaga*. ed. and trans. Hanni Woodbury, Reg Henry, and Harry Webster. Algonquian and Iroquoian Linguistics Memoir 9. Winnipeg, Manitoba.

Goddard, I. 1971. The Ethnohistorical Implications of Early Delaware Linguistic Materials. *Man in the Northeast* 1: 14–26.

—— 1978a. Eastern Algonquian Languages. In *Northeast*, ed. B. G. Trigger (*Handbook of North American Indians*, gen. ed. W. C. Sturtevant, vol. 15), 70–7. Smithsonian Institution, Washington, DC.

—— 1978b. Synonymy. In *Northeast*, ed. B. G. Trigger (*Handbook of North American Indians*, gen. ed. W. C. Sturtevant, vol. 15), 319–21. Smithsonian Institution, Washington, DC.

Gookin, D. 1970. *Historical Collections of the Indians in New England*. Towtaid, Boston.

Graymont, B. 1972. *Iroquois in the American Revolution*. Syracuse University Press, Syracuse.

Greenhalgh, W. 1849–51. Observations of Wentworth Greenhalgh in a Journey from Albany to the Indians Westward begun 28th May and Ended 14th July 1677. In *Documentary History of the State of New York (DNHY)*, vol. 1, 11–12. Weed, Parsons and Company, Albany.

Griffin, J. B. 1944. The Iroquois in American Prehistory. *Papers of the Michigan Academy of Science, Arts, and Letters* 29: 357–74.

Grinde, D. A., Jr, and Johansen, B. E. 1991. *Exemplar of Liberty: Native America and the Evolution of Democracy*. UCLA American Indian Studies Center, Los Angeles.

Haan, R. L. 1987. Covenant and Consensus: Iroquois and English, 1676–1760. In *Beyond the Covenant Chain: The Iroquois and their Neighbors in Indian North America, 1600–1800*, ed. D. K. Richter and J. H. Merrell, 41–57. Syracuse University Press, Syracuse.

Hale, H. E. 1883. *The Iroquois Book of Rites*. D. G. Brinton, Philadelphia. Repr. 1965, University of Toronto Press, Toronto.

—— 1885. The Iroquois Sacrifice of the White Dog. *American Antiquarian* 7: 7–14.

Hall, L. K. n.d. Rebuilding the Iroquois Confederacy. Privately distributed MS.

Hamell, G. 1983. Trading in Metaphors: The Magic of Beads. Another Perspective upon Indian–European Contact in Northeastern North America. In *Proceedings of the 1982 Glass Trade Bead Conference*, ed. C. F. Hayes, III, 5–28. Research Records 16. Rochester Museum and Science Center, Rochester.

—— 1987. Mythical Realities and European Contact in the Northeast during the Sixteenth and Seventeenth Centuries. *Man in the Northeast* 33: 63–87.

—— 1992. The Iroquois and the World's Rim: Speculations on Color, Culture, and Contact. *The American Indian Quarterly* 26: 451–69.

Hauptman, L. M. 1980. Raw Deal: The Iroquois View the Indian Reorganization Act of 1934. In *Studies on Iroquoian Culture*, ed. N. Bonvillain, 15–25. Occasional Publications in Northeastern Anthropology 6. Rindge, New Hampshire.

—— 1981. *The Iroquois and the New Deal*. Syracuse University Press, Syracuse.

—— 1985a. *Iroquois Struggle for Survival: World War II to Red Power*. Syracuse University Press, Syracuse.

—— 1985b. *Historical Background to the Present Day Seneca Nation–Salamanca Lease Controversy: The First Hundred Years, 1851–1951*. Nelson A. Rockefeller Institute of Government, State University of New York, Albany.

—— 1988. *Formulating American Indian Policy in New York State, 1970–1986*. State University of New York Press, Albany.

—— 1993. *The Iroquois in the Civil War: From Battlefield to Reservation*. Syracuse University Press, Syracuse.

Hayden, B. 1979. *Settlement Patterns of the Draper and White Sites: 1973 Excavations*. Department of Archaeology Publication 6. Simon Fraser University, Burnaby, British Columbia.

Hayden, R. 1980. The Patrilineal Determination of Band Membership at the Six Nations Reserve: A Case Study of Semi-Autonomy and Cultural Change. In *Studies on Iroquoian Culture*, ed. N. Bonvillain, 27–36. Occasional Publications in Northeastern Anthropology 6. Rindge, New Hampshire.

Hayes, C. F. (ed.) 1989. *Proceedings of the 1986 Shell Bead Conference: Selected Papers*. Research Records of the Rochester Museum and Science Center 20. Rochester.

Heckewelder, J. G. E. 1819. *An Account of the History, Manners, and Customs of the Indian Nations, who once Inhabited Pennsylvania and the Neighboring States*. Transactions of the Committee of History, Moral Science and General Literature of the American Philosophical Society 1. Philadelphia.

Heidenreich, C. E. 1971. *Huronia: A History and Geography of the Huron Indians 1600–1650*. Ontario Ministry of Natural Resources, Ottawa.

Herrick, J. W. 1977. Iroquois Medical Botany. PhD dissertation, State University of New York at Albany.

Hewitt, J. N. B. 1892a. Legend of the Founding of the Iroquois League. *American Anthropologist* (o.s.) 3: 341–52.

—— 1892b. Iroquois Game of La Crosse. *American Anthropologist* (o.s.) 5: 189–91.

—— 1903. Iroquoian Cosmology; First Part. *Annual Report of the Bureau of American Ethnology for the years 1899–1900*. Washington, DC.

—— 1920. A Constitutional League of Peace in the Stone Age of America: The League of the Iroquois and its Constitution. *Annual Report of the Smithsonian Institution for 1918*, 527–45. Washington, DC.

—— 1928. Iroquoian Cosmology; Second Part, with Introduction and Notes. *Annual Report of the Bureau of American Ethnology for the years 1925–1926*. Washington, DC.

Hodder, I. 1986. *Reading the Past: Current Approaches to Interpretation in Archaeology*. Cambridge University Press, New York.

Hoffecker, J. F., Powers, W. R., and Goebel, T. 1993. The Colonization of Beringia and the Peopling of the New World. *Science* 259: 46–53.

Hornung, R. 1991. *One Nation under the Gun.* Pantheon Books, New York.

Hoskin, N. R. 1990. Death Dark, State Silent. *Capital,* August 1990.

Hubbard, J. M. 1886. *Account of Sa-go-ye-wat-ha, or Red Jacket, and His People.* Munsell, Albany.

Hunt, G. T. 1940. *The Wars of the Iroquois: A Study in Intertribal Trade Relations.* University of Wisconsin Press, Madison.

Ingram, M., Farmer, G., and Wigley, T. 1981. Past Climates and their Impact on Man: A Review. In *Climate and History,* ed. T. Wigley, M. Ingram, and G. Farmer, 3–50. Cambridge University Press, Cambridge.

Jameson, J. F. (ed.) 1909. *Narratives of New Netherland, 1609–1664.* Barnes and Noble, New York.

Jennings, F. 1976. *The Invasion of America: Indians, Colonialism, and the Cant of Conquest.* W. W. Norton, New York.

—— 1984. *The Ambiguous Iroquois Empire.* W. W. Norton, New York.

Jennings, F. (ed.) 1985. *History and Culture of Iroquois Diplomacy: An Interdisciplinary Guide to the Treaties of the Six Nations and their League.* Syracuse University Press, Syracuse.

Johansen, B. E. 1990. Native American Societies and the Evolution of Democracy in America, 1600–1800. *Ethnohistory* 37: 279–90.

—— 1993. *Life and Death in Mohawk Country.* North American Press, Golden, Colorado.

Jones, J. 1990. A Nation Divided. *Metroland,* June 7–13, 1990.

*JP* = Johnson, W. 1921–57. *Papers of Sir William Johnson,* 12 vols, ed. J. Sullivan, A. C. Flick, A. W. Lauber, and M. W. Hamilton. University of the State of New York, Albany.

*JR* = Thwaites, R. G. (ed.) 1959. *The Jesuit Relations and Allied Documents 1610–1791,* 73 vols. Pageant, New York.

Kelsay, I. T. 1984. *Joseph Brant, 1743–1807: Man of Two Worlds.* Syracuse University Press, Syracuse.

Kent, B. C. 1984. *Susquehanna's Indians.* The Pennsylvania Historical and Museum Commission Anthropological Series No. 6. Harrisburg.

Koppedrayer, K. I. 1993. The Making of the First Iroquois Virgin: Early Jesuit Biographies of the Blessed Kateri Tekakwitha. *Ethnohistory* 40: 277–306.

Kraft, H. C. 1975. *The Archaeology of the Tocks Island Area.* Archaeological Research Center, Seton Hall University Museum, South Orange, New Jersey.

Krusche, R. 1986. The Origin of the Mask Concept in the Eastern Woodlands of North America. *Man in the Northeast* 31: 1–47.

Kuhn, R. 1985. Trade and Exchange among the Mohawk-Iroquois:

A Trace Element Analysis of Ceramic Smoking Pipes. PhD dissertation, State University of New York at Albany.

Lafitau, J. F. 1974. *Customs of the American Indians Compared with the Customs of Primitive Times,* vol. 1, ed. W. N. Fenton and E. L. Moore. Publications of the Champlain Society 48. Toronto.

—— 1977. *Customs of the American Indians Compared with the Customs of Primitive Times,* vol. 2, ed. W. N. Fenton and E. L. Moore. Publications of the Champlain Society 49. Toronto.

Landsman, G. H. 1988. *Sovereignty and Symbol: Indian–White Conflict at Ganienkeh.* University of New Mexico Press, Albuquerque.

Landy, D. 1978. Tuscarora among the Iroquois. In *Northeast,* ed. B. G. Trigger (*Handbook of North American Indians,* gen. ed. W. C. Sturtevant, vol. 15), 518–24. Smithsonian Institution, Washington, DC.

Lenig, D. 1965. *The Oak Hill Horizon and Its Relation to the Development of Five Nations Iroquois Culture.* Researches and Transactions of New York State Archaeological Association 15 (1). Buffalo.

—— 1977. Of Dutchmen, Beaver Hats and Iroquois. In *Current Perspectives in Northeastern Archeology: Essays in Honor of William A. Ritchie,* ed. R. E. Funk and C. F. Hayes III, 71–84. Researches and Transactions of New York State Archeological Association 17 (1). Rochester.

Lounsbury, F. G. 1978. Iroquoian Languages. In *Northeast,* ed. B. G. Trigger (*Handbook of North American Indians,* gen. ed. W. C. Sturtevant, vol. 15), 334–43. Smithsonian Institution, Washington, DC.

Lydekker, J. W. 1938. *The Faithful Mohawks.* Macmillan, New York.

MacNeish, R. S. 1952. *Iroquois Pottery Types: A Technique for the Study of Iroquois Prehistory.* National Museum of Canada Bulletin 124, Anthropological Series 31.

—— 1976. The *In Situ* Iroquois Revisited and Rethought. In *Culture Change and Continuity: Essays in Honor of James Bennett Griffin,* ed. C. E. Cleland, 79–98. Academic Press, New York.

Mathews, Z. P. 1980. Seneca Figurines: A Case of Misplaced Modesty. In *Studies on Iroquoian Culture,* ed. N. Bonvillain, 71–90. Occasional Publications in Northeastern Anthropology 6. Rindge, New Hampshire.

—— 1981. Janus and other Multiple-Image Iroquoian Pipes. *Ontario Archaeology* 35: 3–22.

Megapolensis, J. 1909. A Short Account of the Mohawk Indians. In *Narratives of New Netherland, 1609–1664,* ed. J. F. Jameson, 163–80. Barnes and Noble, New York.

Mithun, M. 1984. The Proto-Iroquoians: Cultural Reconstruction from Lexical Materials. In *Extending the Rafters: Interdisciplinary Approaches to Iroquoian Studies*, ed. M. K. Foster, J. Campisi, and M. Mithun, 259–81. State University of New York Press, Albany.

—— 1988. "Maman": L'évolution d'un terme de parenté dans les langues Iroquoiennes. *Recherches amérindiennes au Québec* 14: 17–23.

Morgan, L. H. 1871. *Systems of Consanguinity and Affinity of the Human Family*. Smithsonian Contributions to Knowledge 17. Washington, DC.

—— 1877. *Ancient Society: or, Researches in the Lines of Human Progress from Savagery through Barbarism to Civilization*. Henry Holt, New York.

—— 1881. *Houses and House-life of the American Aborigines*. Contributions to North American Ethnology 4. United States Geographical and Geological Survey of the Rocky Mountain Region, Washington, DC.

—— 1962. *League of the Iroquois*. Corinth Books, New York. Originally published 1851 as *League of the Ho-dé-no-sau-nee or Iroquois*, Sage, New York.

Morrow, L. 1991. Evil. *Time* 137 (23) (June 10): 48–53.

Moulton, A. L., and Abler, T. S. 1991. Lithic Beings and Lithic Technology: References from Northern Iroquoian Mythology. *Man in the Northeast* 42: 1–7.

Nabokov, P., and Easton, R. 1989. *Native American Architecture*. Oxford University Press, New York.

Niemczycki, M. A. P. 1984. *The Origin and Development of the Seneca and Cayuga Tribes of New York State*. Rochester Museum and Science Center Research Records 17.

—— 1988. Seneca Tribalization: An Adaptive Strategy. *Man in the Northeast* 36: 77–87.

Noble, W. 1975. Corn and the Development of Village Life in Southern Ontario. *Ontario Archaeology* 25: 37–46.

NYCD = O'Callaghan, E. B. (ed.) 1853–87. *Documents Relative to the Colonial History of the State of New York; Procured in Holland, England and France, by John R. Brodhead*, 15 vols. Weed and Parsons, New York.

Oswald, A. 1975. *Clay Pipes for the Archaeologist*. British Archaeological Reports 14. Oxford.

Otterbein, K. F. 1968. Internal War: A Cross-Cultural Study. *American Anthropologist* 70: 277–89.

Parker, A. C. 1909. Secret Medicine Societies of the Seneca. *American Anthropologist* 11: 161–85.

—— 1910. Iroquois Uses of Maize and other Food Plants. *New York State Museum Bulletin* 144 (482): 5–113. Repr. in *Parker on the Iroquois*, ed. W. N. Fenton, bk 1, 1968. Syracuse University Press, Syracuse.

—— 1913. *The Code of Handsome Lake, The Seneca Prophet*. New York State Museum Bulletin 163. Albany. Repr. in *Parker on the Iroquois*, ed. W. N. Fenton, bk 2, 1968. Syracuse University Press, Syracuse.

—— 1916a. The Origin of the Iroquois as Suggested by their Archaeology. *American Anthropologist* 18: 479–507.

—— 1916b. The Constitution of the Five Nations. *New York State Museum Bulletin* 184: 7–158. Albany. Repr. in *Parker on the Iroquois*, ed. W. N. Fenton, bk 3, 1968. Syracuse University Press, Syracuse.

—— 1923. *Seneca Myths and Folk Tales*. Buffalo Historical Society Publications 27. Buffalo.

Pearce, R. 1984. Mapping Middleport: A Case Study in Societal Archaeology. PhD dissertation, McGill University.

Peña, E. S. 1990. Wampum Production in New Netherland and Colonial New York: The Historical and Archaeological Context. PhD dissertation, Boston University.

Pendergast, J. F. 1990. Emerging Saint Lawrence Iroquoian Settlement Patterns. *Man in the Northeast* 40: 17–30.

Pilkington, W. (ed.) 1980. *The Journals of Samuel Kirkland*. Hamilton College. Clinton, New York.

Pratt, P. P. 1976. *Archaeology of the Oneida Iroquois*, vol. 1. Occasional Publications in Northeastern Anthropology 1. Rindge, New Hampshire.

Puniello, A. J. 1980. Iroquois Series Ceramics in the Upper Delaware Valley New Jersey and Pennsylvania. In *Proceedings of the 1979 Iroquois Pottery Conference*, ed. C. F. Hayes III, 147–55. Rochester Museum and Science Center Research Records 13.

Radisson, P. E. 1967. *Voyages of Peter Esprit Radisson*. Burt Franklin, New York.

Ramenofsky, A. F. 1987. *Vectors of Death: The Archaeology of European Contact*. University of New Mexico Press, Albuquerque.

Richards, C. 1967. Huron and Iroquois Residence Patterns 1600–1650. In *Iroquois Culture, History, and Prehistory: Proceedings of the 1965 Conference on Iroquois Research*, ed. E. J. Tooker, 51–6. New York State Museum and Science Service, Albany.

Richter, D. K. 1987. Ordeals of the Longhouse: The Five Nations in Early American History. In *Beyond the Covenant Chain: The Iroquois and their Neighbors in Indian North America, 1600–*

*1800*, ed. D. K. Richter and J. H. Merrell, 11–27. Syracuse Univerity Press, Syracuse.

—— 1992. *The Ordeal of the Longhouse: The Peoples of the Iroquois League in the Era of European Colonization*. University of North Carolina Press, Chapel Hill.

Rickard, C. 1973. *Fighting Tuscarora: The Autobiography of Chief Clinton Rickard*, ed. Barbara Graymont. Syracuse University Press, Syracuse.

Rippeteau, B. E. 1978. The Upper Susquehanna Valley Iroquois: An Iroquoian Enigma. In *Essays in Northeastern Anthropology in Memory of Marian E. White*, ed. W. E. Engelbrecht and D. K. Grayson, 123–51. Occasional Publications in Northeastern Anthropology 5. Rindge, New Hampshire.

Ritchie, W. A. 1944. *The Pre-Iroquoian Occupations of New York State*. Rochester Museum of Arts and Sciences Memoir 1. Rochester.

—— 1952. *The Chance Horizon: An Early Stage of Mohawk Iroquois Cultural Development*. New York State Museum Circular 29. Albany.

—— 1961. Iroquois Archeology and Settlement Patterns. In *Symposium on Cherokee and Iroquois Culture*, ed. W. N. Fenton and J. Gulick, 27–38. Bureau of American Ethnology Bulletin 180. Washington, DC.

—— 1965. *The Archaeology of New York State*. Natural History Press, Garden City, New York.

—— 1969. *The Archaeology of New York State*, rev. edn. Natural History Press, Garden City, New York.

Ritchie, W. A., and Funk, R. E. 1973. *Aboriginal Settlement Patterns in the Northeast*. New York State Museum and Science Service Memoir 20. Albany.

Ritchie, W. A., Lenig, D., and Miller, P. S. 1953. *An Early Owasco Sequence in Eastern New York*. New York State Museum Circular 32. Albany.

Ritchie, W. A., and MacNeish, R. S. 1949. The Pre-Iroquoian Pottery of New York State. *American Antiquity* 15: 97–124.

Rustige, R. 1988. *Tyendinaga Tales*. McGill-Queen's University Press, Kingston.

Sagard, G. 1939. *Father Gabriel Sagard: The Long Journey to the Country of the Hurons* [1632], ed. G. M. Wrong. Publications of the Champlain Society, Toronto.

Sahlins, M. D. 1961. The Segmentary Lineage: An Organization of Predatory Expansion. *American Anthropologist* 53: 322–45.

Salisbury, N. 1987. Toward the Covenant Chain: Iroquois and Southern New England Algonquians, 1637–1684. In *Beyond the Covenant*

*Chain: The Iroquois and their Neighbors in Indian North America, 1600–1800*, ed. D. K. Richter and J. H. Merrell, 61–73. Syracuse University Press, Syracuse.

Schoolcraft, H. R. 1847. *Notes on the Iroquois: or, Contributions to the Statistics, Aboriginal History, Antiquities, and General Ethnology of Western New York*. Erastus H. Pease, Albany.

Scott, D. C. (ed.) 1912. Traditional History of the Confederacy of the Six Nations, Prepared by a Committee of the Chiefs. *Transactions of the Royal Society of Canada*, 3rd ser., 5 (2): 195–246.

Seaver, J. E. 1992. *Narrative of the Life of Mrs. Mary Jemison*. University of Oklahoma Press, Norman. Originally published 1824.

Sempowski, M. forthcoming. Preliminary Observations on Early Historic Exchange between the Seneca and Susquehannock. *People to People Conference: Intertribal and Interethnic Relationships in the Northeast during the Early Contact Period*. Rochester Museum and Science Center, Rochester.

Seymour, R. 1991. Letter to the editor. *Time* 137 (26) (July 1): 4.

Shattuck, G. C. 1991. *Oneida Land Claims: A Legal History*. Syracuse University Press, Syracuse.

Shelford, V. E. 1963. *The Ecology of North America*. University of Illinois Press, Urbana.

Smith, E. A. 1883. Myths of the Iroquois. In *Second Annual Report of the Bureau of American Ethnology for the Years 1880–1881*, 47–116. Washington, DC. Repr. 1983 by Iroqrafts, Ohsweken, Ontario.

Snow, D. R. 1976. Abenaki Fur Trade in the Sixteenth Century. *Western Canadian Journal of Anthropology* 6 (1): 3–11.

—— 1980. *The Archaeology of New England*. Academic Press, New York.

—— 1984. Iroquois Prehistory. In *Extending the Rafters: Interdisciplinary Approaches to Iroquoian Studies*, ed. M. K. Foster, J. Campisi, and M. Mithun, 241–57. State University of New York Press, Albany.

—— 1985. *The Mohawk Valley Project: 1982 Field Season Report*. The Institute for Northeast Anthropology, State University of New York at Albany, Albany.

—— 1986. Historic Mohawk Settlement Patterns. Paper presented at the annual meetings of the Canadian Archaeological Association, April 25, 1986. MS in author's possession.

—— 1991a. Dating the Emergence of the Iroquois League: A Reconsideration of the Documentary Evidence. In *A Beautiful and Fruitful Place: Selected Rensselaerswijck Seminar Papers*, ed. N. A. M. Zeller, 139–44. New Netherland Publishing, Albany.

—— 1991b. Population Movement During the Woodland Periods: The Intrusion of Iroquoian Peoples. Paper presented at the annual meetings of the New York State Archaeological Association, Rochester, April 1991.

—— 1992a. L'augmentation de la population chez les groupes Iroquoiens et ses conséquences sur l'étude de leurs origins. *Recherches amérindiennes au Québec* 22: 5–12.

—— 1992b. Paleoecology and the Prehistoric Incursion of Northern Iroquoians into the Lower Great Lakes Region. In *Great Lakes Archaeology and Paleoecology: Exploring Interdisciplinary Initiatives for the Nineties,* ed. B. G. Warner and R. MacDonald. In press.

—— 1992c. Disease and Population Decline in the Northeast. In *Disease and Demography in the Americas,* ed. J. W. Verano and D. H. Ubelaker, pp. 177–186. Smithsonian Press, Washington, DC.

—— 1993a. *Migration in Prehistory: The Northern Iroquoian Case.* MS in the author's possession.

—— 1993b. Mohawk Valley Archaeology: The Sites. MS in the author's possession.

—— forthcoming. Theyanoguin. In *Native Northeastern Culture Brokers,* ed. R. Grumet. In preparation.

Snow, D. R., and Lanphear, K. M. 1988. European Contact and Indian Depopulation in the Northeast: The Timing of the First Epidemics. *Ethnohistory* 35: 15–33.

Snow, D. R., and Starna, W. A. 1989. Sixteenth Century Depopulation: A View from the Mohawk Valley. *American Anthropologist* 91: 142–9.

Snyderman, G. S. 1951. Concepts of Land Ownership among the Iroquois and their Neighbors. In *Symposium on Local Diversity in Iroquois Culture,* ed. W. N. Fenton, Bureau of American Ethnology Bulletin 149. Washington, DC.

Spiess, A. E., and Spiess, B. D. 1987. New England Pandemic of 1616–1622: Cause and Archaeological Implication. *Man in the Northeast* 34: 71–83.

Starna, W. A. 1993. The Repeal of Article 8: Law, Government, and Cultural Politics at Akwesasne. *American Indian Law Review.* In press.

Starna, W. A., and Campisi, J. 1992. *When Two Are One: The Mohawks at St Regis.* MS in the author's possession.

Starna, W. A., and Relethford, J. H. 1985. Deer Densities and Population Dynamics: A Cautionary Note. *American Antiquity* 50: 825–32.

Starna, W. A., and Vecsey, C. (eds) 1988. *Iroquois Land Claims.* Syracuse University Press, Syracuse.

Starna, W. A., and Watkins, R. 1991. Northern Iroquoian Slavery. *Ethnohistory* 38: 34–57.

Stewart, M. 1990. Clemson's Island Studies in Pennsylvania: A Perspective. *Pennsylvania Archaeologist* 60: 79–107.

Stone, W. L. 1838. *Life of Joseph Brant–Thayendanegea*, 2 vols. Alexander V. Glake, New York. Repr. 1969 by Kraus Reprint, New York.

—— 1901. King Hendrick. In *Constitution and By-Laws of the New York State Historical Association, with Proceedings of the Second Annual Meeting*, 28–39. Cooperstown, NY, New York State Historical Association.

Stuiver, M., and Reimer, P. J. 1993. Extended $^{14}$C Data Base and Revised Calib 3.0 $^{14}$C Age Calibration Program. *Radiocarbon* 35: 215–30.

Swiers, G. 1993. Indian Affairs: State still Hurting rather than Helping. *Sunday Gazette*, June 27.

Tehanetorens 1976. *Tales of the Iroquois.* Akwesasne Notes, Rooseveltown.

Tooker, E. J. 1963. The Iroquois Defeat of the Huron: A Review of Causes. *Pennsylvania Archaeologist* 33: 11–123.

—— 1965. The Iroquois White Dog Sacrifice in the Latter Part of the Eighteenth Century. *Ethnohistory* 12: 129–40.

—— 1970. *The Iroquois Ceremonial of Midwinter.* Syracuse University Press, Syracuse.

—— 1978a. Wyandot. In *Northeast*, ed. B: G. Trigger (*Handbook of North American Indians*, gen. ed. W. C. Sturtevant, vol. 15), 398–406. Smithsonian Institution, Washington, DC.

—— 1978b. The League of the Iroquois: Its History, Politics, and Ritual. In *Northeast*, ed. B. G. Trigger (*Handbook of North American Indians*, gen. ed., W. C. Sturtevant, vol. 15), 418–41. Smithsonian Institution, Washington, DC.

—— 1984. Women in Iroquois Society. In *Extending the Rafters: Interdisciplinary Approaches to Iroquoian Studies*, ed. M. K. Foster, J. Campisi, and M. Mithun, 109–23. State University of New York Press, Albany.

—— 1988. The United States Constitution and the Iroquois League. *Ethnohistory* 35: 305–36.

—— 1989. On the Development of the Handsome Lake Religion. *Proceedings of the American Philosophical Society* 133 (1): 35–50.

—— 1990. Rejoinder to Johansen. *Ethnohistory* 37: 291–7.

—— 1992. Lewis H. Morgan and his Contemporaries. *American Anthropologist* 94: 357–75.

Tooker, E. J. (ed.) 1985a. *An Iroquois Source Book*, vol. 1: *Political and Social Organization*. Garland Publishing, New York.

—— 1985b. *An Iroquois Source Book*, vol. 2: *Calendric Rituals*. Garland Publishing, New York.

—— 1986. *An Iroquois Source Book*, vol. 3: *Medicine Society Rituals*. Garland Publishing, New York.

Torok, C. H. 1967. Tyendinaga Acculturation. In *Iroquois Culture, History, and Prehistory: Proceedings of the 1965 Conference on Iroquois Research*, ed. E. J. Tooker, 31–3. New York State Museum and Science Service, Albany.

Trigger, B. G. 1978. Iroquoian Matriliny. *Pennsylvania Archaeologist* 48: 55–65.

—— 1981. Prehistoric Social and Political Organization: An Iroquoian Case Study. In *Foundations of Northeast Archaeology*, ed. D. R. Snow, 1–50. Academic Press, New York.

Trigger, B. G. (ed.) 1978. *Northeast* (*Handbook of North American Indians*, gen. ed., W. C. Sturtevant, vol. 15). Smithsonian Institution, Washington, DC.

Tuck, J. 1971. *Onondaga Iroquois Prehistory: A Study in Settlement Archaeology*. Syracuse University Press, Syracuse.

Turnbaugh, W. H. 1977. *Man, Land and Time: The Cultural Prehistory and Demographic Patterns of North-Central Pennsylvania*. Lycoming County Historical Society, Williamsport, Pennsylvania.

Van den Bogaert, H. M. 1988. *A Journey into Mohawk and Oneida Country, 1634–1635*, trans. and ed. C. T. Gehring and W. A. Starna. Syracuse University Press, Syracuse.

Vanderlaan, S. 1980. The Oakfield Phase – Western New York State. In *Proceedings of the 1979 Iroquois Pottery Conference*, ed. C. F. Hayes III, 95–8. Rochester Museum and Science Center Research Records 13. Rochester.

Wallace, A. F. C. 1969. *The Death and Rebirth of the Seneca*. Alfred A. Knopf, New York.

—— 1978. Origins of the Longhouse Religion. In *Northeast*, ed. B. G. Trigger (*Handbook of North American Indians*, gen. ed. W. C. Sturtevant, vol. 15), 442–8. Smithsonian Institution, Washington, DC.

Wallace, P. A. W. 1945. *Conrad Weiser, Friend of Colonist and Mohawk*. Russell and Russell, New York.

—— 1946. *The White Roots of Peace*. University of Pennsylvania Press, Philadelphia.

Warrick, G. 1984. *Reconstructing Ontario Iroquoian Village Organization*. National Museum of Man, Mercury Series. Archaeological Survey of Canada Paper 124. National Museums of Canada, Ottawa.

—— 1988. Trends in Huron Family, Household, and Community Size, AD 900–AD 1650. Paper presented at the 21st Annual Chacmool Conference, University of Calgary, Calgary.

—— 1990. A Population History of the Huron-Petun, AD 900–1650. PhD dissertation, McGill University.

Waugh, F. W. 1912. Cosmogonic Myth. Anthony Day (Oneida): Oneidatown, Ontario; Nov., 1912. #100. MS in Frederick Wilderson Waugh, Collection of Iroquois Folklore [1915–1918]. American Philosophical Society Library, Philadelphia.

—— 1916. *Iroquois Foods and Food Preparation.* Memoirs of the Canadian Geological Survey 86, Anthropological Series 12. Ottawa.

Weaver, S. M. 1984. Seth Newhouse and the Grand River Confederacy at Mid-Nineteenth Century. In *Extending the Rafters: Interdisciplinary Approaches to Iroquoian Studies,* ed. M. K. Foster, J. Campisi, and M. Mithun, 165–82. State University of New York Press, Albany.

Whallon, R., Jr 1968. Investigations of Late Prehistoric Social Organization in New York State. In *New Perspectives in Archaeology,* ed. S. R. Binford and L. R. Binford, 223–44. Aldine, Chicago.

White, M. E. 1967. *An Early Historic Niagara Frontier Iroquois Cemetery in Erie County, New York.* Researches and Transactions of the New York State Archaeological Association 17 (1). Buffalo.

White, M. E., Engelbrecht, W. E., and Tooker, E. J. 1978. Cayuga. In *Northeast,* ed. B. G. Trigger (*Handbook of North American Indians,* gen. ed. W. C. Sturtevant, vol. 15), 500–4. Smithsonian Institution, Washington, DC.

White, R. 1991. *The Middle Ground.* Cambridge University Press, New York.

Williams, R. 1643. *A Key into the Language of America.* Gregory Dexter, London.

—— 1863. To John Winthrop [1643]. *Collections of the Massachusetts Historical Society,* 4th ser., 6: 229.

Wilson, E. 1992. *Apologies to the Iroquois.* Syracuse University Press, Syracuse.

Wray, C. F., and Schoff, H. L. 1953. A Preliminary Report on the Seneca Sequence in Western New York. *Pennsylvania Archaeologist* 23: 53–63.

Wray, C. F., Sempowski, M. L., Saunders, L. P., and Cervone, G. C. 1987. *The Adams and Culbertson Sites.* Rochester Museum and Science Center Research Records 19. Rochester.

—— 1991. *Tram and Cameron: Two Early Contact Era Seneca Sites.* Rochester Museum and Science Center Research Records 21. Rochester.

Wright, J. V. 1966. *The Ontario Iroquois Tradition.* National Museum of Canada Bulletin 210. Ottawa.

—— 1974. *The Nodwell Site.* National Museum of Man, Mercury Series. Archaeological Survey of Canada Paper 22. National Museums of Canada, Ottawa.

Wright, Q. 1968. War: The Study of War. In *International Encyclopedia of the Social Sciences,* vol. 16, ed. D. L. Sills, 453–68. Macmillan, New York.

Wykoff, M. W. 1989. Iroquoian Prehistory and Climate Change: Notes for Empirical Studies of the Eastern Woodlands. PhD dissertation, Cornell University.

# Index